# iPad®
# For Seniors

2025–2026 Edition

## by Dwight Spivey

# iPad® For Seniors For Dummies®, 2025–2026 Edition

Published by: **John Wiley & Sons, Inc.,** 111 River Street, Hoboken, NJ 07030-5774, www.wiley.com

For general information on our other products and services, please contact our Customer Care Department within the U.S. at 877-762-2974, outside the U.S. at 317-572-3993, or fax 317-572-4002. For technical support, please visit https://hub.wiley.com/community/support/dummies.

Wiley publishes in a variety of print and electronic formats and by print-on-demand. Some material included with standard print versions of this book may not be included in e-books or in print-on-demand. If this book refers to media that is not included in the version you purchased, you may download this material at http://booksupport.wiley.com. For more information about Wiley products, visit www.wiley.com.

Library of Congress Control Number: 2025930867

ISBN 978-1-394-31340-2 (pbk); ISBN 978-1-394-31342-6 (ebk); ISBN 978-1-394-31341-9 (ebk)

SKY10098492_021425

# Contents at a Glance

**Introduction** . . . . . . . . . . . . . . . . . . . . . . . . . . . . . . . . . . . . . . . . . . . . . . . . . . . . . . .1

**Part 1: Getting to Know Your iPad** . . . . . . . . . . . . . . . . . . . . . . . . . . . . . . .5
CHAPTER 1: Buying Your iPad . . . . . . . . . . . . . . . . . . . . . . . . . . . . . . . . . . 7
CHAPTER 2: Exploring Your iPad . . . . . . . . . . . . . . . . . . . . . . . . . . . . . . 25
CHAPTER 3: Beyond the Basics . . . . . . . . . . . . . . . . . . . . . . . . . . . . . . . 65

**Part 2: Beginning to Use Your iPad** . . . . . . . . . . . . . . . . . . . . . . . . . . . .81
CHAPTER 4: Making Your iPad More Accessible . . . . . . . . . . . . . . . . . . .83
CHAPTER 5: Conversing with Siri . . . . . . . . . . . . . . . . . . . . . . . . . . . . . .117
CHAPTER 6: Expanding Your iPad Horizons with Apps . . . . . . . . . . . . .135
CHAPTER 7: Organizing Contacts. . . . . . . . . . . . . . . . . . . . . . . . . . . . . .151
CHAPTER 8: Getting Social with Your iPad . . . . . . . . . . . . . . . . . . . . . .165
CHAPTER 9: Browsing with Safari . . . . . . . . . . . . . . . . . . . . . . . . . . . . .191
CHAPTER 10: Working with Email in Mail . . . . . . . . . . . . . . . . . . . . . . . .213

**Part 3: Enjoying Media** . . . . . . . . . . . . . . . . . . . . . . . . . . . . . . . . . . . . . .237
CHAPTER 11: Shopping the iTunes Store and Apple TV. . . . . . . . . . . . . .239
CHAPTER 12: Reading Books . . . . . . . . . . . . . . . . . . . . . . . . . . . . . . . . . .249
CHAPTER 13: Enjoying Music and Podcasts. . . . . . . . . . . . . . . . . . . . . . .265
CHAPTER 14: Taking and Sharing Photos. . . . . . . . . . . . . . . . . . . . . . . . .287
CHAPTER 15: Creating and Watching Videos. . . . . . . . . . . . . . . . . . . . . .305

**Part 4: Living with Your iPad** . . . . . . . . . . . . . . . . . . . . . . . . . . . . . . . . .319
CHAPTER 16: Keeping on Schedule with Calendar and Clock. . . . . . . . . .321
CHAPTER 17: Working with Reminders and Notifications. . . . . . . . . . . . .343
CHAPTER 18: Making Notes . . . . . . . . . . . . . . . . . . . . . . . . . . . . . . . . . . .367
CHAPTER 19: Using Utilities . . . . . . . . . . . . . . . . . . . . . . . . . . . . . . . . . . .385
CHAPTER 20: Troubleshooting and Maintaining Your iPad . . . . . . . . . . .407

**Index** . . . . . . . . . . . . . . . . . . . . . . . . . . . . . . . . . . . . . . . . . . . . . . . . . . . . .421

# Table of Contents

INTRODUCTION. . . . . . . . . . . . . . . . . . . . . . . . . . . . . . . . . . . . . . . .1
    About This Book . . . . . . . . . . . . . . . . . . . . . . . . . . . . . 1
    Foolish Assumptions . . . . . . . . . . . . . . . . . . . . . . . . . . 3
    Beyond the Book . . . . . . . . . . . . . . . . . . . . . . . . . . . . . 3
    Where to Go from Here. . . . . . . . . . . . . . . . . . . . . . . . . 3

PART 1: GETTING TO KNOW YOUR IPAD . . . . . . . . . . . . . . . .5

CHAPTER 1:  **Buying Your iPad**. . . . . . . . . . . . . . . . . . . . . . 7
    Discover the Newest iPads and iPadOS 18. . . . . . . . . . . . . 8
    Choose the Right iPad for You . . . . . . . . . . . . . . . . . . . 12
    Decide How Much Storage Is Enough . . . . . . . . . . . . . . . 13
    Know What Else You May Need: Internet and Computer . . . . . 15
        Use basic internet access for your iPad. . . . . . . . . . . . 15
        Pair your iPad with a computer . . . . . . . . . . . . . . . . 16
    Choose Wi-Fi Only or Wi-Fi + Cellular . . . . . . . . . . . . . . 16
    Consider iPad Accessories . . . . . . . . . . . . . . . . . . . . . 18
    Explore What's in the Box . . . . . . . . . . . . . . . . . . . . . 19
    Take a First Look at the Gadget . . . . . . . . . . . . . . . . . . 19

CHAPTER 2:  **Exploring Your iPad**. . . . . . . . . . . . . . . . . . . . 25
    See What You Need to Use the iPad . . . . . . . . . . . . . . . 26
    Turn On Your iPad for the First Time . . . . . . . . . . . . . . . 26
    Meet the Multitouch Screen. . . . . . . . . . . . . . . . . . . . 28
    Say Hello to Tap and Swipe. . . . . . . . . . . . . . . . . . . . . 31
    Browsing the App Library . . . . . . . . . . . . . . . . . . . . . 36
    The Dock . . . . . . . . . . . . . . . . . . . . . . . . . . . . . . . 40
    Display and Use the Onscreen Keyboard. . . . . . . . . . . . . 40
        Keyboard shortcuts . . . . . . . . . . . . . . . . . . . . . . . 42
        QuickPath. . . . . . . . . . . . . . . . . . . . . . . . . . . . . 44
    Use the Small Keyboard . . . . . . . . . . . . . . . . . . . . . . 44
    Flick to Search. . . . . . . . . . . . . . . . . . . . . . . . . . . . 46
    Easily Switch Between Apps . . . . . . . . . . . . . . . . . . . . 47
    Use Slide Over and Split View. . . . . . . . . . . . . . . . . . . 48
        Starting with Slide Over . . . . . . . . . . . . . . . . . . . . 49

Moving to Split View . . . . . . . . . . . . . . . . . . . . . . . . . . 50
Examine the iPad Cameras. . . . . . . . . . . . . . . . . . . . . . . 52
Discover Control Center . . . . . . . . . . . . . . . . . . . . . . . . 52
Understand Touch ID . . . . . . . . . . . . . . . . . . . . . . . . . 55
Take a Look at Face ID. . . . . . . . . . . . . . . . . . . . . . . . . 56
Lock Screen Rotation. . . . . . . . . . . . . . . . . . . . . . . . . . 57
Explore the Status Bar. . . . . . . . . . . . . . . . . . . . . . . . . 58
Wonderful Widgets . . . . . . . . . . . . . . . . . . . . . . . . . . . 59
Take Inventory of Preinstalled Apps . . . . . . . . . . . . . . . . . 60
Lock iPad, Turn It Off, or Unlock It. . . . . . . . . . . . . . . . . . 63

CHAPTER 3:  **Beyond the Basics** . . . . . . . . . . . . . . . . . . . . . . . . . . 65
Keep Your iPad's Operating System Updated . . . . . . . . . . . . 66
Charge the Battery. . . . . . . . . . . . . . . . . . . . . . . . . . . 67
Sign into an Apple Account for Music, Movies, and More . . . . . 68
Sync Wirelessly . . . . . . . . . . . . . . . . . . . . . . . . . . . . . 71
Understand iCloud. . . . . . . . . . . . . . . . . . . . . . . . . . . . 72
Turn On iCloud Drive . . . . . . . . . . . . . . . . . . . . . . . . . . 75
Set Up iCloud Sync Settings . . . . . . . . . . . . . . . . . . . . . . 76
Browse Your iPad's Files . . . . . . . . . . . . . . . . . . . . . . . . 77

PART 2: BEGINNING TO USE YOUR IPAD . . . . . . . . . . . . . . . . . . . .81

CHAPTER 4:  **Making Your iPad More Accessible** . . . . . . . . . . . . . 83
Use Magnifier . . . . . . . . . . . . . . . . . . . . . . . . . . . . . . 84
Set Brightness and Night Shift . . . . . . . . . . . . . . . . . . . . 86
Change the Wallpaper. . . . . . . . . . . . . . . . . . . . . . . . . . 88
Set Up VoiceOver . . . . . . . . . . . . . . . . . . . . . . . . . . . . 90
Use VoiceOver. . . . . . . . . . . . . . . . . . . . . . . . . . . . . . 93
Make Additional Vision Settings. . . . . . . . . . . . . . . . . . . . 95
Use iPad with Hearing Aids. . . . . . . . . . . . . . . . . . . . . . . 98
Adjust the Volume . . . . . . . . . . . . . . . . . . . . . . . . . . . 99
Set Up Subtitles and Captioning . . . . . . . . . . . . . . . . . . 100
Say It with Live Speech and Personal Voice . . . . . . . . . . . . 102
Turn On and Work with AssistiveTouch . . . . . . . . . . . . . . . 103
Turn On Additional Physical and Motor Settings. . . . . . . . . . 106
Focus Learning with Guided Access . . . . . . . . . . . . . . . . . 106
Control Your iPad with Voice Control . . . . . . . . . . . . . . . . 109
Control Your iPad with Your Eyes . . . . . . . . . . . . . . . . . .111

Control Your iPad with Vocal Shortcuts . . . . . . . . . . . . . . . . . . . 113
Adjust Accessibility Settings on a Per-App Basis . . . . . . . . . . . 114

CHAPTER 5:  **Conversing with Siri** . . . . . . . . . . . . . . . . . . . . . . . . . . . . . . . . . . . 117
Activate Siri . . . . . . . . . . . . . . . . . . . . . . . . . . . . . . . . . . . . . . . . . . . . 119
Discover All That Siri Can Do . . . . . . . . . . . . . . . . . . . . . . . . . . . . 121
Get Suggestions . . . . . . . . . . . . . . . . . . . . . . . . . . . . . . . . . . . . . . . . 125
Call Contacts via FaceTime . . . . . . . . . . . . . . . . . . . . . . . . . . . . . . 125
Create Reminders and Alerts . . . . . . . . . . . . . . . . . . . . . . . . . . . . . 126
Add Events to Your Calendar . . . . . . . . . . . . . . . . . . . . . . . . . . . . . 127
Play Music . . . . . . . . . . . . . . . . . . . . . . . . . . . . . . . . . . . . . . . . . . . . . 128
Get Directions . . . . . . . . . . . . . . . . . . . . . . . . . . . . . . . . . . . . . . . . . . 129
Ask for Facts . . . . . . . . . . . . . . . . . . . . . . . . . . . . . . . . . . . . . . . . . . . 130
Search the Web . . . . . . . . . . . . . . . . . . . . . . . . . . . . . . . . . . . . . . . . 130
Send Email, Messages, or Tweets . . . . . . . . . . . . . . . . . . . . . . . . 131
Use Dictation . . . . . . . . . . . . . . . . . . . . . . . . . . . . . . . . . . . . . . . . . . 131
Translate Words and Phrases . . . . . . . . . . . . . . . . . . . . . . . . . . . . 132

CHAPTER 6:  **Expanding Your iPad Horizons with Apps** . . . . . . . . . . . . . 135
Search the App Store . . . . . . . . . . . . . . . . . . . . . . . . . . . . . . . . . . . 136
Get Applications from the App Store . . . . . . . . . . . . . . . . . . . . . 138
Organize Your Applications on Home Screen Pages . . . . . . . . 139
Organize Apps in Folders . . . . . . . . . . . . . . . . . . . . . . . . . . . . . . . 142
Delete Apps You No Longer Need . . . . . . . . . . . . . . . . . . . . . . . . 143
Update Apps . . . . . . . . . . . . . . . . . . . . . . . . . . . . . . . . . . . . . . . . . . . 145
Purchase and Download Games . . . . . . . . . . . . . . . . . . . . . . . . . 147

CHAPTER 7:  **Organizing Contacts** . . . . . . . . . . . . . . . . . . . . . . . . . . . . . . . . . 151
Add a Contact . . . . . . . . . . . . . . . . . . . . . . . . . . . . . . . . . . . . . . . . . . 152
Sync Contacts with iCloud . . . . . . . . . . . . . . . . . . . . . . . . . . . . . . . 155
Add Photos to Contacts . . . . . . . . . . . . . . . . . . . . . . . . . . . . . . . . . 157
Designate Related People . . . . . . . . . . . . . . . . . . . . . . . . . . . . . . . 160
Set Individual Ringtones and Text Tones . . . . . . . . . . . . . . . . . . 161
Delete a Contact . . . . . . . . . . . . . . . . . . . . . . . . . . . . . . . . . . . . . . . 163

CHAPTER 8:  **Getting Social with Your iPad** . . . . . . . . . . . . . . . . . . . . . . . . 165
What You Need to Use FaceTime . . . . . . . . . . . . . . . . . . . . . . . . . 166
An Overview of FaceTime . . . . . . . . . . . . . . . . . . . . . . . . . . . . . . . 167
Make a FaceTime Call with Wi-Fi or Cellular . . . . . . . . . . . . . . . 168

Use a Memoji with FaceTime . . . . . . . . . . . . . . . . . . . . . . . . . . . 170
Accept, Enjoy, and End a FaceTime Call . . . . . . . . . . . . . . . . 170
Switch Views . . . . . . . . . . . . . . . . . . . . . . . . . . . . . . . . . . . . . . . . 172
Set Up an iMessage Account . . . . . . . . . . . . . . . . . . . . . . . . . . 172
Use Messages to Address, Create, and Send Messages. . . . . 174
Read Messages. . . . . . . . . . . . . . . . . . . . . . . . . . . . . . . . . . . . . . . 176
Clear a Conversation . . . . . . . . . . . . . . . . . . . . . . . . . . . . . . . . . 177
Send Emojis with Your Text . . . . . . . . . . . . . . . . . . . . . . . . . . . 178
Use Messages Apps and Tools. . . . . . . . . . . . . . . . . . . . . . . . . . 179
Send and Receive Audio . . . . . . . . . . . . . . . . . . . . . . . . . . . . . . . 181
Send a Photo or Video. . . . . . . . . . . . . . . . . . . . . . . . . . . . . . . . . 181
Send a Map of Your Location . . . . . . . . . . . . . . . . . . . . . . . . . . 182
Understand Group Messaging. . . . . . . . . . . . . . . . . . . . . . . . . . 183
Find and Install Social Media Apps . . . . . . . . . . . . . . . . . . . . . 185
Create a Facebook Account . . . . . . . . . . . . . . . . . . . . . . . . . . . . 187
Create an X Account. . . . . . . . . . . . . . . . . . . . . . . . . . . . . . . . . . 188
Create an Instagram Account. . . . . . . . . . . . . . . . . . . . . . . . . . . 189

CHAPTER 9:  **Browsing with Safari** . . . . . . . . . . . . . . . . . . . . . . . . . . . . . 191
Connect to the Internet. . . . . . . . . . . . . . . . . . . . . . . . . . . . . . . . 192
Explore Safari . . . . . . . . . . . . . . . . . . . . . . . . . . . . . . . . . . . . . . . 193
Navigate Web Pages . . . . . . . . . . . . . . . . . . . . . . . . . . . . . . . . . . 195
Use Tabbed Browsing . . . . . . . . . . . . . . . . . . . . . . . . . . . . . . . . . 197
Organize with Tab Groups . . . . . . . . . . . . . . . . . . . . . . . . . . . . 199
View Browsing History. . . . . . . . . . . . . . . . . . . . . . . . . . . . . . . . 202
Search the Web . . . . . . . . . . . . . . . . . . . . . . . . . . . . . . . . . . . . . . 204
Add and Use Bookmarks. . . . . . . . . . . . . . . . . . . . . . . . . . . . . . . 204
Save Links and Web Pages to Safari Reading List . . . . . . . . . . 208
Enable Private Browsing . . . . . . . . . . . . . . . . . . . . . . . . . . . . . . 209
Download Files . . . . . . . . . . . . . . . . . . . . . . . . . . . . . . . . . . . . . . . 210
Translate Web Pages . . . . . . . . . . . . . . . . . . . . . . . . . . . . . . . . . 211

CHAPTER 10:  **Working with Email in Mail** . . . . . . . . . . . . . . . . . . . . . . . 213
Add an Email Account . . . . . . . . . . . . . . . . . . . . . . . . . . . . . . . . 214
Manually Set Up an Email Account . . . . . . . . . . . . . . . . . . . . . 216
Open Mail and Read Messages . . . . . . . . . . . . . . . . . . . . . . . . . 218
Reply To or Forward Email . . . . . . . . . . . . . . . . . . . . . . . . . . . . 220
Create and Send a New Message . . . . . . . . . . . . . . . . . . . . . . . . 222
Format Email. . . . . . . . . . . . . . . . . . . . . . . . . . . . . . . . . . . . . . . . 224

Search Email . . . . . . . . . . . . . . . . . . . . . . . . . . . . . . . . . . . . 228
Mark Email as Unread or Flag for Follow-Up . . . . . . . . . . . . . . . 229
Create an Event from Email Contents. . . . . . . . . . . . . . . . . . . . 231
Delete Email . . . . . . . . . . . . . . . . . . . . . . . . . . . . . . . . . . . . 232
Organize Email . . . . . . . . . . . . . . . . . . . . . . . . . . . . . . . . . . 233
Create a VIP List . . . . . . . . . . . . . . . . . . . . . . . . . . . . . . . . . 235

**PART 3: ENJOYING MEDIA** . . . . . . . . . . . . . . . . . . . . . . . . . . 237

CHAPTER 11: **Shopping the iTunes Store and Apple TV** . . . . . . . . . . . 239
Explore the iTunes Store. . . . . . . . . . . . . . . . . . . . . . . . . . . . 240
Buy a Selection . . . . . . . . . . . . . . . . . . . . . . . . . . . . . . . . . . 242
Rent or Buy Movies and TV Shows . . . . . . . . . . . . . . . . . . . . . 243
Use Apple Pay and Wallet . . . . . . . . . . . . . . . . . . . . . . . . . . . 245
Set Up Family Sharing . . . . . . . . . . . . . . . . . . . . . . . . . . . . . 246

CHAPTER 12: **Reading Books** . . . . . . . . . . . . . . . . . . . . . . . . . . . 249
Find Books with Apple Books . . . . . . . . . . . . . . . . . . . . . . . . . 250
Explore Other E-Book Sources . . . . . . . . . . . . . . . . . . . . . . . . 253
Buy Books . . . . . . . . . . . . . . . . . . . . . . . . . . . . . . . . . . . . . 255
Navigate a Book . . . . . . . . . . . . . . . . . . . . . . . . . . . . . . . . . 256
Customize Your Reading Experience. . . . . . . . . . . . . . . . . . . . . 259
Select and customize themes. . . . . . . . . . . . . . . . . . . . . . 259
Modify your book's font. . . . . . . . . . . . . . . . . . . . . . . . . . 260
Adjust Accessibility & Layout options . . . . . . . . . . . . . . . . 261

CHAPTER 13: **Enjoying Music and Podcasts** . . . . . . . . . . . . . . . . . . 265
View the Music Library . . . . . . . . . . . . . . . . . . . . . . . . . . . . . 266
Create Playlists . . . . . . . . . . . . . . . . . . . . . . . . . . . . . . . . . . 269
Search for Music. . . . . . . . . . . . . . . . . . . . . . . . . . . . . . . . . 270
Play Music . . . . . . . . . . . . . . . . . . . . . . . . . . . . . . . . . . . . . 271
Shuffle Music . . . . . . . . . . . . . . . . . . . . . . . . . . . . . . . . . . . 276
Listen with Your Earbuds . . . . . . . . . . . . . . . . . . . . . . . . . . . . 276
Listen with Spatial Audio. . . . . . . . . . . . . . . . . . . . . . . . . . . . 277
Use AirPlay . . . . . . . . . . . . . . . . . . . . . . . . . . . . . . . . . . . . . 279
Play Music with Radio . . . . . . . . . . . . . . . . . . . . . . . . . . . . . . 279
Find and Subscribe to Podcasts . . . . . . . . . . . . . . . . . . . . . . . 281
Play Podcasts . . . . . . . . . . . . . . . . . . . . . . . . . . . . . . . . . . . 284

CHAPTER 14: **Taking and Sharing Photos** . . . . . . . . . . . . . . . . . . . . . . . . .287
Take Pictures with the iPad Cameras . . . . . . . . . . . . . . . . . . . .288
View Your Photos . . . . . . . . . . . . . . . . . . . . . . . . . . . . . . . . . . . .292
Edit Photos . . . . . . . . . . . . . . . . . . . . . . . . . . . . . . . . . . . . . . . . . .295
Organize Photos . . . . . . . . . . . . . . . . . . . . . . . . . . . . . . . . . . . . .296
Share Photos via Mail, Social Media, or Other Apps . . . . . . . .298
Share a Photo Using AirDrop . . . . . . . . . . . . . . . . . . . . . . . . . . .300
Share Photos Using iCloud Photo Sharing . . . . . . . . . . . . . . . .300
Print Photos . . . . . . . . . . . . . . . . . . . . . . . . . . . . . . . . . . . . . . . . .301
Delete Photos . . . . . . . . . . . . . . . . . . . . . . . . . . . . . . . . . . . . . . . .302

CHAPTER 15: **Creating and Watching Videos** . . . . . . . . . . . . . . . . . . . . . . .305
Capture Your Own Videos with the Built-In Cameras . . . . . . .306
Edit Videos . . . . . . . . . . . . . . . . . . . . . . . . . . . . . . . . . . . . . . . . . . .308
Play Movies or TV Shows with the TV App . . . . . . . . . . . . . . . .310
Content from third-party providers . . . . . . . . . . . . . . . . . . . .310
Content from Apple . . . . . . . . . . . . . . . . . . . . . . . . . . . . . . . . .312
Turn On Closed-Captioning . . . . . . . . . . . . . . . . . . . . . . . . . . . .315
Delete a Video from the iPad . . . . . . . . . . . . . . . . . . . . . . . . . . .316

PART 4: LIVING WITH YOUR IPAD . . . . . . . . . . . . . . . . . . . . . . . . . .319

CHAPTER 16: **Keeping on Schedule with Calendar and Clock** . . . . . . .321
View Your Calendar . . . . . . . . . . . . . . . . . . . . . . . . . . . . . . . . . . .322
Add Calendar Events and Reminders . . . . . . . . . . . . . . . . . . . .326
Add Events or Reminders with Siri . . . . . . . . . . . . . . . . . . . . . .327
Create Repeating Events . . . . . . . . . . . . . . . . . . . . . . . . . . . . . . .328
View an Event . . . . . . . . . . . . . . . . . . . . . . . . . . . . . . . . . . . . . . . .329
Add an Alert to an Event . . . . . . . . . . . . . . . . . . . . . . . . . . . . . . .330
Select a default Calendar alert . . . . . . . . . . . . . . . . . . . . . . . .330
Set up an alert for an event . . . . . . . . . . . . . . . . . . . . . . . . . . .330
Search for an Event . . . . . . . . . . . . . . . . . . . . . . . . . . . . . . . . . . .332
Add a Calendar Account . . . . . . . . . . . . . . . . . . . . . . . . . . . . . . .333
Use a Family Calendar . . . . . . . . . . . . . . . . . . . . . . . . . . . . . . . . .335
Delete an Event . . . . . . . . . . . . . . . . . . . . . . . . . . . . . . . . . . . . . .337
Display the Clock App . . . . . . . . . . . . . . . . . . . . . . . . . . . . . . . . .338
Delete a Clock . . . . . . . . . . . . . . . . . . . . . . . . . . . . . . . . . . . . . . . .339
Set an Alarm . . . . . . . . . . . . . . . . . . . . . . . . . . . . . . . . . . . . . . . . .340
Use Stopwatch and Timer . . . . . . . . . . . . . . . . . . . . . . . . . . . . . .342

CHAPTER 17: **Working with Reminders and Notifications** . . . . . . . . . . . 343

Create a Reminder . . . . . . . . . . . . . . . . . . . . . . . . . . . . . . . . . 344

Edit Reminder Details . . . . . . . . . . . . . . . . . . . . . . . . . . . . . . 345

Schedule a Reminder by Time, Location, or When
Messaging . . . . . . . . . . . . . . . . . . . . . . . . . . . . . . . . . . . . . . . . 347

Create a List . . . . . . . . . . . . . . . . . . . . . . . . . . . . . . . . . . . . . . . 350

Sync with Other Devices and Calendars . . . . . . . . . . . . . . . . 352

Mark as Complete or Delete a Reminder . . . . . . . . . . . . . . . 353

Get Notified! . . . . . . . . . . . . . . . . . . . . . . . . . . . . . . . . . . . . . . 355

Notification summaries . . . . . . . . . . . . . . . . . . . . . . . . . . . 356

Set notification types . . . . . . . . . . . . . . . . . . . . . . . . . . . . 358

View Notification Center . . . . . . . . . . . . . . . . . . . . . . . . . 360

Stay Focused and Undisturbed . . . . . . . . . . . . . . . . . . . . . . 362

Set up a focus . . . . . . . . . . . . . . . . . . . . . . . . . . . . . . . . . . . 363

Turn on a focus . . . . . . . . . . . . . . . . . . . . . . . . . . . . . . . . . 364

CHAPTER 18: **Making Notes** . . . . . . . . . . . . . . . . . . . . . . . . . . . . . . . . . . 367

Open a Blank Note . . . . . . . . . . . . . . . . . . . . . . . . . . . . . . . . . 368

Use Copy and Paste . . . . . . . . . . . . . . . . . . . . . . . . . . . . . . . . 371

Insert Attachments . . . . . . . . . . . . . . . . . . . . . . . . . . . . . . . . 373

Add a Drawing or Handwriting . . . . . . . . . . . . . . . . . . . . . . 374

Apply a Text Style . . . . . . . . . . . . . . . . . . . . . . . . . . . . . . . . . 376

Create a Checklist . . . . . . . . . . . . . . . . . . . . . . . . . . . . . . . . . 377

Delete a Note . . . . . . . . . . . . . . . . . . . . . . . . . . . . . . . . . . . . . 379

Speeding Along with Quick Notes . . . . . . . . . . . . . . . . . . . . 380

Smarten Things Up . . . . . . . . . . . . . . . . . . . . . . . . . . . . . . . . 382

CHAPTER 19: **Using Utilities** . . . . . . . . . . . . . . . . . . . . . . . . . . . . . . . . . . 385

Use the Calculator App . . . . . . . . . . . . . . . . . . . . . . . . . . . . . 385

Record Voice Memos . . . . . . . . . . . . . . . . . . . . . . . . . . . . . . . 389

Measure Distances . . . . . . . . . . . . . . . . . . . . . . . . . . . . . . . . . 392

Find a Missing Apple Device . . . . . . . . . . . . . . . . . . . . . . . . . 395

Get the Latest Weather Updates and Alerts . . . . . . . . . . . . . 398

Translate Words and Phrases . . . . . . . . . . . . . . . . . . . . . . . . 400

Manage Passwords and Other Stuff . . . . . . . . . . . . . . . . . . . 404

CHAPTER 20: **Troubleshooting and Maintaining Your iPad** . . . . . . . . . 407

Keep the iPad Screen Clean . . . . . . . . . . . . . . . . . . . . . . . . . . 408

Protect Your Gadget with a Case . . . . . . . . . . . . . . . . . . . . . 409

Extend Your iPad's Battery Life . . . . . . . . . . . . . . . . . . . . . . . . . 410
What to Do with a Nonresponsive iPad . . . . . . . . . . . . . . . . . . 412
Update the iPadOS Software . . . . . . . . . . . . . . . . . . . . . . . . . . . 413
Restore the Sound . . . . . . . . . . . . . . . . . . . . . . . . . . . . . . . . . . . 414
Get Support. . . . . . . . . . . . . . . . . . . . . . . . . . . . . . . . . . . . . . . . 415
Back Up to iCloud. . . . . . . . . . . . . . . . . . . . . . . . . . . . . . . . . . . . 416

INDEX . . . . . . . . . . . . . . . . . . . . . . . . . . . . . . . . . . . . . . . . . . . . . 421

# Introduction

**B**ecause you bought this book (or are thinking about buying it), you've probably already made the decision to buy an iPad. The iPad is designed to be easy to use, but you can still spend hours exploring the preinstalled apps, configuring settings, getting help from Apple Intelligence, and finding out how to sync the device to your computer or through iCloud. I've invested those hours so that you don't have to — and I've added advice and tips for getting the most from your iPad.

This book helps you get going with your iPad quickly and painlessly so that you can move directly to the fun part.

# About This Book

If you're a mature person who is relatively new to using a tablet, or you want to update to iPadOS 18 and learn about all the new features of that version, you need this book. In *iPad For Seniors For Dummies*, you discover the basics of buying an iPad, working with its preinstalled apps, getting on the internet, and using social media.

This book uses a few conventions to assist you:

» **Bold:** I use bold type to make figure references stand out in the text.

» **Italics:** I use italics for emphasis and for placeholder text that substitutes for what you might be seeing onscreen, such as *Price* when the actual price is what you would be seeing.

» **Command sequences:** When you need to follow a series of actions, you might see it presented like this: Tap Settings ⇨ General ⇨ Date & Time. That means to first tap the Settings icon, and then tap General on the screen that appears, and then tap the Date & Time option.

- » **URLs:** Web addresses appear in monofont type in the printed book and as clickable links in the e-book, like this: `www.dummies.com`.

**TIP**

The Tip icon in the margin of a page alerts you to brief pieces of advice to help you to take a skill further, provide an alternative way of doing something, or, occasionally, to be aware of a problem an action might cause.

This book uses nontechnical language, like all *Dummies* books, as it guides you through the basic steps of working with your iPad. To make the content of this book easily accessible, it's organized into sets of tasks in the following parts:

- » **Part 1: Getting to Know Your iPad:** The first chapter in this part guides you through buying an iPad, in case you don't have one yet, as well as any accessories you might need. Also in this part, you learn what buttons to push and screen elements to tap, and what movements to make to turn on and use your iPad effectively. If you need to update your iPad's operating system to the latest version, you can find out about that and more in this part.

- » **Part 2: Beginning to Use Your iPad:** This part begins by showing you how to enable accessibility features that may help you use your iPad more easily. You then learn more about Apple's virtual assistant, Siri, and how to manage apps and contacts and use communication tools such as FaceTime, Messages, and social media apps. Finally, I give you a good start on surfing the web and sending and receiving email.

- » **Part 3: Enjoying Media:** Your iPad will quickly become indispensable for all things media related. From reading books to watching movies and television shows to listening to your favorite tunes and podcasts, this part shows you the ropes for acquiring and enjoying new content. You also find out how to take stunning pictures and videos using your iPad's built-in cameras.

- » **Part 4: Living with Your iPad:** Finally, this part of the book helps you to stay on top of your busy life by taking notes and by setting calendar events, appointments, and reminders of important items on your to-do lists. You also explore several helpful utilities that come with iPadOS 18 and learn how to troubleshoot and maintain your iPad.

# Foolish Assumptions

This book assumes that you are a mature iPad user who wants to get straight to the basics of using an iPad. It assumes also that you may not be familiar with using a tablet, or that you are updating to iPadOS 18 and want to discover all the new features that come with that update. In writing this book as a quinquagenarian myself, I've tried to consider the types of activities that might interest someone who is 50 years old or older.

# Beyond the Book

Like every *Dummies* book, this one comes with a cheat sheet that brings together some of the most commonly needed information for people learning to use, in this case, the iPad. To get the cheat sheet, head to www.dummies.com and enter *iPad For Seniors For Dummies Cheat Sheet* in the Search box.

# Where to Go from Here

You can work through this book from beginning to end or simply open a chapter to solve a problem or acquire a specific new skill whenever you need it. The steps in every task quickly get you to where you want to go without a lot of technical explanation.

At the time I wrote this book, all the information it contained was accurate for the 13-inch iPad Pro (M4), 12.9-inch iPad Pro (third through sixth generations), 11-inch iPad Pro (first through fifth generations), iPad (seventh through tenth generations), 13-inch iPad Air (M2), iPad Air (third through sixth generations), iPad mini (fifth and sixth generations), version 18 of iPadOS (the operating system used by the iPad), and version 12.8 (for Macs) or 12.12 (for PCs) or later of iTunes. Apple may introduce new iPad models and new versions of iOS and iTunes between book editions. If you've bought a new iPad and found that its hardware, user interface, or the version of iTunes on your computer looks a little different, be sure to check out what Apple has to say at www.apple.com/ipad. You'll no doubt find updates there on the company's latest releases.

# 1

# Getting to Know Your iPad

**IN THIS PART . . .**

Choosing and purchasing your iPad

Navigating the Home screen, discovering preinstalled apps, and customizing your experience

Updating and synchronizing your iPad and understanding iCloud

IN THIS CHAPTER

» Discover what's new in iPads
and iPadOS 18

» Choose the right iPad for you

» Understand what you need to
use your iPad

» Explore what's in the box

» Take a look at the gadget

Chapter **1**

# Buying Your iPad

You've read about it. You've seen the lines at Apple Stores on the day a new version of the iPad is released. You're so intrigued that you've decided to get your own iPad. Perhaps you're not new to tablet computers but are ready to make the switch to the ultimate in such devices. With your iPad, you can have fun with apps, such as games and exercise trackers; explore the online world; read e-books, magazines, and other periodicals; take and organize photos and videos; listen to music and watch movies; and a lot more.

Trust me: You've made a good decision, because the iPad redefines the tablet computing experience in an exciting way. It's also a perfect fit for seniors.

In this chapter, you learn about the advantages of the iPad, as well as where to buy this little gem and associated data plans from providers for iPads that support cellular data. After you have one in your hands, I help you explore what's in the box and get an overview of the little buttons and slots you'll encounter. Luckily, the iPad has very few of them.

# Discover the Newest iPads and iPadOS 18

Apple's iPad gets its features from a combination of hardware and its software operating system, which is called iPadOS (short for iPad operating system). The most current version of the operating system is iPadOS 18. It's helpful to understand which new features the latest iPad models and iPadOS 18 bring to the table (all of which are covered in more detail in this book).

The iPad is currently available in a variety of sizes and configurations, depending on the version of iPad:

» **iPad:** The tenth-generation model takes the iPad up a notch with a touchscreen that measures 10.9 inches diagonally and boasts a fast 64-bit desktop-class A14 Bionic processor.

» **iPad Air:** The sixth-generation iPad Air sports a powerful M2 processor and comes in two touchscreen sizes, one measuring 11 inches diagonally and the other at 13 inches diagonally.

» **iPad mini:** The iPad mini 7's touchscreen measures 8.3 inches diagonally. This iPad uses an A17 Pro processor to do the behind-the-scenes work.

» **iPad Pro:** The two seventh-generation iPad Pro models are the fastest of the bunch. One's touchscreen measures 11 inches diagonally, and the other's is 13 inches; they both come with blazing-fast M4 processors, which are the same processors used in many of Apple's newest Mac desktop and laptop computers.

TIP

Dimensions of devices are typically shown in the units of measurement commonly used in a region. This means, for example, that the basic tenth-generation iPad is shown on Apple's U.S. site as being 9.79 inches (248.6 mm) high and 7.07 inches (179.5 mm) wide. In metric-system countries, both dimensions are given, but the order is reversed. When it comes to screen sizes, however, the dimensions are given in inches.

In addition to the features of previous iPads, the latest iPad models offer the following:

» **Ultra Retina XDR and Liquid Retina displays:** In addition to screen size, screen resolution has evolved so that Apple's Ultra Retina XDR and Liquid Retina displays, both of which support very high-resolution graphics, now appear across the line. The name derives from the concept that individual pixels on the screen are so small that they can't be distinguished at normal viewing distance.

» **Apple Pencil:** Originally designed exclusively for use with iPad Pro models, the Apple Pencil now works with all the latest iPad models. (Be sure to check which version of Apple Pencil will work with your iPad by visiting www.apple.com/apple-pencil.) Apple Pencil lets you draw and write on the screen with a familiar pencil-style tool rather than with your finger. The Apple Pencil contains a battery and sophisticated processing powers that make the experience of using it very much like (and sometimes better than) a traditional pencil. Third-party pencils and drawing tools exist, but Apple's integration of Apple Pencil is remarkably smooth; the product has taken off quickly among graphic artists, illustrators, and designers. As other people have discovered its usability for marking up documents, it is becoming more and more common in business environments.

» **Neural Engine:** The Neural Engine is a component of the processor in every iPad that focuses on handling specialized tasks related to artificial intelligence, image and speech processing, and more cool things.

» **Touch ID:** This security feature is included on several iPad models. Sensors in the Home button (ninth-generation iPad) or top button (iPad Air, iPad mini, and tenth-generation iPad) allow you to train the iPad to recognize your fingerprint and grant you access with a finger press. Touch ID also allows you to use the Apple Pay feature to buy items without having to enter your payment information every time.

» **Facial recognition:** Touch ID is replaced with Face ID on certain iPad models. Using Face ID and the front-facing camera, your iPad unlocks when it recognizes your face. It can be used also for purchases and other tasks.

- » **Barometric sensor:** On all iPad models, this sensor makes it possible for your iPad to sense air pressure around you. This feature is especially cool when you're hiking a mountain, where the weather may change as you climb. Perhaps more to the point, the changes in barometric pressure can be sensed on a smaller scale so that elevation can be measured as you move normally.

- » **Smart Connector for Smart Keyboard:** In addition to the onscreen keyboard, you can use a Smart Connector to hook up a Smart Keyboard, an external keyboard that makes getting complex work done much easier. Smart Connector is supported for all iPad models, with the exception of iPad mini.

- » **Live photos:** Using the 3D Touch feature, you can press a photo on the screen to make it play like a short video. The Camera app captures 1.5 seconds on either side of the moment when you capture the photo, so anything moving in the image you photographed, such as water flowing in a stream, seems to move when you press and hold the still photo.

The iPadOS 18 update to the operating system adds many features, including (but definitely not limited to) the following:

- » **Apple Intelligence:** Apple Intelligence is Apple's spin on generative artificial intelligence. This gamechanger includes a greater understanding of personal context for Siri, which will be able to better understand and interact intelligently when you ask something like, "When is my granddaughter's plane landing?" Apple Intelligence can assist with writing just about anything and includes built-in access to the latest incarnation of ChatGPT (a ChatGPT account is not required!). Information you request will never leave the comfort of your iPad and Apple's servers without your explicit permission. Some Apple Intelligence features are available now but more will be released in future updates of iPadOS. Apple Intelligence is available only for iPad mini (A17 Pro), iPad Pro 11-inch (3rd and 4th generations) and 12.9-inch (5th and 6th generations), iPad Air (5th generation), or newer. For much more information than I can squeeze in here, please visit www.apple.com/apple-intelligence.

» **Notes:** This gem of an app is getting better all the time, with new features such as live audio transcription and Smart Script. With live audio transcription, you can record audio in a note and have Notes generate a transcription on the fly! Smart Script re-creates your own handwriting style from your notes when you jot them down using an Apple Pencil (or even your finger), smoothing and straightening the text.

» **Customization:** You can customize your iPad more than ever before. Move apps and widgets anywhere you want on the Home screen pages. Lock and hide apps such as financial or medical apps to prevent other people from accessing them. Use custom colors for your app icons and text. Even Control Center has been given a big upgrade.

» **Photos:** The Photos app has been heavily redesigned, making it easier for you to find photos based on a range of topics. A carousel helps you browse your photos and videos with ease.

» **Built-in apps have been updated:** iPadOS 18 provides performance enhancements and interface upgrades for all the apps that come preinstalled with it, bringing many into the realm of their desktop computer counterparts.

TIP

Don't need all the built-in apps? You can remove them from your Home screen. (Note that built-in apps take up very little of your iPad's storage space.) When you remove a built-in app from your Home screen, you aren't deleting it — you're hiding it. And if you change your mind, you can easily add them back to your Home screen by searching for them in the App Store and tapping the Get button.

These are but a very few of the improvements made to the latest version of iPadOS. I highly suggest visiting www.apple.com/ipados to find out more.

# Choose the Right iPad for You

The most obvious differences among iPad models (the current 11-inch and 13-inch iPad Air models are shown in **Figure 1-1**) are their size and weight, with the Pro being biggest, followed by iPad Air, then iPad, and finally the smallest, iPad mini. All models come in a variety of colors to suit everyone's taste.

*Photo courtesy of Apple Inc.*

**FIGURE 1-1**

All models come either with Wi-Fi only, so you access a Wi-Fi network for internet access, or with Wi-Fi + Cellular for connecting to the internet through Wi-Fi or a cellular network (as your cellphone does). The iPad models also differ in available memory and price based on that memory (prices are accurate as of this writing and are subject to change):

>> **iPad Pro 11-inch:** Wi-Fi models come in 256GB for $999, 512GB for $1,199, 1TB for $1,599, and 2TB for $1,999; Wi-Fi + Cellular

models of each memory configuration cost $200 more than their Wi-Fi–only counterparts.

» **iPad Pro 13-inch:** Wi-Fi models come in 256GB for $1299, 512GB for $1,499, 1TB for $1,899, and 2TB for $2,299; Wi-Fi + Cellular models of each memory configuration cost $200 more than their Wi-Fi–only counterparts.

» **iPad Air 11-inch:** Wi-Fi models come in 128GB for $599, 256GB for $699, 512GB for $899, and 1TB for $1,099; Wi-Fi + Cellular models of each memory configuration cost $150 more than their Wi-Fi-only counterparts.

» **iPad Air 13-inch:** Wi-Fi models come in 128GB for $799, 256GB for $899, 512GB for $1,099, and 1TB for $1,299; Wi-Fi + Cellular models of each memory configuration cost $150 more than their Wi-Fi-only counterparts.

» **iPad (tenth generation):** Wi-Fi models come in 64GB for $349 and 256GB for $499; Wi-Fi + Cellular models of each memory configuration cost $150 more than their Wi-Fi-only counterparts.

» **iPad mini:** The Wi-Fi model comes in 128GB for $499, 256GB for $599, and 512GB for $799; Wi-Fi + Cellular models of each memory configuration cost $150 more than their Wi-Fi-only counterparts.

iPad models vary in screen quality and resolution, camera quality, and so on. Logically, the bigger the iPad, the bigger the price and (usually) the higher the quality.

# Decide How Much Storage Is Enough

Storage is a measure of how much information — for example, movies, photos, and software applications (apps) — you can store on a computing device. Storage can also affect your iPad's performance when handling such tasks as streaming favorite TV shows from the web or downloading music.

*Streaming* refers to playing video or music content from the web (or from other devices) rather than playing a file stored on your iPad. You can enjoy a lot of material online without ever downloading its full content to your iPad — and given that some iPad models have relatively small amounts of storage, streaming is a good idea. See Chapters 11, 13, and 15 for more about getting your music and movies online.

Your storage options with the various iPad models range from 64 gigabytes (GB) to 2 terabytes (TB), which is equivalent to 2,000GB. You must choose the right amount of storage because you can't open the unit and add more as you typically can with a desktop computer. However, Apple has thoughtfully provided iCloud, a service you can use to store content on the internet. (You can read more about iCloud in Chapter 3.)

How much storage is enough for your iPad? Here's a guideline:

» If you regularly work with large media files, such as movies or TV shows, you might need 512GB or higher. For example, if you shoot 4K video at 60 frames per second, that will take roughly 1GB of storage space for every two-and-a-half minutes of footage. In light of this fact, at least 1TB of storage may be more appealing if you shoot a lot of video.

» If you like lots of media, such as movies or TV shows, you may need at least 256GB or 512GB.

» For most people who manage a reasonable number of photos, download some music, and watch heavy-duty media (such as movies) online, 128GB or 256GB is probably sufficient.

» If you simply want to check email, browse the web, and write short notes to yourself, 64GB is likely plenty.

Do you know how big a gigabyte (GB) is? Consider this: Just about any computer you buy today comes with a minimum of 256GB of storage. Computers have to tackle larger tasks than iPads, so that number makes sense. The iPad, which uses a technology called *flash storage* for storing data, is meant (to a great extent) to help you experience online media and email; it doesn't have to store much since it pulls lots of content from the internet. In the world of storage, 64GB for any kind of storage is puny if you keep lots of content (such as audio, video, and photos) on the device. As mentioned earlier, some iPad models are offering *terabytes* (TB) of storage; 1TB is equal to 1,000GB.

# Know What Else You May Need: Internet and Computer

Although you can use your iPad on its own without any internet or Wi-Fi access and without a computer to pair it with, it's easier if you have internet access and a computer that you can (occasionally) use with your iPad.

## Use basic internet access for your iPad

You need to be able to connect to the internet to take advantage of most iPad features. If you have an Apple Account, you can have an iCloud account, Apple's online storage service, to store and share content online, and you can use a computer to download photos, music, or applications from non-Apple online sources (such as stores, sharing sites, or your local library) and transfer them to your iPad through a process called syncing, which you learn about in Chapter 3. You can also use a computer or iCloud to register your iPad the first time you start it, although you can have the folks at the Apple Store handle registration for you if you have an Apple Store nearby. If you don't have a store nearby, visit www.apple.com/shop/help for assistance.

You can set up your iPad without an internet connection and without going to an Apple Store: The best way to find out more information is to contact https://support.apple.com/ through an internet connection on another device or at a public library or internet cafe.

Can you use your iPad without owning a computer and just use public Wi-Fi hotspots to go online (or a cellular connection, if you have such a model)? Yes. To go online using a Wi-Fi–only iPad and to use many of its built-in features at home, however, you need to have a home Wi-Fi network available.

## Pair your iPad with a computer

For syncing with a computer, Apple's iPad User Guide recommends that you have

» A Mac or PC with a USB 2.0 or 3.0 port and one of these operating systems:

- macOS version 10.13 (High Sierra) or newer
- Windows 10 or newer

» iTunes 12.9 or newer on a Mac running macOS El Capitan (10.11.6) through macOS Mojave (10.14.6), Finder on Mac's running macOS Catalina (10.15) and newer, and iTunes 12.12.10 or newer on a PC, available at www.apple.com/itunes/download or via the Microsoft Store

» Internet access

» An Apple Account

Apple has set up its iTunes software and the iCloud service to give you two ways to manage content for your iPad — including movies, music, or photos you've downloaded — and to specify how to sync your calendar and contact information.

There are a lot of tech terms to absorb here (iCloud, iTunes, syncing, and so on). Don't worry: Chapters 2 and 3 cover these in more detail.

# Choose Wi-Fi Only or Wi-Fi + Cellular

You use Wi-Fi to connect to a wireless network at home or at locations such as an internet cafe, a library, a grocery store, or any public transportation that offers Wi-Fi. This type of network uses short-range radio to connect to the internet; its range is reasonably limited, so if you leave home or walk out of the coffee shop, you can't use it anymore. (These limitations may change, however, as towns install community-wide Wi-Fi networks.)

The cellular technologies allow an iPad to connect to the internet via a widespread cellular network. You use it in much the same way that you make calls from just about anywhere with your cellphone. A Wi-Fi + Cellular iPad costs more than the basic Wi-Fi–only model, but it also includes GPS (Global Positioning System) service, which pinpoints your location so that you can get more accurate location information and driving directions.

Also, to use your cellular network in the United States, you must pay a monthly fee. The good news is that no carrier requires a long-term contract, which you probably had to have when you bought your cellphone and its service plan. You can pay for a connection during the month you visit your grandkids or friends, for example, and get rid of it when you arrive home. Features, data allowance (which relates to accessing email or downloading items from the internet, for example), and prices vary by carrier and could change at any time, so visit each carrier's website to see what it offers. Note that if you intend to stream videos (watch them on your iPad from the internet), you can eat through your data plan allowance quickly.

How do you choose? If you want to wander around the woods or town — or take long drives with your iPad continually connected to the internet to get step-by-step navigation info from the Maps app — get Wi-Fi + Cellular and pay the additional costs. Don't bother with cellular if you'll use your iPad mainly at home or via a Wi-Fi hotspot (a location where Wi-Fi access to the internet is available, such as a local coffee shop or bookstore). You can find lots of hotspots at libraries, restaurants, hotels, airports, and other locations.

If you have a Wi-Fi–only iPad, you can use the hotspot feature on a smartphone, which allows the iPad to use your phone's cellular connection to go online if you have a data-use plan that supports hotspot use with your phone service carrier. Check out the features of your phone to turn on the hotspot feature.

# Consider iPad Accessories

At present, Apple and many other companies offer some accessories that you may want to check out when you purchase your iPad, including the following:

» **iPad cases and covers:** Your iPad isn't cheap, and unlike a laptop computer, it has a constantly exposed screen that can be damaged if you drop or scratch it. Investing in a good iPad case or cover is a good idea if you intend to take your iPad out of your house.

» **Printers:** Various HP, Brother, Canon, and Epson printers support the wireless AirPrint feature. At this writing, prices range from $129 to $399, and discounts are often available. Be sure to check whether your current printer will work before going out to purchase a new one.

» **Smart Keyboards:** You can buy an attachable keyboard for certain iPad models, which will make working with productivity apps much easier. These keyboards connect to your iPad to provide power and transmit data between the devices. Also, the Magic Keyboard from Apple for iPad Pro includes a trackpad for easy navigation without using your finger on the screen.

» **Apple Pencil:** For $79 (Apple Pencil) or $129 (Apple Pencil Pro), you can buy the highly sophisticated stylus for use with the iPad. The Apple Pencil makes it easy to draw on your iPad screen or manage complex interactions more precisely.

» **Apple Digital AV Adapter:** To connect devices to output high-definition media, you can buy this adapter for about $40 and use it with an HDMI cable. More and more devices are using this technology, such as projectors and TVs. But remember that wireless connections such as Bluetooth and Wi-Fi are less expensive and can eliminate all those cables and cords. In some circumstances, a wired connection is faster and more reliable than wireless.

# Explore What's in the Box

After you fork over your hard-earned money for your iPad, you'll be holding one box. Besides your iPad and a small documentation package, here's a rundown of what you'll find when you take off the shrink wrap and open the box:

» **iPad:** Your iPad is covered in a thick plastic sleeve-film that you can take off and toss (unless you think there's a chance that you'll return the device, in which case you may want to keep all packaging for 14 days — Apple's standard return period).

» **Documentation:** Under the iPad itself is a small, white envelope about the size of a half-dozen index cards. Open it and you'll find the iconic Apple stickers and some very brief instructions on how to use your iPad. Apple feels that using an iPad should be so intuitive that you don't really need instructions. But folks are buying this book (thanks!), so Apple may not be right about that.

» **A USB-C cable:** Use this cable to connect the iPad to your computer or use it with the last item in the box, which is the USB-C power adapter.

» **USB-C power adapter:** The power adapter attaches to the cable so that you can plug it into the wall and charge the battery.

That's all you'll find in the box, a study in Zen-like simplicity.

# Take a First Look at the Gadget

The little card contained in the documentation that comes with your iPad gives you a picture of the iPad with callouts to the buttons you'll find on it. In this section, I give you a bit more information about those buttons and other physical features of the iPad. **Figure 1-2** shows you the layout for the tenth-generation iPad, and **Figure 1-3** gives you the rundown for features pertaining to the iPad Air. **Figure 1-4** lays out the iPad mini, and the iPad Pro models are mapped out in **Figure 1-5.**

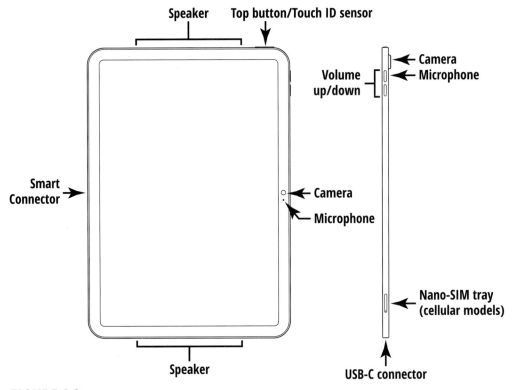

## Tenth-generation iPad

FIGURE 1-2

Here's the rundown on what the various hardware features are and what they do:

» **Top button:** You can use this button (whose functionality I cover in more detail in Chapter 2) to power up your iPad, put it in sleep mode, wake it up, or power it down. The top button also includes a Touch ID sensor on the tenth-generation iPad, iPad Air, and iPad mini.

» **Lightning/USB-C Connector slot:** Plug the Lightning or USB-C connector into this port on the iPad, and plug the other end of the cable into the power adapter to charge your battery or use it without the power adapter to sync your iPad with your computer (which you find out more about in Chapter 3).

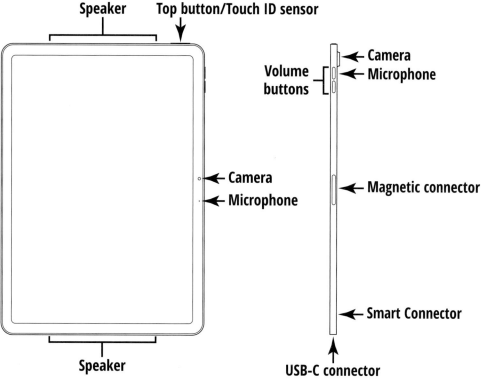

**iPad Air**

FIGURE 1-3

» **Cameras:** iPads offer front- and rear-facing cameras, which you can use to shoot photos or video. Be careful not to put your thumb over the rear camera when taking shots. (I have several very nice photos of my fingers already.)

» **Smart Connector:** iPad Pro, iPad Air, and iPad include this feature to support accessories such as the Smart Keyboard.

» **SIM tray:** This tray comes only with Wi-Fi + Cellular models. The SIM is what allows your iPad to connect and authenticate to a cellular network.

» **(Tiny, mighty) speakers:** One nice surprise when I first got my iPad was hearing what a great little stereo sound system it has — and how much sound can come from these tiny speakers.

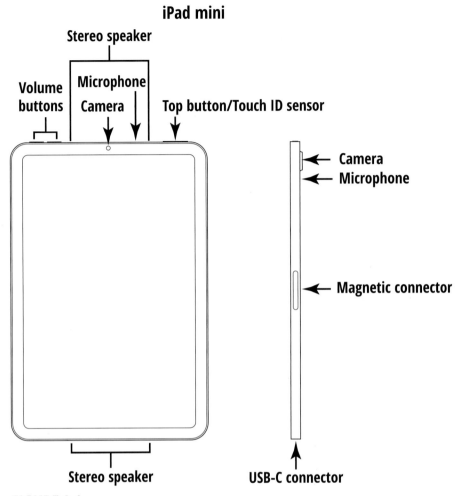

**iPad mini**

Stereo speaker

Volume buttons

Microphone

Camera

Top button/Touch ID sensor

Camera

Microphone

Magnetic connector

Stereo speaker

USB-C connector

**FIGURE 1-4**

TIP

» **Volume:** Tap the volume switch, called a rocker, up for more volume and down for less.

You can use this rocker as a camera shutter button when the camera is activated.

» **Microphones:** Microphones make it possible to speak into your iPad to deliver commands or enter content using the Siri personal-assistant feature. Using Siri, you can do things such as make phone calls using the internet, use video-calling services, dictate your keyboard input, or work with other apps that accept audio input.

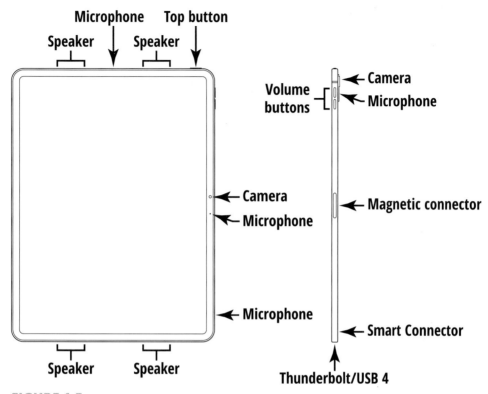

**FIGURE 1-5**

IN THIS CHAPTER

» See what's needed to use
your iPad

» Turn on your iPad and use the
multitouch screen

» Display and use the keyboard

» Switch between apps and
adjust views

» Identify yourself to your iPad

» Discover Control Center

» Get to know the apps that
are already installed

Chapter **2**

# Exploring Your iPad

G ood news! Getting anything done on the iPad is simple when
you know the ropes. In fact, using your fingers to do things is
an intuitive way to communicate with your computing device,
which is just what the iPad is.

In this chapter, you turn on your iPad and then take your first look at
the Home screen. You also practice using the onscreen keyboard, see
how to interact with the touchscreen in various ways, learn how to
use Touch ID or Face ID, get pointers on working with the cameras,
get an overview of built-in applications (more commonly referred to
as *apps*), and more.

TIP

Although the iPad's screen has been treated to repel oils, you're
about to deposit a ton of fingerprints on it — one downside of a
touchscreen device. So you'll need to clean the screen from time
to time. A soft cloth, such as the microfiber cloth you might use to

clean eyeglasses, is usually all you'll need to clean things up. Never use harsh chemicals. Please check out Chapter 20 for more on keeping your screen clean.

## See What You Need to Use the iPad

At a minimum, you need to be able to connect to the internet to take advantage of most iPad features, which you can do using a Wi-Fi network (a wireless network that you set up in your own home or office through an internet service provider or access in a public place such as a library or coffee shop) or a cellular data connection from your cellular provider (if your iPad model supports cellular data).

You may want to have a computer handy so that you can connect your iPad to it to download photos, videos, music, or applications and transfer them to or from your iPad through a process called *syncing* (see Chapter 3 for more about syncing). An Apple service called iCloud syncs content from all your Apple devices (such as the iPad, iPhone, or Mac), so anything you buy on your iPhone that can be run on an iPad, for example, will automatically be pushed to your iPad. In addition, you can sync without connecting a cable to a computer using a Wi-Fi connection to your computer.

Your iPad will probably arrive registered and activated, or if you buy it in a store, the person helping you can handle those procedures.

## Turn On Your iPad for the First Time

When you're ready to get going with your new toy, be sure you're within range of a Wi-Fi network that you can connect with, and then hold the iPad. Plug the charging cable that came with your device (the type depends on the iPad model you have) into your iPad and plug the other end into a USB or USB-C port on your computer or into the charging block that came with your iPad, just in case you lose your battery charge during the setup process.

Now follow these steps to set up and register your iPad:

1. Press and hold the top button on the top (fancy that) of your iPad until the Apple logo appears.

   A screen appears with a cheery greeting on it.

2. Follow the series of prompts to make choices about your language and location, using iCloud (Apple's online sharing service), and more.

   After you deal with all the setup screens, a Welcome to iPad screen appears.

3. Tap Get Started to display the Home screen.

**TIP**

If you set up iCloud during or after registering (see Chapter 3), updates to your operating system will be downloaded to your iPad without plugging it into a computer. Apple refers to this feature as *PC Free*, simply meaning that your device has been liberated from having to use a physical connection to a computer to get upgrades.

**TIP**

You can choose to have personal items transferred to your iPad from your computer when you sync the two devices using iTunes or Finder (depending on your computer's operating system), including music, videos, downloaded apps, audiobooks, e-books, podcasts, and browser bookmarks. Contacts and Calendars are downloaded via iCloud, or (if you're moving to iPad from an Android device) you can download an app from the Google Play Store called Move to iOS (developed by Apple) to copy your current Android settings to your iPad. (See this support article from Apple for more info: https://support.apple.com/en-us/118670.) You can also transfer to your computer any content you download directly to your iPad by using iTunes, the App Store, or non-Apple stores.

# Meet the Multitouch Screen

The iPad has more than one Home screen page. By default, the first Home screen page contains preinstalled apps, and the second contains a few more preinstalled apps. After those initial pages are fully populated with app icons, other pages are created to contain any further apps you download or sync to your iPad.

When the iPad Home screen appears, you see a colorful background, two sets of icons, and perhaps a couple of widgets, as shown in **Figure 2-1**.

FIGURE 2-1

One set of icons appears on the dock, along the bottom of the screen. The *dock* contains the Messages, Safari, Music, Mail, Calendar, Photos, and Notes app icons by default, though you can swap one app for another. The dock appears on every Home screen page and can even be accessed from within apps. You can add new apps to your iPad to populate additional Home screens, too.

Other icons appear above the dock and are closer to the top of the screen. Some of these icons are for widgets, which are snippets of information from apps and other sources; see the section "Wonderful Widgets," later in this chapter. Other icons above the dock are for apps. I cover all these icons in the "Take Inventory of Preinstalled Apps" task, later in this chapter. Different icons appear in this area on each Home screen page. You can also nest apps in folders, which gives you the possibility of storing almost limitless apps on your iPad. You are, in fact, limited — but only by your iPad's memory.

Treat the iPad screen carefully. It's made of glass and will break if an unreasonable amount of force is applied, if it's dropped, or if the kids in your life throw it against the wall (yes, that's actually happened in our house).

The iPad uses *touchscreen technology:* When you swipe your finger across the screen or tap it, you're providing input to the device just as you do to a computer using a mouse or keyboard. You hear more about the touchscreen in the next task, but for now, go ahead and play with it for a few minutes — really, you can't hurt anything. Use the pads of your fingertips (not your fingernails) and try these tasks:

» **Tap the Settings icon.** The various Settings categories appear, as shown in **Figure 2-2.** (You read more about these categories throughout this book.)

To return to the Home screen, swipe up from the very bottom of the screen (if your iPad doesn't have a Home button), or press the Home button.

» **Swipe a finger from right to left on the Home screen.** This action moves you to the next Home screen page.

The little dots at the bottom of the screen, above the dock icons, indicate which Home screen page is displayed. Gray dots indicate the number of Home screen pages, and the white or black dot (depending on the wallpaper color) indicates the current page.

**FIGURE 2-2**

» **To experience the screen rotation feature, hold the iPad firmly while turning it sideways.** The screen flips to the landscape (horizontal) orientation, if the app you're in supports it.

To flip the screen back to portrait (vertical) orientation, just turn the device so that it's oriented like a pad of paper again. (Some apps force iPad to stay in one orientation or the other.)

» **Drag your finger down from the very top center edge of the screen to reveal items such as notifications, reminders, and calendar entries.** Drag up from the very bottom edge of the Home screen to hide these items.

» **Drag your finger down from the top-right corner of the screen to display Control Center (containing commonly used controls and tools and discussed later in this chapter).** Swipe up from the bottom of the screen or touch an area outside Control Center to hide it.

**TIP**

You can customize the Home screen by changing its *wallpaper* (background picture) and brightness. You can read about making these changes in Chapter 4.

# Say Hello to Tap and Swipe

You can use several methods for getting around and getting things done with your iPad using its multitouch screen, including

» **Tap once.** To open an app, choose a field (such as a search box), choose an item in a list, use an arrow to move back or forward one screen, or follow an online link, simply tap the item once with your finger.

» **Tap twice.** Use this method to enlarge or reduce the display of a web page (see Chapter 9 for more about using the Safari web browser) or to zoom in or out while in the Maps app.

» **Pinch.** As an alternative to the tap-twice method, you can pinch your fingers together or move them apart on the screen (see **Figure 2-3**) when you're looking at photos, maps, web pages, or email messages to quickly reduce or enlarge them, respectively. This method allows you to grow or contract the image on the screen to a variety of sizes rather than a fixed size, as with the double-tap method.

**TIP**

Use the three-finger tap to zoom your screen to be even larger or use multitasking gestures to swipe with four or five fingers. This method is handy if you have vision challenges. Go to Chapter 4 to discover how to turn on this feature using Accessibility settings.

» **Drag to scroll (known as *swiping*).** When you touch your finger to the screen and drag to the right or left, the screen moves (see **Figure 2-4**). Swiping to the left on the Home screen, for example, moves you to the next Home screen page. Swiping up while reading an online newspaper moves the page up; swiping down moves the page back down.

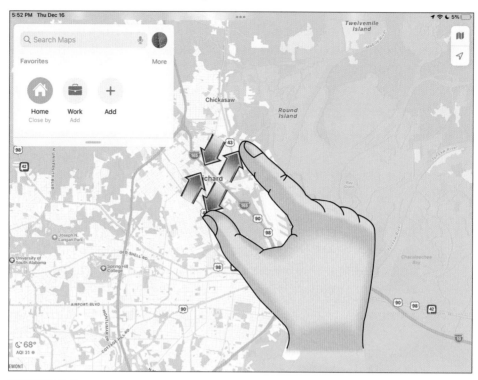

**FIGURE 2-3**

» **Flick.** To scroll a page more quickly, quickly flick your finger up or down on the screen.

» **Tap the status bar.** To move quickly to the top of a list, a web page, or an email message, tap the status bar at the top of the iPad screen. (For some sites, you have to tap the status bar twice to get this to work.)

» **Press and hold.** If you're using Notes or Mail or any other application that lets you select text, or if you're on a web page, pressing and holding down on text selects a word and displays editing tools that you can use to select, cut, or copy and paste the text. You can also press and hold an icon on the Home screen to view a list of options you can use with it.

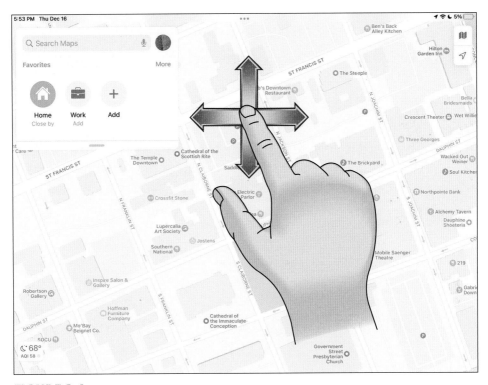

**FIGURE 2-4**

When you rock your iPad backward or forward, the background moves as well (a feature called *parallax*). You might want to disable this feature if it makes you queasy. From the Home screen, tap Settings ⇨ Accessibility ⇨ Motion and then tap and turn on the Reduce Motion setting by tapping the toggle switch (it turns green when the option is enabled).

You can try these methods now:

» Tap the Safari button on the dock at the bottom of any iPad Home screen page to display the Safari web browser.

» Tap a link to move to another web page.

» Double-tap the page to enlarge it; then pinch your thumb and finger together on the screen to reduce its size.

» Drag one finger up and down the page to scroll.

» Flick your finger quickly up or down on the page to scroll more quickly.

» Press and hold your finger on a word that isn't a link (links take you to another location on the web).

The word is selected, and the tools shown in **Figure 2-5** are displayed. (You can use these tools for getting a definition of a word, copying it, and more.)

» Press and hold your finger on a link or an image.

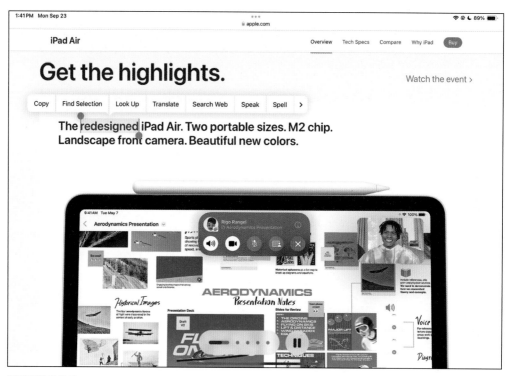

FIGURE 2-5

A menu appears (shown in **Figure 2-6**) with commands that let you do things like open the link or picture, open it in a new tab or window, open it in a new tab group, download a linked file, add it to your Reading List, copy it, share it, and possibly others; these options may be different, depending on what you're pressing and holding. If you press and hold an unlinked image, the menu also offers the Add to Photos command.

Tap outside the menu to close it without making a selection.

» Position your thumb and finger slightly apart on the screen, and then pinch them together to reduce the page. With your thumb and finger already pinched together on the screen, move them apart to enlarge the page.

» Swipe up from the bottom of the screen or press the Home button (depending on your iPad model) to go back to the Home screen.

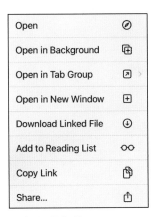

**FIGURE 2-6**

# Browsing the App Library

App Library is an organizational tool that houses every app on your iPad and organizes them automatically according to categories (defined by Apple). This allows you to hide apps from your Home screen pages, reducing the number of them that you have to scroll through to find an app. You can even hide entire Home screen pages, too! And if you want to display the apps or Home screen pages again, it's simple to do so. Follow these steps to get around in App Library:

1. Swipe from right to left on any Home screen page until the App Library screen appears.

    App Library (shown in **Figure 2-7**) always resides on the last Home screen page.

**FIGURE 2-7**

App Library organizes apps according to categories, such as Suggestions, Recently Added, Social, Games, Entertainment, and Utilities. Note that each category displays three larger app icons and up to four smaller app icons, with the exception of Suggestions, which displays four larger icons.

2. Tap one of the larger icons to open the app. When finished, swipe up from the bottom of the screen or press the Home button to switch to the App Library screen.

3. Tap one of the smaller icons to expand the category, and then tap the app you want to open. Tap near the top or bottom of the screen when viewing an expanded category to return to App Library's main screen.

4. Tap the search field at the top of App Library to see all apps listed alphabetically, as shown in **Figure 2-8.** To find a specific app, start typing its name using the keyboard.

**FIGURE 2-8**

5. To perform a quick action on an app icon in App Library, press and hold down on an app icon to open the quick actions menu, the contents of which will vary depending on what options the app offers.

   For example, **Figure 2-9** shows the Instagram quick actions menu, which offers some options that aren't available in the Camera app's quick actions menu.

FIGURE 2-9

6. To remove an app from your Home screen (leaving it in App Library) or delete it from your iPad, press and hold an app's icon on the Home screen until the quick actions menu appears. Tap Remove App and then tap one of the selections shown in **Figure 2-10.** Tap Delete App to delete the app from your iPad altogether, or tap Remove from Home Screen to remove the app from the Home screen but retain it in App Library.

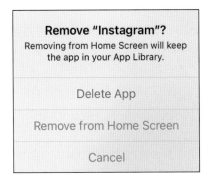

**FIGURE 2-10**

7. To hide an entire Home screen page, press and hold down on any area on a Home screen page until all the icons begin to jiggle. Tap one of the small white dots just above the dock to view thumbnails of each of your Home screen pages, as shown in **Figure 2-11.** Tap the circle below a Home screen page to hide or display it. (A visible Home screen page displays a check mark in the circle.) Tap Done when you're finished.

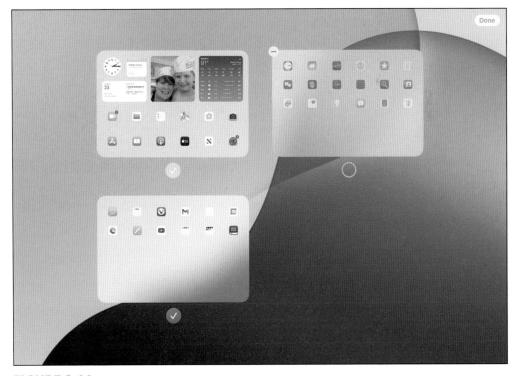

**FIGURE 2-11**

The Home screen page remains in App Library, and you can display it again later by using the same technique.

# The Dock

The dock at the bottom of your iPad's screen houses apps you use most often. You can remove or add apps from it simply by dragging and dropping their icons in or out of the dock. You can also reorder icons within the dock using the same drag-and-drop method. To drag and drop, press and hold down on an app icon until it pulsates (essentially tagging it to your finger) and then drag it to a new location and drop it by removing your finger from the screen.

The dock is divided between left and right sides by a thin line. The icons on the right side of the dock are those you've used most recently but don't keep on the dock at all times. This makes it easier to access these apps when you're using them more heavily. You can enable or disable this behavior by going to Settings ⇨ Home Screen & App Library and toggling the Show Suggested and Recent Apps in Dock switch on (green) or off.

# Display and Use the Onscreen Keyboard

The onscreen iPad keyboard appears whenever you're in a text-entry location, such as a search field or a text message. Follow these steps to display and use the keyboard (I'm using the Notes app for this example):

1. Tap the Notes icon on the Home screen to open the Notes app.
2. Open a note you want to work in:
   - Tap the new note icon in the top-right to create a new note.
   - If you've already created some notes, tap one to display the page and then tap anywhere on the note.
3. Type a few words using the keyboard, as shown in **Figure 2-12**.

**Tap to start a new note**

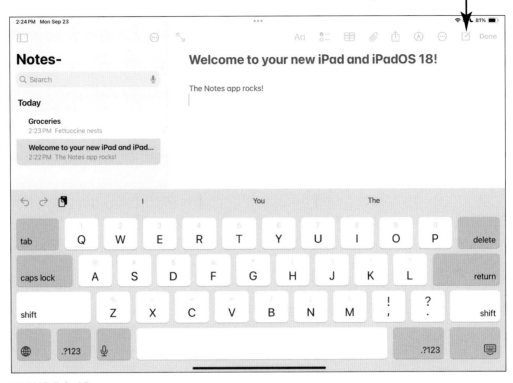

**FIGURE 2-12**

TIP

To make the keyboard display as widely as possible, rotate your iPad to landscape (horizontal) orientation. (If you've locked the screen orientation in Control Center, you have to unlock the screen to do this; just swipe down from the right corner of the screen to open Control Center, and then tap the lock icon.)

TIP

QuickType provides suggestions above the keyboard as you type. You can turn this feature off or on by pressing and holding down on either the emoji icon (smiley face) or the international icon (globe) on the keyboard to display a menu. Tap Keyboard Settings and toggle the Predictive Text switch to turn the feature off or on (green). To quickly return to Notes from Keyboard Settings, tap the word Notes in the upper left of your screen.

# Keyboard shortcuts

After you open the keyboard, you're ready to use it for editing text. You'll find a number of shortcuts for editing text:

>> If you make a mistake while using the keyboard — and you will, especially when you first use it — tap the delete key (it's to the right of the *p* key) to delete text to the left of the insertion point.

To quickly type a period and space together at the same time, just double-tap the spacebar.

>> To create a new paragraph, tap the Return key (just like the keyboard on a Mac or the Enter key on a PC's keyboard).

>> To type numbers and symbols, tap the number key (labeled .?123) on the left side of the spacebar (refer to **Figure 2-12**). The characters on the keyboard change (see **Figure 2-13**).

If you type a number and then tap the spacebar, the keyboard returns to the letter keyboard automatically. To return to the letter keyboard at any time, simply tap the key labeled ABC on the left side of the spacebar.

You can easily type the alternative character marked on a key by tapping and dragging down on the key. For example, if you need an exclamation mark (!), simply tap and drag the comma (,) key downward, and an exclamation mark will be inserted (because it's the alternate character on the comma key).

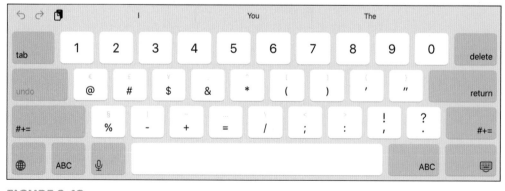

**FIGURE 2-13**

» Use the shift key to type capital letters:

- Tapping the shift key once causes only the next letter you type to be capitalized.

- Double-tap (rapidly tap twice) the shift key to turn on the caps lock feature so that all letters you type are capitalized until you turn off the feature. Tap the shift key once to turn off caps lock.

  You can control whether caps lock is enabled by opening the Settings app, tapping General and then Keyboard, and toggling the Enable Caps Lock switch.

» To type a variation on a symbol or letter (for example, to see alternative presentations for the letter *A* when you press the A key on the keyboard), hold down on the key; a set of alternative letters or symbols appears (see **Figure 2-14**).

This trick works with only certain letters and symbols.

» Tap the smiley-faced emoji key to display the emoji keyboard, which contains illustrations that you can insert, including numerical, symbol, and arrow keys, as well as a row of symbol sets along the bottom of the screen.

Tapping one of these displays a portfolio of icons from smiley faces and hearts to pumpkins, cats, and more. Tap the ABC key to close the emoji keyboard and return to the letter keyboard.

**FIGURE 2-14**

**TIP**

A small globe symbol appears instead of the emoji key on the keyboard if you've enabled multilanguage functionality in the iPad Settings app. To access the emoji keyboard, press and hold down on the globe key until a menu opens, and then tap Emoji. Return to the normal keyboard by tapping ABC in the lower-left when ready.

» Swipe up from the bottom of the screen or press the Home button (depending on your iPad model) to return to the Home screen.

**TIP**

You can buy one of three Magic Keyboards for your iPad. These physical keyboards from Apple attach to your iPad and allow both power and data exchange. Check out the options and which ones work for your iPad at www.apple.com/ipad-keyboards.

## QuickPath

QuickPath allows you to zip your finger from key to key to quickly spell words without ever lifting your finger from the screen. For example, spell the word *path* by touching *p* on the keyboard and then quickly moving to *a* and then *t* and then *h*. Ta-da! You've spelled *path* without your finger leaving the screen.

# Use the Small Keyboard

The *small keyboard* feature allows you to shrink the keyboard to make more of the screen visible and to assist with one-handed typing. Open an application in which you can use the onscreen keyboard, such as Notes, and then follow these steps:

1. Tap an entry field or page to display the onscreen keyboard.

2. Spread two fingers apart, place them on the keyboard, and then quickly pinch your fingers together on the keyboard to shrink it, as shown in **Figure 2-15.**

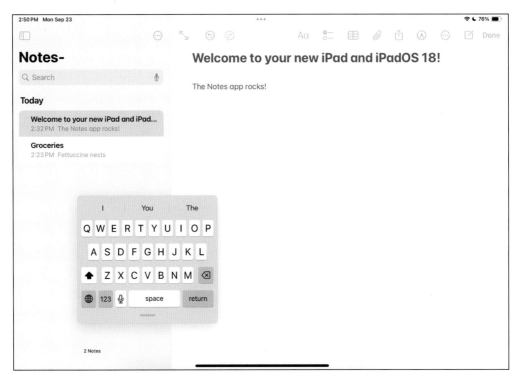

**FIGURE 2-15**

This feature can be finicky, so you may have to try it a few times.

3. Now hold the iPad with a hand on either side and practice using your thumbs to enter text. You may also move the small keyboard around the screen by tapping and dragging the dark gray handle at the bottom of the keyboard (under the spacebar).

4. To restore the original keyboard, pinch two fingers together, place them on the keyboard, and then quickly spread them apart.

**TIP**

Be sure to double-check that you didn't inadvertently type unnecessary characters in your text when pinching.

# Flick to Search

The search feature in iPadOS helps you find suggestions from the web, Music, and the App Store as well as suggestions for nearby locations and more. Here's how to use search:

1. Swipe down on any area of any Home screen page (except the far edges) to reveal the search feature (see **Figure 2-16**).

FIGURE 2-16

2. Begin entering a search term.

   In the example in **Figure 2-17,** after I typed the word *coffee,* the search feature displayed maps and other search results. As you continue to type a search term or phrase, the results narrow to match it.

3. Scroll down to view more results.

4. Tap an item in the search results to open it in its appropriate app or player.

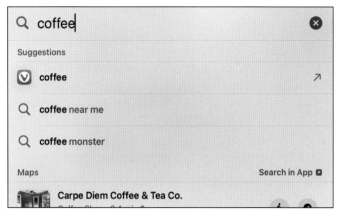

FIGURE 2-17

# Easily Switch Between Apps

App Switcher lets you easily switch from one app to another without returning to the Home screen. You simply preview any open app and move from one to another; you can quit an app by simply swiping it upward. To learn the ropes of App Switcher, follow these steps:

1. Open App Switcher by doing one of the following, depending on your iPad model:

   - Swipe up from the bottom edge of any screen with one finger, pause in the middle of the screen, and then lift your finger.

   - Press the Home button twice.

   App Switcher appears (see **Figure 2-18**).

2. To locate another app that you want to switch to, flick to scroll to the left or right.

3. Tap an app to open it.

**TIP** Swipe up from the bottom of the screen or press the Home button once (depending on your iPad model) to return to the app that you were working in.

FIGURE 2-18

# Use Slide Over and Split View

iPadOS 18 allows you to be more productive than ever before with your iPad with features like Slide Over and Split View.

Slide Over lets you view one app in a floating panel, while viewing and working with other apps behind it. Split View allows two apps to share the screen between them, splitting the screen so that one app is on the left and the other is on the right. You can even adjust the amount of space each app is allocated by dragging a divider between them.

Make sure the Slide Over and Split View options are enabled on your iPad by going to Settings ⇨ Multitasking & Gestures. Tap the circle below Split View & Slide Over, if necessary, to enable the features.

TIP

# Starting with Slide Over

To use the Slide Over feature, follow these steps:

1. From an app you're already using, tap the three dots at the top of the screen.

2. Tap Slide Over in the menu that appears.

   The app slides across to the right edge of the screen, so only its left edge is visible. A prompt at the top of the screen asks you to choose another app.

3. Tap another app to open it.

   The second app opens and the first app floats above it; the two apps are now in Slide Over mode, as illustrated with Notes and Safari in **Figure 2-19.**

FIGURE 2-19

4. Simply swipe up from the bottom of the screen or tap the Home button (depending on your iPad model) to close Slide Over. You can also tap the three dots at the top of the floating app and then tap Close in the menu that appears.

## Moving to Split View

If you want to use two apps at the same time, you can use Split View. If you're already using two apps with Slide Over, tap the three small dots at the top of the floating window, tap Split View, and then tap either Left Split or Right Split, as shown in **Figure 2-20.** To exit Split View, simply tap the three dots at the top of the window of one of the apps and then tap Full Screen.

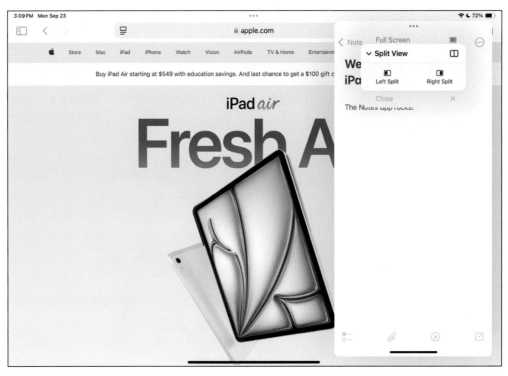

**FIGURE 2-20**

As mentioned, you can easily move between Slide Over, Split View, and even Full Screen by tapping the three dots at the top of any app window and then tapping the icon for one of those options.

While you're in Split View, you can drag the heavy black divider (see **Figure 2-21**) left or right to change the sizes of the panes, or you can have equal space for both apps. Both apps are fully functional, although in some special cases, the app may not show certain noncritical elements to adjust to the narrower width of the split view when compared to the full screen.

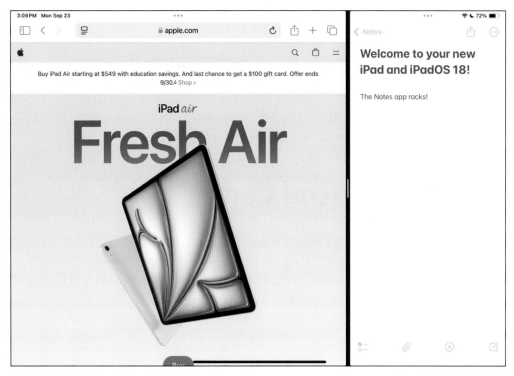

**FIGURE 2-21**

**TIP**

You can drag and drop items between apps in Slide Over and Split View. For example, with Photos and Notes open, drag and drop a picture from Photos into a note in the Notes window. Another example might be dragging a link from a text document into the Safari web browser to open it.

# Examine the iPad Cameras

iPads have front- and back-facing cameras. You can use the cameras to take still photos (covered in more detail in Chapter 14) or shoot videos (covered in Chapter 15).

For now, take a quick look at your camera by tapping the Camera app icon on the Home screen. You can use the controls on the screen to take pictures and video, switch between front and rear cameras, turn the flash on and off, and so much more. See Chapters 14 and 15 for more detail about using the iPad cameras.

# Discover Control Center

Control Center is a one-stop screen for common features and settings, such as connecting to a network and increasing screen brightness or volume. iPadOS 18 has given Control Center a new look and added several features. Here's how to use it:

1. To display Control Center, swipe down from the upper-right corner of the screen.

   The Control Center screen appears to the right.

2. In Control Center (highlighted in **Figure 2-22**), tap a button or press and drag a slider to access or adjust a setting.

**FIGURE 2-22**

To switch to one of the other Control Center screens, swipe up and down on the Control Center screen or simply tap one of the icons on the far right of the Control Center screen (as shown in Figure 2-22).

3. After you make a change, tap anywhere on the screen outside Control Center to exit it.

Some options in Control Center are hidden from initial view but may be accessed by tapping and holding a button in Control Center. For example, press and hold on the brightness slider to reveal the Dark Mode, Night Shift, and True Tone buttons (as shown in **Figure 2-23**).

**TIP**

Try pressing and holding other buttons in Control Center to see what other options are waiting for you to discover. If you press and hold an item and its icon just pulses once, no further options are available for the item.

FIGURE 2-23

iPadOS 18 allows you to customize Control Center (a feature I love):

1. Open Control Center and tap + in the upper-left corner to enter edit mode.

   Icons and controls now all sport a minus sign (–) and most have a curved gray handle in their lower-right corner, as shown in **Figure 2-24**.

2. Edit items in Control Center:

   • To add an item, tap the Add a Control button at the bottom of the screen. Swipe through all the options and tap the one you want. You'll now see the item in Control Center.

   • To resize an item, drag the gray handle in the lower-right corner of its icon or group.

**FIGURE 2-24**

- To reorganize items, touch-and-hold an icon until it appears to lift off the screen, and then drag it into another position.

- To remove an item, tap the – in a gray circle to the upper left of the item. No worries if you accidentally remove something; you can add it back by tapping the Add a Control button at the bottom of the screen.

# Understand Touch ID

Certain iPad models sport a feature called Touch ID, which allows you to unlock your iPad by touching the Home button or top button (depending on the model). The button contains a sophisticated fingerprint sensor. Because your fingerprint is unique, this feature is one of the most foolproof ways to protect your data.

If you're going to use Touch ID (it's optional), you must educate the iPad about your fingerprint on your finger of choice by tapping Settings ⇨ Touch ID & Passcode, entering your passcode, and choosing what to use Touch ID for — for example, unlocking the iPad, using Apple Pay (Apple's electronic wallet service), or making purchases. You can change these preferences anytime you like.

Then, if you did not set up a fingerprint previously or you want to add another one, tap Add a Fingerprint from Touch ID & Passcode. Follow the instructions and press your finger lightly on the Home button several times to allow Touch ID to sense and record your fingerprint. (You will be guided through this process and told when to touch and when to lift your finger.) With the iPad Unlock option turned on, press the power button to go to the lock screen and touch the Home button or top button. The iPad unlocks. If you chose the option for using Touch ID with Apple Pay or for purchasing an item in the Apple stores, you simply touch your finger to the Home button or top button rather than enter your Apple ID and password to complete a purchase.

# Take a Look at Face ID

Some iPad models use a different — and very cool — method of authenticating a user: Face ID. Face ID uses your iPad's built-in cameras and scanners to scan your face and save a profile of it. It then remembers the information and compares it to whoever is facing the iPad. If the face doesn't match the profile, the person can't access the iPad (unless they know and use your passcode, which you have to set up to use Face ID). Face ID is so advanced that it can even work in total darkness.

To set up Face ID:

1. Go to Settings and tap Face ID & Passcode.
2. Tap Set Up Face ID.

3. Hold the iPad a few inches in front of your face (in portrait mode, not landscape).

4. Tap the Get Started button and then follow the prompts to slowly move your head in a complete circle.

   If you have difficulty moving your head, tap the Accessibility Options button at the bottom of the screen and follow the prompts from there.

5. Tap Continue and follow the prompts to perform the circle step again.

6. Tap Done when finished.

The next time you want to use your iPad, simply hold it up in front of you, swipe up from the bottom of the screen when the lock icon unlocks, and you'll jump right to the Home screen or whatever app you were last using.

For more information on using Face ID and its capabilities, visit `https://support.apple.com/en-us/108411`.

# Lock Screen Rotation

Sometimes you don't want your screen orientation to flip when you move your iPad around. Use these steps to lock the iPad into portrait orientation (narrow and tall, not low and wide):

1. Swipe down from the upper-right corner of any screen to open Control Center.

2. Tap the lock screen icon (a padlock with an arrow encircling it).

3. Tap anywhere on the screen outside Control Center to exit it.

Perform the steps again to unlock the screen, if desired.

# Explore the Status Bar

Across the top of the iPad screen is the status bar. Tiny icons in this area can provide useful information, such as the time, battery level, and wireless-connection status. **Table 2-1** lists some of the most common items you find on the status bar.

**TIP**

If you have GPS, cellular (if your iPad supports it), Bluetooth service, or a connection to a virtual private network (VPN), a corresponding symbol appears on the status bar whenever a feature is active. (If you don't know what a virtual private network is, there's no need to worry about it.)

**TABLE 2-1**   Common Status Bar Icons

| Icon | Name | What It Indicates |
|------|------|-------------------|
| 📶 Wi-Fi | Wi-Fi | You're connected to a Wi-Fi network. |
| Activity | Activity | A task is in progress — a web page is loading, for example. |
| 2:30 PM | Time | You guessed it: You see the time. |
| Screen rotation lock | Screen rotation lock | The screen is locked in portrait orientation and doesn't rotate when you turn the iPad. |
| Do not disturb | Do not disturb | Your iPad's communications are disabled during scheduled times. |
| Battery life | Battery life | The charge percentage remaining in the battery. The indicator changes to a lightning bolt when the battery is charging. |

# Wonderful Widgets

Widgets provide at-a-glance snippets of information, such as the weather and calendar appointments so that you don't have to open individual apps. You can add widgets to any Home screen page.

To add a widget:

1.  Press and hold down on any Home screen page until all the icons are jiggling.

2.  Tap Edit in the upper-left corner of the screen and then tap Add Widget in the menu that appears.

3.  Scroll through the list of widgets and tap the one you want to add, or use the Search Widgets field to find a specific widget.

4.  If the widget has several styles (as indicated by dots at the bottom of the screen), such as Weather's Forecast widget in **Figure 2-25,** swipe right or left to see those styles. Then tap to select one.

**FIGURE 2-25**

**5.** Tap the blue Add Widget button.

You can move your widget by dragging it, or remove it and start over by tapping the minus sign (–) button in the upper-left corner of the widget.

**6.** When you're finished, tap Done in the upper right.

# Take Inventory of Preinstalled Apps

The iPad comes with many applications — or apps, for short — built right in. When you look at the Home screen, you see an icon for each app. This task gives you an overview of what each app does.

By default, the following icons appear on the dock at the bottom of every Home screen (refer to **Figure 2-1**), from left to right:

» **Messages:** If you love to instant message, the Messages app comes to the rescue. You can engage in live text- and image-based conversations with others on their phones or other devices that use email. You can also send video or audio messages.

» **Safari:** You use the Safari web browser to navigate on the internet, create and save bookmarks of favorite sites, and add web clips to your Home screen so that you can quickly visit favorite sites from there. You may have used this web browser (or others, such as Google Chrome) on your desktop computer.

» **Music:** Music is the name of your media player. Although its main function is to play music, you can use it to play other audio files, as well.

» **Mail:** Access email accounts that you've set up in iPad. Move among the preset mail folders, read and reply to email, and download attachments to your iPad. Read more about email accounts in Chapter 10.

» **Calendar:** Use this handy onscreen daybook to set up appointments and send alerts to remind you about them.

- » **Photos:** Organize pictures in folders, send photos in an email message, use a photo as your iPad wallpaper, and assign pictures to contact records. You can also run slideshows of your photos, open albums, pinch or unpinch to shrink or expand photos, respectively, and scroll photos with a simple swipe.

  You can use the photo-sharing feature to share photos among your friends. The Photos app displays images by collections, including years and moments.

- » **Notes:** Enter text, format text, or cut and paste text and objects (such as images) from a website into this easy-to-use notepad app.

Apps with icons above the dock on Home screen pages include the following:

- » **FaceTime:** Engage in phone calls using video of the sender and receiver.

- » **Camera:** The Camera app allows you to take photos and videos using the still and video cameras built into the iPad.

- » **Weather:** Get the latest weather for your location instantly. You can easily add other locations so you can check the weather where you're going or where you've been.

- » **Files:** This app allows you to browse files that you've stored not only on your iPad but also on other services, such as iCloud Drive, Google Drive, Dropbox, and the like.

- » **Clock:** Display clocks from around the world, set alarms, and use timer and stopwatch features.

- » **Maps:** View conventional maps or aerial views of addresses and get directions from one place to another whether traveling by car, by bicycle, on foot, or on public transportation. You can even get your directions read aloud by a spoken narration feature.

- » **TV:** This media player is similar to Music but specializes in playing videos, and it offers a few features specific to this type of media, such as information about a movie's plot and cast.

» **Contacts:** In this address-book feature, you can enter contact information (including photos, if you like, from your Photos or Cameras app) and share contact information by email. You can also use the search feature to find your contacts easily.

» **Reminders:** This useful app allows you to create and be alerted to your to-do lists.

» **News:** News is a customizable aggregator for stories from your favorite news sources.

» **iTunes Store:** Tapping this icon takes you to the iTunes store, where you can shop 'til you drop (or until your iPad battery runs out of juice) for music, movies, TV shows, and audiobooks and then download them directly to your iPad. (See Chapter 11 for more about how the iTunes Store works.)

» **App Store:** Buy and download apps that do everything from enabling you to play games to building business presentations. Many of these apps and games are free!

» **Books:** The Books app is bundled with the iPad out of the box. Because the iPad has been touted as being a good e-reader — a device that enables you to read books on an electronic device — you should definitely check this one out. (To work with the Books e-reader app itself, go to Chapter 12.)

» **Home:** Control most (if not all) of your home automation devices in one convenient app.

» **Photo Booth:** Enjoy snapping fun pictures of yourself and others with this app that adds a little flair to the standard Camera app.

» **Stocks:** Keep track of the stock market, including stocks that you personally follow, in real time.

» **Translate:** The Translate app translates text or voice between supported languages.

» **Voice Memos:** Record your thoughts and save or share them.

» **Measure:** Use your iPad to measure distances using its built-in camera.

» **Magnifier:** Zoom in on anything to get a better look.

- » **Podcasts:** Use this app to find and listen to recorded informational programs. Think of podcasts as downloadable radio broadcasts that you can listen to anytime you like.

- » **Find My:** The Find My app helps you locate Apple devices that you own (see Chapter 19 for more info) and track down friends who also own an Apple device.

- » **Shortcuts:** This app helps you string together multiple iPad actions into single commands that you can run either manually or by using Siri.

- » **Freeform:** Get creative, gather ideas, and add files of just about any kind using this online whiteboard app.

- » **Passwords:** Store and access all your passwords in one convenient and (very) secure app.

- » **Settings:** Settings is the central location on the iPad where you can specify settings for various functions and do administrative tasks, such as set up email accounts or create a password.

# Lock iPad, Turn It Off, or Unlock It

*Sleep* is a state in which the screen goes black, though you can quickly wake up the iPad. You can also turn off the power to give your new toy a rest.

Here are the procedures you use to put the iPad to sleep or turn it off:

- » **Sleep:** Press the sleep/wake or top button (depending on your iPad model), and the iPad goes to sleep. The screen goes black and is locked.

TIP

The iPad automatically enters sleep mode after a brief period of inactivity. You can change the time interval at which it sleeps by adjusting the auto-lock feature in Settings ⇨ Display & Brightness.

» **Power Off:** For models without a Home button, press and hold the top button and either volume button at the same time until the Slide to Power Off bar appears, and then swipe the bar. For models with a Home button, press and hold the top button until the Slide to Power Off bar appears, then swipe the bar. You've just turned off your iPad.

» **Force Off:** For iPad models without a Home button, press and release the volume up button, press and release the volume down button, and then press and hold the top button. For models with a Home button, hold the top button and Home button simultaneously. Let go of all buttons, regardless of model, when the Apple logo appears on the screen.

To wake the iPad up from sleep mode, simply tap the screen or press the Home button once.

If you have the passcode feature enabled, you need to enter your passcode before proceeding to unlock your screen. However, if you have Touch ID enabled, you need to press the top button or Home button only once and rest your finger on it for it to scan your fingerprints; the iPad will automatically unlock. If you have Face ID, your iPad will scan your face and unlock when you swipe up from the bottom of the screen.

TIP

Want a way to shut down your iPad without having to press buttons? Go to Settings ⇨ General and scroll all the way to the bottom of the screen. Tap the Shut Down button, slide the Power Off slider, and your iPad will turn off.

## IN THIS CHAPTER

» **Update iPadOS**

» **Charge your iPad's battery**

» **Sign into an iTunes account**

» **Sync your iPad wirelessly**

» **Understand how to use iCloud**

» **Store and browse files**

Chapter **3**

# Beyond the Basics

n this chapter, you look first at updating your iPad OS version (the operating system that your iPad uses) and making sure that your iPad's battery is charged.

Next, you discover how to get an Apple Account. You'll need one if you want to find free or paid content for your iPad from Apple, from movies to music to e-books to audiobooks.

You also find out how to use the wireless sync feature to exchange content between your computer and iPad over a wireless network.

Another feature you might take advantage of is the iCloud service from Apple to store and push all kinds of content and data to all your Apple devices — wirelessly. You can pick up where you left off from one device to another through iCloud Drive, an online storage service that enables sharing content among devices so that edits that you make to documents in iCloud are reflected on all of your iPads and iPhones, and Macs running OS X Yosemite (version 10.10) or later. (Note that some features may not be supported as well or at all if you're using an older version of the operating system.)

TIP

The operating system for Apple's Mac computers used to be called OS X. These days, it's referred to as macOS. The Mac operating system is mentioned a few times throughout this book, and you should know that macOS is the new and improved version of OS X.

# Keep Your iPad's Operating System Updated

This book is based on the latest version of the iPad operating system at the time: iPadOS 18. To be sure that you have the latest and greatest features, update your iPad to the latest iPadOS now (and do so periodically to receive minor updates to iPadOS 18 or future versions of iPadOS). If you've set up an iCloud account on your iPad, you'll receive an alert and can choose to install the update or not, or you can update manually:

1. Tap Settings.

   Be sure that you have Wi-Fi enabled and that your iPad is connected to a Wi-Fi network to perform these steps.

2. Tap General.

3. Tap Software Update.

   Your iPad checks to find the latest iPadOS version and walks you through the updating procedure if an update is available.

TIP

You can also allow your iPad to perform automatic updates overnight. Go to Settings ⇨ General ⇨ Software Update ⇨ Automatic Updates and toggle all available switches on (green). Your iPad must be connected to Wi-Fi and its charger to automatically update. I highly recommend doing this so that you don't miss updates or cool new features.

# Charge the Battery

My iPad showed up in the box almost fully charged, and I hope yours did, too — when you open a new toy it dulls the thrill if you have to charge it before you can do anything with it. But all batteries run down eventually, so one of your first priorities is to know how to recharge your iPad's battery.

Gather your iPad along with its charging cable and power adapter (be sure to use the proper cable and adapter).

Here's how to charge your iPad:

1. Gently plug the correct end of the charging cable into the iPad. What kind of connector it is depends on which model iPad you have.

2. Plug the other end of the charging cable into the Apple power adapter.

3. Plug the adapter into an electric outlet.

   The charging icon appears onscreen, indicating that your iPad is getting power.

You can charge your iPad also by using your Mac or PC, assuming it has the correct ports to match your charging cable. Mind you, though, this method is anywhere from a tad to much slower than using your iPad's charger.

If you need a replacement charger cable or power adapter, get it from Apple. It's tempting to buy a less expensive product, but take it from me: I did so for my previous iPad and fried the internal components because the cables weren't up to spec for my device.

# Sign into an Apple Account for Music, Movies, and More

The terms *iTunes account* and *Apple Account* are interchangeable: Your Apple Account *is* the credential for your iTunes account, but you'll need to be signed in with your Apple Account to download items from the App Store and the iTunes Store.

**TIP** If you've never set up an Apple Account, please visit `https://support.apple.com/en-us/108647` on your computer, iPhone, or iPad for help in setting one up.

To be able to buy or download free items from the iTunes Store or the App Store on your iPad, you must open an Apple Account. Here's how to sign in to an account after you've created it:

1. Tap Settings on your iPad.

2. At the top left of the Settings list, tap Apple Account, as shown in **Figure 3-1,** and then tap Sign In Manually when the Apple Account window pops up.

**TIP** Your iPad must be connected to a Wi-Fi or cellular network to sign in.

3. Enter the email address or phone number of your Apple Account in the field provided (see **Figure 3-2**) and then tap the Continue button. Enter the password of your Apple Account in the field provided and tap the Continue button again. When prompted to enter a verification code, do so, and then you'll be signed in to your Apple Account.

FIGURE 3-1

**TIP**

Your Apple Account will require a payment method if you intend on purchasing content from the App Store or the iTunes Store. If you prefer not to leave your credit card info with Apple, one option is to buy an Apple gift card and provide that as your payment information. You can replenish the card periodically through the Apple Store.

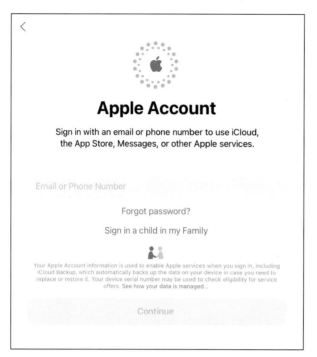

**FIGURE 3-2**

# SIGN IN WITH APPLE

Sign In with Apple is a privacy feature that allows you to use your Apple Account to sign in to many social media accounts or websites. This service provides a simple and secure way to sign in to accounts without having to remember a unique password for each one. Think of it as Apple's more secure replacement for Sign In with Google or Sign In with Facebook, both of which you've probably seen online. The Sign In with Apple button will show up in apps and websites when an account login is required. Check out `https://support.apple.com/en-us/102609` for more information on what I consider to be an important and effective privacy feature from Apple.

# Sync Wirelessly

You can connect your iPad to a computer and use the tools there to sync content on your computer to your iPad. Or, with Wi-Fi turned on in Settings, you can use Wi-Fi to allow cordless syncing if you're within range of a Wi-Fi network that has a computer connected to it.

**TIP**

If you have a Mac running macOS Mojave (10.14) or earlier, or a Windows-based PC, you'll need iTunes installed on your computer to sync content with your iPad. You can download iTunes by visiting `www.apple.com/itunes`; Windows 10 and 11 users will be better served by downloading iTunes by using the Microsoft Store app that comes with those versions of Windows. If you have a Mac running macOS Catalina (10.15) or later, you use Finder to sync with your iPad.

Before you can perform a wireless sync, you need to perform a few steps with your iPad connected to your computer:

1. If you're charging with an electrical outlet, remove the power adapter.

2. Use your iPad's charging cable to connect your iPad to your computer.

3. If you have a Mac running macOS Mojave or earlier, or a Windows-based PC running iTunes:

   a. Open iTunes and click the icon of your iPad, which appears in the tools in the upper-left corner of the window.

   b. Select the Sync with This iPad over Wi-Fi check box; you may need to scroll down a bit to see it.

   c. Skip to Step 5.

   You can click any item on the left side of the screen to handle settings for syncing such items as movies, music, and books. You can also tap the list of items in the On My Device section on the left side to view and even play content directly from your iPad.

4. If you have a Mac running macOS Catalina or later:

   a. Open a Finder window and then click the icon of your iPad, which appears in the left sidebar.

   b. At the top of the Finder window, click General, and then select the Show This iPad When on Wi-Fi check box.

5. In the lower-right corner of the iTunes or Finder window, click Apply.

6. Disconnect your iPad from your computer.

After you complete the preceding steps, you'll be able to wirelessly sync your iPad with your computer.

TIP

Backing up over a wireless connection is slower than with a cable connected to your computer. If you need to speed things up, simply connect your iPad to your computer and the sync will continue seamlessly. However, if you then disconnect the iPad from your computer, the sync will stop. Reconnect to the computer with the cable or with Wi-Fi to pick up where you left off.

TIP

If you have your iPad set up to sync wirelessly to your Mac or PC and both are connected to the same Wi-Fi network, your iPad will appear in your devices list (if you're using iTunes) or in Locations (if you're using Finder). This setup allows you to sync and manage syncing from iTunes or Finder (depending on which is required for your computer).

# Understand iCloud

There's an alternative to syncing content with a computer. iCloud is a service offered by Apple that allows you to back up most of your content to online storage. That content is then pushed automatically to all your Apple devices wirelessly. All you need to do is get an iCloud account, which is free (again, simply using your Apple Account), and choose settings on your devices and in iTunes for which types of content you want pushed to each device. After you've done that, content you create or purchase on one device — such as music, apps, and TV shows, as well as documents created in Apple's iWork apps (Pages, Keynote, and Numbers), photos, and so on — is synced among your devices automatically.

You can stick with iCloud's default storage capacity, or you can increase it if you need more:

» Your iCloud account includes 5GB of free storage. You may be fine with the free 5GB of storage.

  Content that you purchase from Apple (such as apps, books, music, iTunes Match content, Photo Sharing contents, movies and shows) isn't counted against your storage.

» If you want additional storage, you can buy an upgrade to iCloud+. Currently, 50GB costs only 99¢ per month, 200GB is $2.99 per month, and 2TB (a large amount of storage) is $9.99 per month. Two more options are simply too much for most of us (in terms of both size and cost): 6TB for $29.99 per month and 12TB for $59.99 per month. Most likely, 50GB will satisfy the needs of folks who just like to take and share pictures, but if videos are your thing, you may eventually want to consider the larger capacities.

## WHAT INFORMATION DOES iCLOUD BACK UP?

It's helpful to know what iCloud backs up on your iPad or other Apple devices, such as your iPhone or Mac. Apple's happy to share that with us iPad fans:

- Device settings
- Home screen settings and app organization
- Photos and videos
- Text messages
- Data from the apps you've installed
- Your purchase history from Apple: apps, music, ringtones, movies, and TV shows

*(continued)*

*(continued)*

- Apple Watch data
- Your Visual Voicemail password

For more information, please see Apple's support site at https://support.apple.com/en-us/108770.

To upgrade your storage, go to Settings, tap your Apple Account at the top of the screen, go to iCloud ⇨ Storage, and then tap Change Storage Plan, Buy More Storage, or Upgrade. On the Change Storage Plan screen, tap the amount you need and then tap Buy (in the upper-right corner), as shown in **Figure 3-3.**

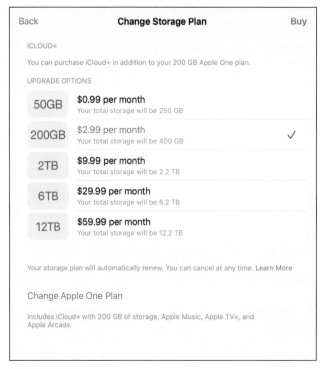

**FIGURE 3-3**

If you change your mind, you can get in touch with Apple within 15 days to cancel your upgrade.

**TIP**

# Turn On iCloud Drive

iCloud Drive is the online storage space that comes free with iCloud (as covered in the preceding section). Before you can use iCloud Drive, you need to be sure that it's turned on.

Here's how to turn on iCloud Drive:

1. Tap Settings and then tap your Apple Account at the top of the screen.

2. Tap iCloud to open the iCloud screen, and then tap See All in the Saved to iCloud section.

3. Tap iCloud Drive in the Saved to iCloud screen to display the iCloud Drive screen.

4. Tap the Sync This iPad switch on (green) to turn on iCloud Drive (see **Figure 3-4**).

FIGURE 3-4

# Set Up iCloud Sync Settings

When you have an iCloud account up and running, you have to specify which type of content iCloud should sync with your iPad. Follow these steps:

**1.** Open Settings, tap your Apple Account at the top of the screen, and then tap iCloud.

**2.** In the Saved to iCloud section, tap See All.

**3.** As shown in **Figure 3-5,** tap the switch for any item that's turned off that you want to turn on (or vice versa). If you don't see a switch on this screen, tap the item to view its options on a separate screen.

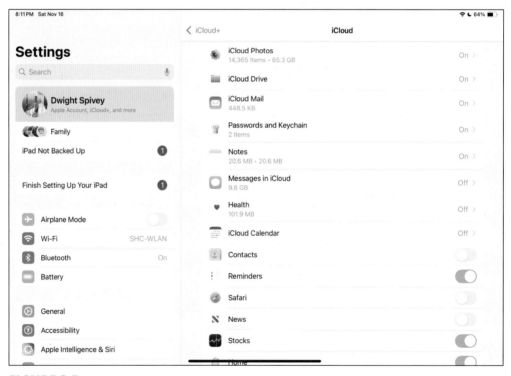

**FIGURE 3-5**

You can sync Photos, Mail, Contacts, Calendars, Reminders, Safari, Notes, News, Wallet, and more. The listing of apps on this screen isn't alphabetical, so scroll down if you don't see what you're looking for at first glance.

If you want to allow iCloud to provide a service for locating a lost or stolen iPad, tap your Apple Account in Settings, tap Find My, tap Find My iPad, and then toggle the on/off switch in the Find My iPad field on (green) to activate it. While you're there, it's a great idea to toggle on the switches for Find My Network and Send Last Location. This service helps you locate, send a message to, or delete content from your iPad if it falls into other hands.

# Browse Your iPad's Files

Longtime iPad users once pined for a way to browse files stored on their devices, as opposed to being limited to finding documents and other files within the apps they're intended for or created by. Finally, a few iPadOS iterations back, the Files app came along to allow you to browse not only for files stored on your iPad and iCloud Drive but also for stuff you've stored on other online (cloud) services, such as Google Drive, Dropbox, OneDrive, and others.

To use other services with the Files app, first download their apps from the App Store and then sign in to your respective account for that service. Once that's done, the service will appear in the sidebar of the Files app.

## USE EXTERNAL STORAGE

You can connect external storage devices, such as an SD card, a USB device, or a hard drive, to your iPad by using your iPad's Lightning or USB-C port (depending on your model). Make sure that your external device will connect to the charging port on your iPad; this connection may require an adapter. (Apple sells various types of adapters that will enable you to use external storage with your iPad.)

*(continued)*

*(continued)*

Every external storage device uses a file format, and Apple supports ExFAT, FAT32, FAT, HFS+, APFS, and APFS (encrypted) formats in the Files app. Be sure your external devices support one of those file formats before attempting to use them with your iPad. The external device must also only have a single partition. Additionally, some devices may need to be connected to an external power source. Again, check with the manufacturer of the device to find out if this is necessary.

You'll find the Files app on the first Home screen, by default.

**1.** Tap the Files icon to open the app.

**2.** On the Browse screen (see **Figure 3-6**):

- Tap the Search icon (magnifying glass in the upper right) to search for items by title or content.

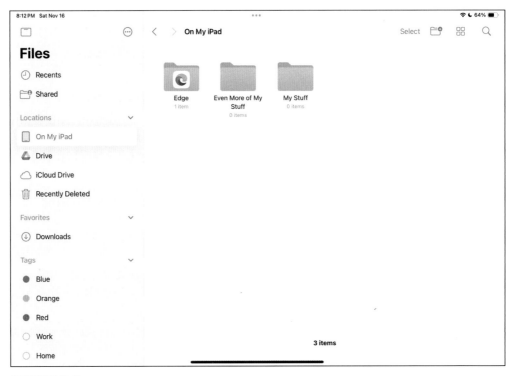

**FIGURE 3-6**

- Tap a source in the Locations or Favorites sections (in the sidebar) to browse a particular service or your iPad.

- Tap a tag in the Tags section (in the sidebar) to search for files you've tagged according to categories.

3. Once in a source (see **Figure 3-7**), you can tap files to open or preview them, and you can tap folders to open them and view their contents.

4. To perform an action on a file or folder (such as duplicating or moving it), tap Select in the upper-right corner of the screen and then tap items to select them for an action.

Available actions, which are at the bottom of the screen, include

- **Duplicate:** Make copies of selected items.

- **Move:** Move selected items to other locations.

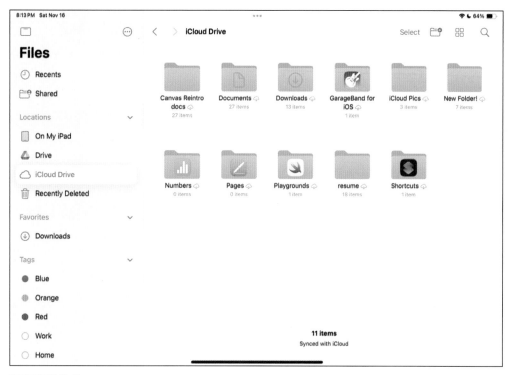

**FIGURE 3-7**

- **Share:** Share selected items with other people in a variety of ways (Messages and Mail, for example), and you can even invite them to make edits, if you like.

- **Delete:** Trash items you no longer need.

TIP

If you need to retrieve an item you've deleted (you have 30 days to do so before it disappears forever into the digital ether), go to the Browse screen (if you're not already there) and tap Recently Deleted in the sidebar. Tap Select in the upper-right corner, tap the item you'd like to retrieve, and tap the Recover button at the bottom of the screen. The item will be placed back in the location from which it was originally deleted. Please note that some services may not allow you to retrieve an item you've deleted, so if you don't see the item you're looking for, contact that particular service for help.

# 2

# Beginning to Use Your iPad

**IN THIS PART . . .**

Understanding accessibility features

Getting to know Siri

Discovering new apps and games

Managing your contacts

Reaching out with FaceTime and Messages

Engaging with social media and the internet

Working with email

**IN THIS CHAPTER**

» Use Magnifier

» Set brightness and wallpapers

» Set up and use accessibility features

» Set up subtitles, captioning, and other hearing settings

» Learn with Guided Access

» Control your iPad with your voice

» Customize settings for individual apps

Chapter **4**

# Making Your iPad More Accessible

iPad users are a diverse group, and some face visual, motor, or hearing challenges. If you're one of these folks, you'll be glad to know that Apple offers some handy accessibility features for your iPad.

To make your screen easier to read, you can use the Magnifier app, adjust the brightness, or change the wallpaper. You can also set up the VoiceOver feature to read onscreen elements out loud. Voice Control, Numbers, and Grids are welcome accessibility features to help you navigate more easily. And you can turn on or off a slew of features, including Zoom, Invert Colors, Speak Selection, Assistive Access, Live Speech, and Large Type.

If hearing is your challenge, you can do the obvious thing and adjust the system volume. The iPad also allows you to use mono audio (useful when you're wearing headphones) and to set an LED to flash when an alert sounds.

Features that help you deal with physical and motor challenges include an AssistiveTouch feature for those who have difficulty using the iPad touchscreen, Switch Control for working with adaptive accessories, and Call Audio Routing settings.

The Guided Access feature helps if you have difficulty focusing on one task. It also provides a handy mode for showing presentations of content in settings where you don't want users to flit off to other apps, as in school or a public kiosk.

This chapter covers these and more accessibility features of iPadOS 18.

# Use Magnifier

The Magnifier app uses your iPad's camera to help you magnify objects. Magnifier is considered an accessibility feature, but almost everyone needs a magnifier at one time or another. To utilize Magnifier:

1. Tap the Magnifier app icon to open it.

   By default, the app resides on the second Home screen page.

2. Point your iPad's camera at the object you want to magnify.

3. Drag the magnification slider (shown in **Figure 4-1**) to increase or decrease magnification.

By default, Magnifier offers an advanced controls pane (refer to **Figure 4-1**) with more controls to help customize your experience. You can select which camera to use, adjust brightness and contrast levels, and apply color filters. You can also take freeze frames (to freeze something onscreen momentarily) by tapping the large round Capture button.

**Advanced controls pane**          **Magnification slider**

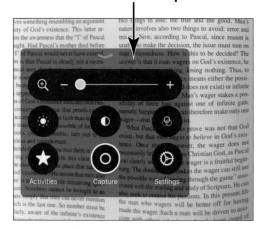 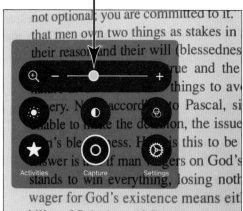

FIGURE 4-1

Freeze frames are not automatically saved to Photos; they disappear into the ether when you close the Magnifier app. However, you can save them by tapping the Share icon (which appears after you take a freeze frame) and then tapping Save Image.

Tap the settings icon (gear) in the lower right of the advanced controls pane to open the Settings dialog, shown in **Figure 4-2.** From here, you can determine which controls appear in the advanced controls pane and the order in which they appear. To remove a control, tap the red circle containing the minus sign (−) found to the left of the control name; then tap the Remove button that appears on the right. To add a control you've removed, simply tap the green circle containing the plus sign (+).

You can combine magnification with your iPad's portability so that you can reach up to (or behind) an object and magnify something that is not only too small to see otherwise but also out of view entirely.

FIGURE 4-2

# Set Brightness and Night Shift

Especially when using your iPad as an e-reader, you may find that a slightly dimmer screen reduces strain on your eyes. To manually adjust screen brightness, follow these steps:

**1.** Tap the Settings icon on the Home screen.

**TIP**

If glare from the screen is a problem for you, consider getting a screen protector. This thin film both protects your screen from damage and reduces glare. You can easily find them on Amazon, and just about any cellphone dealer or tech store carries them.

**2.** In Settings, go to Accessibility ⇨ Display & Text Size.

**3.** Tap the Auto-Brightness switch (see **Figure 4-3**) to turn off this feature (the button turns white when off).

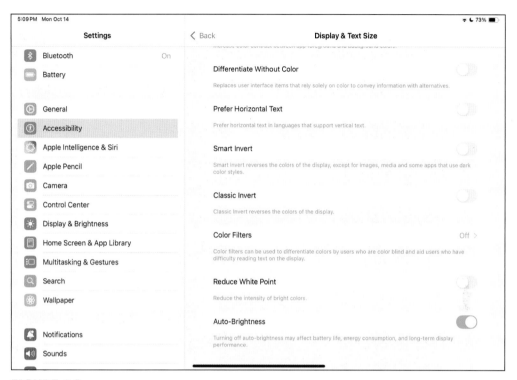

FIGURE 4-3

You may need to scroll down to the bottom of the Display & Text Size list to find this option.

4. Tap Display & Brightness on the left side of the screen, and then tap and drag the Brightness slider (see **Figure 4-4**) to the right to make the screen brighter or to the left to make it dimmer.

5. Press the Home button or swipe up on the screen (for iPad models without a Home button) to return to the Home screen.

TIP

In the Apple Books e-reader app, you can set a sepia tone for the page, which might be easier on your eyes. See Chapter 12 for more about using the Apple Books app.

Night Shift is another option in Display & Brightness that you can use during hours of darkness. It changes the screen colors to reduce the amount of blue in the images on your iPad. Bright blue light seems to interfere with sleep in some people, so turning on Night Shift if you read before bed (or in bed) may help you sleep better.

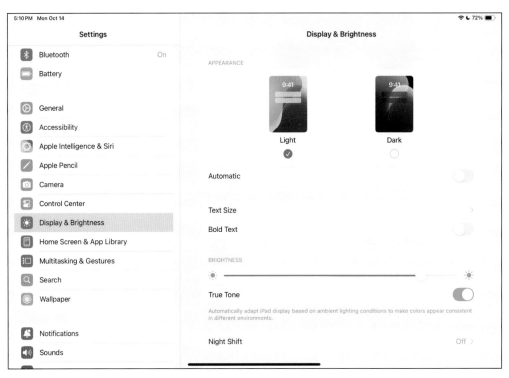

FIGURE 4-4

TIP

You can schedule Night Shift to be automatically enabled at certain times, or you can manually enable it when needed.

# Change the Wallpaper

The default background image on your iPad may be pretty, but it may not be the one that works best for you. Choosing different wallpaper may help you to more easily see all the icons on your Home screen. Follow these steps to change the wallpaper:

1. Tap the Settings icon on the Home screen.

2. In Settings, tap Wallpaper.

3. In the Wallpaper settings, tap +Add New Wallpaper.

4. Tap a wallpaper category, shown in **Figure 4-5,** to view choices.

5. Tap a sample to select it.

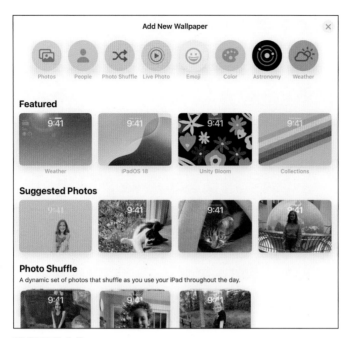

**FIGURE 4-5**

**TIP**

If you prefer to use a picture that's on your iPad, tap Photos in the Add New Wallpaper sheet to locate a picture, and then tap to use it as your wallpaper.

6. In the preview that appears (see **Figure 4-6**), tap any options on the screen that you'd like to customize (what you see depends on the wallpaper you're previewing), and then tap Add in the upper-right corner to select the new wallpaper. To use the wallpaper for both your lock screen and Home screen (my choice for this example), tap Set as Wallpaper Pair. Or to select a different wallpaper for the Home screen, tap Customize Home Screen.

7. Back on the Wallpaper screen, where your new wallpaper has been applied to your lock and Home screens, tap the Customize button under either if you'd like to make any changes.

8. Press the Home button or swipe up from the bottom of the screen (for iPad models without a Home button).

   You return to your Home screen with the new wallpaper set as the background. And the next time you view your lock screen, the new wallpaper will appear there, too.

**FIGURE 4-6**

**TIP**

You can quickly make changes to the wallpaper also when viewing the lock screen. Simply touch and hold the screen to view a list of your wallpapers. Find the wallpaper you'd like to use and tap to change to it. You can also make changes from here by tapping the Customize button under the wallpaper you'd like to change.

# Set Up VoiceOver

VoiceOver reads the names of screen elements and settings to you, but it also changes the way you provide input to the iPad. In Notes, for example, you can have VoiceOver read the name of the Notes buttons to you, and when you enter notes, it reads words or characters that you've entered. It can also tell you whether such features as Auto-Correction are on.

VoiceOver is even smarter in iPadOS 18 than in previous incarnations. It includes support for apps and websites that may not have built-in accessibility support. It can read descriptions of images in apps and on the web, and it can identify and speak text it finds in images.

To turn on VoiceOver, follow these steps:

**1.** Tap the Settings icon on the Home screen.

**2.** In Settings, tap Accessibility.

**3.** In the Accessibility pane, tap VoiceOver.

**4.** In the VoiceOver pane, shown in **Figure 4-7,** tap the VoiceOver switch to turn on this feature (the button becomes green).

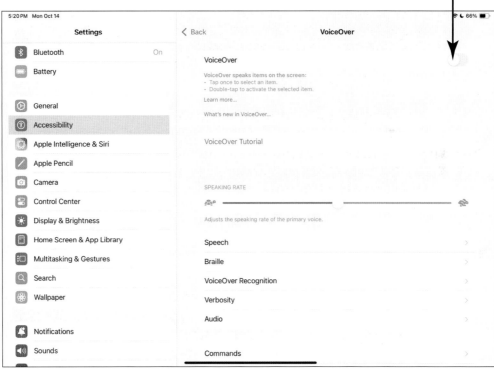

**FIGURE 4-7**

**TIP**

With VoiceOver on, you must first single-tap to select an item such as a button, which causes VoiceOver to read the name of the button to you. Then you double-tap the button to activate its function.

5. Tap the VoiceOver Practice button to select it, double-tap the button to open VoiceOver Practice, and then tap VoiceOver Practice in the middle of the screen to begin. Practice using gestures (such as pinching or flicking left), and VoiceOver tells you what action each gesture initiates.

6. Tap the Done button and then double-tap the same button to return to the VoiceOver dialog.

7. Tap the Verbosity button once and then double-tap to open its options:

   - Tap the Speak Hints switch and then double-tap the switch to turn the feature on (or off). VoiceOver speaks the name of each tapped item.

   - Tap once and then double-tap the VoiceOver button in the upper-left corner of the Verbosity window to go back to the VoiceOver screen.

**TIP**

You can change the language that VoiceOver speaks. In General settings, tap Language & Region, tap Add Language, select another language, and then choose which language to use as your primary language. However, this action also changes the language used for labels on Home icons and various settings and fields in iPad. Be careful with this setting, lest you choose a language you don't understand by accident and have a difficult time figuring out how to change it back.

8. If you would like VoiceOver to speak descriptions of images in apps or on the web, swipe up with three fingers to scroll down and then tap and double-tap VoiceOver Recognition, tap and double-tap Image Descriptions, and finally tap and double-tap the Image Descriptions switch to toggle the setting on (green).

**TIP**

Don't ignore the Sensitive Content Output setting in the Image Descriptions page. If the content of an image is something you'd like to keep everyone in the room from hearing, select any option other than Speak.

9. Return to the main VoiceOver screen.

10. If you want VoiceOver to read words or characters to you (for example, in the Notes app), scroll down (use a three-finger swipe to do so), tap and double-tap Typing, and then tap and double-tap Typing Feedback.

11. In the Typing Feedback dialog, tap and then double-tap to select the option you prefer in both the Software Keyboards section and the Hardware Keyboards section.

    The Words option causes VoiceOver to read words to you but not individual characters you type, such as the dollar sign ($). The Characters and Words option causes VoiceOver to read both the individual characters as you type them and each word as you complete it.

12. Press the Home button or swipe up from the bottom of the screen (iPad models without a Home button) to return to the Home screen.

The following section shows how to navigate your iPad after you've turned on VoiceOver.

TIP

You can use the Accessibility Shortcut setting to help you more quickly turn the VoiceOver, Zoom, Switch Control, AssistiveTouch, Live Captions, and Increase Contrast, and a host of other features on and off. In the Accessibility screen, tap Accessibility Shortcut (near the very bottom of the screen). In the screen that appears, choose what you want with three presses of the Home button (or top button, for iPads without a Home button) to activate. Now three presses with a single finger on the Home button or top button (depending on your iPad model) provide you with the option you selected wherever you go in iPad.

# Use VoiceOver

After VoiceOver is turned on (see preceding section), you need to figure out how to use it. I won't kid you — using it is awkward at first, but you'll get the hang of it.

Here are the main onscreen gestures you should know how to use:

» **Tap an item to select it.** VoiceOver then speaks its name.

» **Double-tap the selected item.** This action activates the item.

» **Flick three fingers.** It takes three fingers to scroll around a page with VoiceOver turned on.

The first time my iPad locked when using VoiceOver, I had no idea how to unlock it. Luckily, I found the answer by consulting Apple's support site from a computer. If your iPad has a Home button, just press it to unlock — simple. However, if your iPad doesn't have a Home button, you need to look at your iPad (for Face ID to recognize you) and then slowly move your finger up from the bottom of the screen until you hear two tones, which indicate that your screen is unlocked.

If tapping with two or three fingers is difficult, try tapping with one finger from one hand and one or two from the other. When double- or triple-tapping, you have to perform these gestures as quickly and as precisely as you can for them to work.

Table 4-1 provides additional gestures to help you use VoiceOver. If you want to use this feature often, I recommend the VoiceOver section of the iPad User Guide, which goes into great detail about using VoiceOver. You can find the User Guide at `https://support. apple.com/en-us/docs`. When there, just click or tap iPad, and then click or tap the model of iPad or the version of iPadOS you have to read its manual. You can also get an Apple Books version of the manual through that app in the Book Store (see Chapter 12 for more information). iPadOS 18 also includes a VoiceOver Tutorial, which is helpful in getting started. You'll find the VoiceOver Tutorial button in VoiceOver settings.

Check out some of the settings for VoiceOver, including a choice for Braille, Language Rotor for making language choices, the ability to navigate images, and a setting to have iPad speak notifications.

**TABLE 4-1**  **VoiceOver Gestures**

| Gesture | Effect |
|---|---|
| Flick right or left | Select the next or preceding item |
| Tap with two fingers | Stop or continue speaking the current item |
| Flick two fingers up | Read everything from the top of the screen |
| Flick two fingers down | Read everything from the current position |
| Flick three fingers up or down | Scroll one page at a time |
| Flick three fingers right or left | Go to the next or preceding page |
| Tap three fingers | Speak the scroll status (for example, line 20 of 100) |
| Flick four fingers up or down | Go to the first or last element on a page |
| Flick four fingers right or left | Go to the next or preceding section (as on a web page) |

# Make Additional Vision Settings

Several Vision features are simple settings that you can turn on or off after you tap Settings ⇨ Accessibility:

» **Zoom:** The Zoom feature enlarges the contents displayed on the iPad screen when you double-tap the screen with three fingers. The Zoom feature works almost everywhere in iPad: in Photos, on web pages, on your Home screens, in your Mail, in Music, and in Apple TV. Give it a try!

» **Spoken Content:** Options here include the ability to have your iPad speak items you've selected or to hear the content of an entire screen and highlight content as it's spoken.

» **Display & Text Size:** Includes such features as

•  **Color Filters** (aids in case of color blindness)

•  **Reduce White Point** (helps reduce the intensity of bright colors)

TIP

- **Invert Colors** (which reverses colors on your screen so that white backgrounds are black and black text is white): Classic Invert inverts all colors, and Smart Invert does not invert colors for items like images, multimedia, and some apps that may use darker color styles.

  The Invert Colors feature works well in some places and not so well in others. For example, in the Photos application, pictures appear almost as photo negatives (which is a really cool trick to try). Your Home screen image likewise looks a bit strange. And don't even think of playing a video with this feature turned on! However, if you need help reading text, White on Black can be useful in several apps.

» **Larger Text (under Accessibility ⇨ Display & Text Size):** If having larger text in such apps as Contacts, Mail, and Notes would be helpful to you, you can turn on the Larger Text feature and choose the text size that works best for you.

» **Bold Text (under Accessibility ⇨ Display & Text Size):** Turning on this setting restarts your iPad (after asking you for permission to do so) and then causes text in various apps and in Settings to be bold.

» **Button Shapes (under Accessibility ⇨ Display & Text Size):** This setting applies shapes to buttons so that they're more easily distinguishable. For an example, check out the Accessibility button near the top of the screen after you enable Button Shapes by toggling its switch on. Turn it back off and notice the difference (shown in **Figure 4-8;** the button name is underlined).

» **Reduce Transparency (under Accessibility ⇨ Display & Text Size):** This setting helps increase legibility of text by reducing blurring and transparency effects that make up a good deal of the iPad user interface.

» **Increase Contrast (under Accessibility ⇨ Display & Text Size):** Use this setting to set up backgrounds in some areas of the iPad and apps with greater contrast, which should improve visibility.

» **On/Off Labels (under Accessibility ⇨ Display & Text Size):** If you have trouble making out colors and therefore find it hard to tell when a setting is on (green) or off (white), use this setting to add a circle to the right of a setting when it's off and a white vertical line to a setting when it's on.

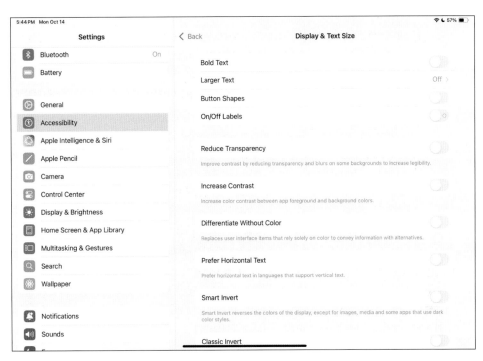

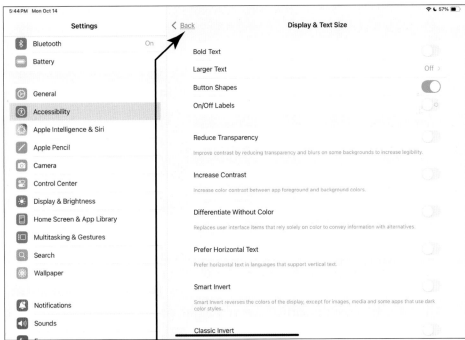

**With Button Shapes enabled**

FIGURE 4-8

>> **Reduce Motion (under Accessibility ⇨ Motion):** Tap this accessibility feature and then tap the on/off switch to turn off the parallax effect, which causes the icons and widgets to appear to float above the background as you move the iPad around.

>> **Audio Descriptions:** This option allows your iPad to describe scenes in videos that support audio descriptions. To learn how to know if a video supports audio descriptions, check out `https://support.apple.com/en-us/118409`.

# Use iPad with Hearing Aids

If you have Bluetooth enabled, your iPad may be able to detect your hearing aid and work with its settings to improve sound. Follow these steps to connect your hearing aid to your iPad. (You should also consult the hearing aid manufacturer's documentation.)

1. Tap Settings on the Home screen.

2. Tap Accessibility, scroll down to the Hearing section, and tap Hearing Devices.

   On the next screen, shown in **Figure 4-9,** your iPad searches for MFi (Made for iPhone) hearing aid devices.

   If you have a non-MFi hearing aid, add your hearing aid in Bluetooth settings. To do so, go to Settings ⇨ Bluetooth, make sure that the Bluetooth toggle switch is set on (green), and select your hearing aid in the list of devices.

3. When your device appears, tap it.

Using the stereo effect in headphones or a headset breaks up sounds so that you hear a portion in one ear and a portion in the other ear. The purpose is to simulate the way your ears process sounds. If there is only one channel of sound, that sound is sent to both ears. However, if you're hard of hearing or deaf in one ear, you're hearing only a portion of the sound in your hearing ear, which can be frustrating. If you have such hearing challenges and want to use iPad with a headset connected, you should turn on Mono Audio (go to Settings ➪ Accessibility ➪ Audio & Visual). When it's turned on, all sound is combined and distributed to both ears.

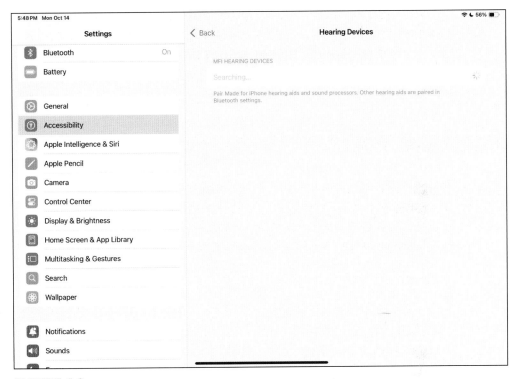

FIGURE 4-9

# Adjust the Volume

Although individual apps (such as Music and TV) have their own volume settings, you can also set your iPad system volume for your ringer and alerts to help you better hear what's going on. Follow these steps:

1. Tap Settings on the Home screen and then tap Sounds.

In the Sounds settings, you can turn on or off the sounds that iPad makes when certain events occur (such as receiving new Mail or Calendar alerts). Some sounds are turned on by default.

TIP

2. In the Sounds settings that appear (see **Figure 4-10**), tap and drag the Ringtone and Alerts slider to adjust the volume of these audible attention grabbers:

- Drag to the right to increase the volume.

- Drag to the left to lower the volume.

3. Press the Home button or swipe up from the bottom of the screen to return to the Home screen.

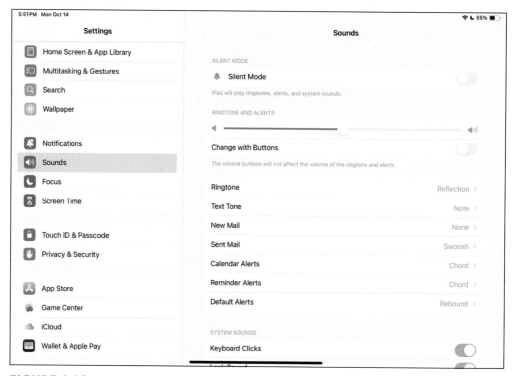

FIGURE 4-10

# Set Up Subtitles and Captioning

Closed captioning and subtitles help folks with hearing challenges enjoy entertainment and educational content. Follow these steps:

1. Tap Settings on the Home screen and then tap Accessibility.

2. Scroll down to the Hearing section and tap Subtitles & Captioning.

3. On the following screen, tap the switch to turn on Closed Captions + SDH (Subtitles for the Deaf and Hard of Hearing).

   You can also tap Style and choose a text style for the captions, as shown in **Figure 4-11.** A neat video shows you what your style will look like when the feature is in use. Tap the black box in the lower right of the video to expand it to full screen. Tap the screen to return to the Style screen.

4. Press the Home button or swipe up from the bottom of the screen to return to the Home screen.

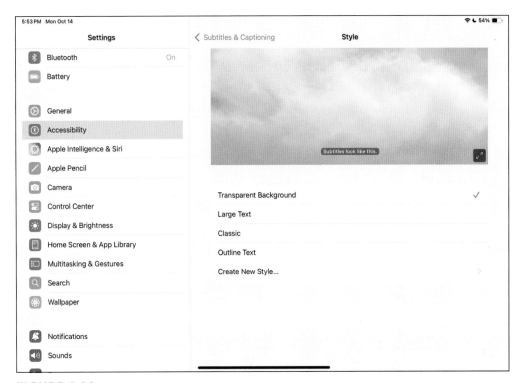

FIGURE 4-11

# Say It with Live Speech and Personal Voice

Live Speech gives your iPad the capability to speak what you type! If you are on a FaceTime call and having difficulty speaking, this feature will allow you to type what you want to say.

To enable Live Speech, go to Settings ➪ Accessibility ➪ Live Speech and toggle the Live Speech switch on (green). From here, you can also create a few of your favorite phrases to save time in a conversation and select a voice you'd like to use.

To launch Live Speech, triple-tap the top button on your iPad to open the Live Speech interface and keyboard, shown in **Figure 4-12**. Simply type what you want to say and tap Speak to have your text spoken.

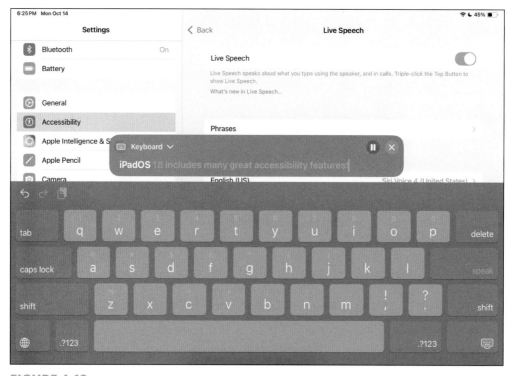

FIGURE 4-12

Don't like the predefined voices in the Live Speech settings? Use the Personal Voice feature to create a voice that sounds much like your own. When you create a personal voice, other features such as live speech will use it to speak to others. This feature is especially wonderful for folks who are faced with the prospect of losing their ability to speak. With Personal Voice, they can still speak to friends and loved ones using their own voice.

To create a personal voice, go to Settings ⇨ Accessibility ⇨ Personal Voice and tap Create a Personal Voice. You will be prompted through a series of steps to record your voice, which allows iPadOS 18 to build a close representation of what you sound like. Be patient: The process of creating your personal voice may take 15 to 60 minutes.

# Turn On and Work with AssistiveTouch

If you have difficulty using buttons, the AssistiveTouch menu aids input using the touchscreen.

1. To turn on AssistiveTouch, tap Settings on the Home screen and then tap Accessibility.

2. In the Accessibility pane, scroll down and tap Touch; then tap AssistiveTouch. In the pane that appears, tap the switch for AssistiveTouch to turn it on (see **Figure 4-13**).

    A black square (called the AssistiveTouch menu button) appears on the right side of the screen; you see it on your iPad's screen, but it doesn't appear in screenshots, such as **Figure 4-13**. This button now appears in the same location in whatever apps you display on your iPad, though you can move it around with your finger.

3. Tap the AssistiveTouch menu button to display options, as shown in **Figure 4-14.** The panel includes Notification Center and Control Center options.

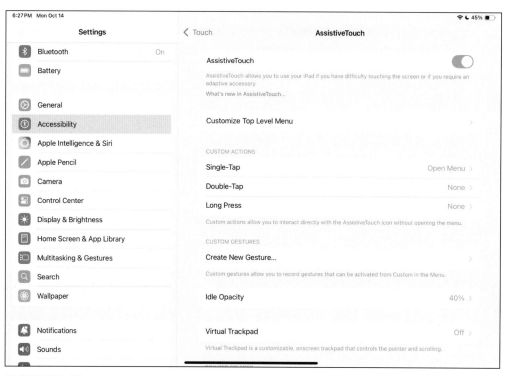

**FIGURE 4-13**

**FIGURE 4-14**

4. Tap Custom or Device to see additional choices; tap Siri to activate the personal assistant feature; tap Notification Center or Control Center to display those panels; or tap Home to go directly to the Home screen.

   After you choose an option, pressing the Home button or swiping up from the bottom of the screen (iPad models without a Home button) takes you back to the Home screen.

Table 4-2 shows the major options available in the AssistiveTouch Control panel and their purposes.

**TABLE 4-2** **AssistiveTouch Controls**

| Control | Purpose |
| --- | --- |
| Siri | Activates the Siri feature, which allows you to speak questions and make requests of your iPad. |
| Custom | Displays a set of gestures, with pinch and rotate, long press, double-tap, and hold and drag gestures preset; you can tap any of the other blank squares to add your own favorite gestures. |
| Device | Displays presets that enable you to rotate the screen, lock the screen, lock rotation of the screen, turn the volume up or down, shake iPad to undo an action, and more. |
| Scroll | Displays preset scroll actions. |
| Dwell | Displays preset dwell controls. |
| Home | Sends you to the Home screen. |
| Control Center | Open the Control Center common commands. |
| Notification Center | Open Notification Center with reminders, Calendar appointments, and so on. |

# Turn On Additional Physical and Motor Settings

Use the options in the Accessibility settings to help you deal with how fast you tap and how you answer incoming calls:

» **Home Button (appears only for iPad models that have one):** Sometimes if you have dexterity challenges, it's hard to double-press or triple-press the Home button fast enough to make an effect. Choose the Slow or Slowest option when you tap this setting to allow you a bit more time to make that second or third press. Also, the Rest Finger to Open feature at the bottom of the screen allows you to simply rest your finger on the Home button to unlock your iPad using Touch ID (if enabled), as opposed to needing to press the Home button.

» **Call Audio Routing (under Accessibility ⇨ Touch):** If you pre-fer to use your speaker phone to receive incoming calls, or you typically use a Bluetooth headset with your iPad that allows you to tap a button to receive a call, tap this option and then choose Bluetooth Headset or Speaker. Speakers and headsets can both provide a better hearing experience for many.

TIP

If you have certain adaptive accessories that allow you to control devices with head gestures, you can use them to control your iPad, highlighting features in sequence and then selecting one of those features. Use the Switch Control feature in the Accessibility settings to turn this mode on and make settings.

# Focus Learning with Guided Access

Guided Access is a feature that you can use to limit a user's access to iPad to a single app, and even limit access in that app to certain features. Guided Access can be useful in a classroom, for someone with attention deficit disorder, and even in a public setting (such as a kiosk where you don't want users to be able to open other apps).

1. Tap Settings and then tap Accessibility.

2. Scroll down and tap Guided Access; on the screen that appears, tap the Guided Access switch to turn the feature on (green). While you're here, also tap the Accessibility Shortcut switch to enable it.

3. Tap Passcode Settings and then tap Set Guided Access Passcode to activate a passcode so that those using an app can't return to the Home screen to access other apps.

   You may also activate Touch ID or Face ID (for iPad models without a Home button) to perform the same function.

4. In the dialog that appears (see **Figure 4-15**), enter a passcode using the numeric pad. Enter the number again when prompted.

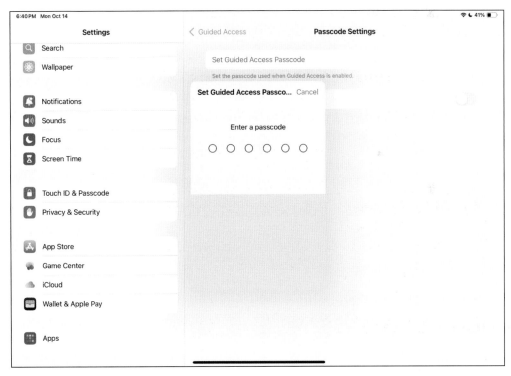

FIGURE 4-15

5. Press the Home button or swipe up from the bottom of the screen (for iPad models without a Home button) to return to the Home screen, then tap an app to open it.

6. Rapidly press the Home button or top button (for iPad models without a Home button) three times. Tap the Options button in the lower-left corner of the screen to display these options in a dialog:

   - **Sleep/Wake Button or Top Button (depending on your iPad model):** You can put your iPad to sleep or wake it up with three presses of the sleep/wake button or top button.

   - **Volume Buttons:** If you don't want users to be able to adjust volume using the volume toggle on the side of the iPad, for example, tap this switch on.

   - **Motion:** Turn this setting off if you don't want users to move the iPad around or switch viewing orientations — for example, to play a race car driving game in landscape mode.

   - **Software Keyboards:** Use this setting to prohibit people using this app from entering text using the keyboard.

   - **Touch:** If you don't want users to be able to use the touchscreen, turn this off.

   - **Time Limit:** Tap this and use the controls that are displayed to set a time limit for the use of the app.

7. Tap outside the dialog to hide the options.

TIP

At this point, you can also use your finger to circle areas of the screen that you want to disable, such as a Store button in the Music app.

8. Tap the Start button (upper-right corner) and then press the Home button or top button (for iPad models without a Home button) three times. Enter your passcode, if you set one, and tap End.

9. Tap the Home button or swipe up from the bottom of the screen (for iPad models without a Home button) again to return to the Home screen.

# Control Your iPad with Voice Control

Another exciting accessibility feature is the ability to control your iPad using your voice! The Voice Control feature also enables you to use numbers and grid overlays to command your iPad to perform tasks. This feature is a real game changer for a lot of folks.

1. Tap Settings and then tap Accessibility.

2. Tap Voice Control. Do one of the following:

   - If you haven't used Voice Control before, on the screen that follows, tap Set Up Voice Control (shown in **Figure 4-16**). Read through the information screens, tapping Continue to advance through them. At the end, you'll see that the Voice Control toggle switch is set on (green).

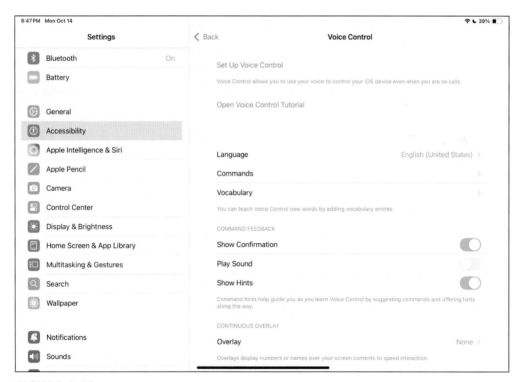

**FIGURE 4-16**

**TIP**

Pay particular attention to the What Can I Say? screen. It tells you in simple terms the commands you can use to get started with Voice Control, such as "Go home" and "Show grid." iPadOS 18 also includes a Voice Control Tutorial that you can access in Voice Control settings.

- If you've used Voice Control before but have since disabled it, toggle the Voice Control switch on (green).

**TIP**

You can easily tell when Voice Control is on because there will be a blue circle containing a waveform in the upper-right corner of your iPad's screen.

3. Tap Commands to see what commands are built in to Voice Control (shown in **Figure 4-17**), enable or disable commands, and even create your own custom commands.

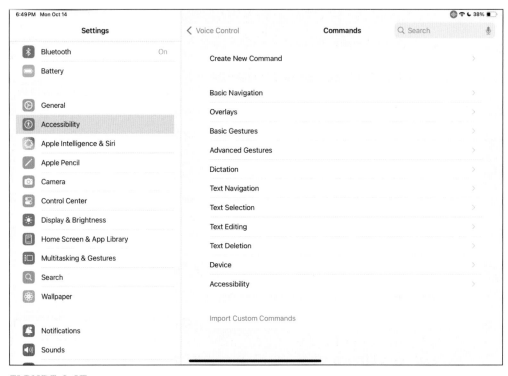

FIGURE 4-17

I suggest taking your time in this section of the Voice Control options because you'll be surprised by how much you can do out of the gate with this amazing tool.

4. Tap the Voice Control button in the upper-middle of the screen to return to the main Voice Control options.

5. In the Voice Control options, tap Vocabulary, tap Vocabulary again, and then tap + in the upper right. In the Add Custom Vocabulary window, type the word or phrase, and then tap the Next button. You then have the chance to teach Voice Control how to say the word so that it gets the pronunciation right. To do so, tap the record button (red circle) and say the word, then tap the blue Save button. You could also skip the recording and simply tap the Save without Recording button at the bottom of the screen.

6. Tap Vocabulary in the upper left, and then tap Voice Control in the upper left to return to the main Voice Control screen.

Tap Overlay at the bottom of the Voice Control screen and then select one of the four options for hiding or displaying an overlay. Overlays are a fantastic accessibility feature in iPadOS. If you use them, tap-pable items on the screen are labeled with numbers, names, or a numbered grid. When you want to tap an item, simply execute a command such as "tap three" to tap the item with your voice. Each of the three overlays are displayed in **Figure 4-18.**

**TIP**

When you're not actively using the feature, the number and name labels fade to a light gray so that you can more clearly see the screen. They darken again when you use the feature.

# Control Your iPad with Your Eyes

iPadOS 18 adds some great accessibility features, but one that's a game changer for many is Eye Tracking. This feature uses the front-facing camera of your iPad to track your eye movement. When you focus on a control or another item on the screen for a specific duration, your iPad acts the same as though you tapped it. This is an incredible leap forward, in my opinion!

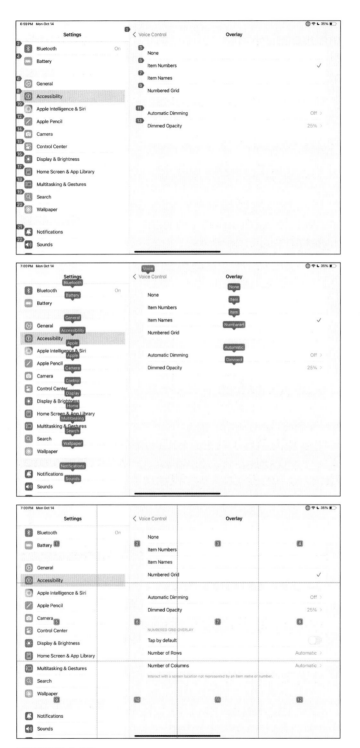

**FIGURE 4-18**

**TIP**

Ensure that you have adequate lighting and that the front-facing camera has a clear view of your face. The iPad should be on a stable surface about one and a half feet away from your face.

To set up Eye Tracking:

1. Tap Settings ⇨ Accessibility ⇨ Eye Tracking.

2. Toggle the Eye Tracking switch on (green).

3. Calibrate Eye Tracking by following the dots on the screen with your eyes.

   Once calibrated, Eye Tracking displays a pointer on the area of the screen that you're looking at.

4. Focus (or *dwell*) on a control for a specific period of time; your iPad will act as though you tapped the item.

   You'll see a line around the sections of the screen that Eye Tracking thinks you're looking at.

You can tap or touch your screen while using Eye Tracking.

Dwell Control is the feature that determines how long you must focus, or dwell, on an onscreen item to interact with it. The default duration is 1.5 seconds. You can adjust that and other Dwell Control settings by going to Settings ⇨ Accessibility ⇨ Touch ⇨ AssistiveTouch ⇨ Dwell Control.

# Control Your iPad with Vocal Shortcuts

Vocal Shortcuts is a new feature that allows a user to say a particular phrase and automatically perform whatever action is assigned to that phrase. For example, if you create a vocal shortcut using the phrase "open Safari," your iPad will open the Safari browser when you speak that phrase. Vocal Shortcuts can complete simple and complex tasks!

To get going with Vocal Shortcuts:

1. Tap Settings ⇨ Accessibility ⇨ Vocal Shortcuts.

2. Tap Set Up Vocal Shortcuts and then tap the blue Continue button on the next screen.

3. Tap an item in the Choose Action screen, and then follow the prompts to finish creating your vocal shortcut.

   For example, I tapped Control Center as my action and assigned it the phrase "Open Control Center." Now I can say "Open Control Center" to both open and close Control Center on my iPad.

4. Tap the Add Action button to continue adding more actions, if you like. When finished, test your actions to make sure they behave as expected.

# Adjust Accessibility Settings on a Per-App Basis

iPadOS 18's iteration of Accessibility features allows you to customize individually how each app handles display and text size settings, such as Bold Text, Larger Text, Increase Contrast, Smart Invert, and Reduce Motion. No need to settle for a one-setting-fits-all approach.

To customize Accessibility options on a per-app basis:

1. Tap Settings and then tap Accessibility.

2. Swipe down to the very bottom of the screen and tap Per-App Settings.

3. Tap Add App, and then tap an app in the list provided.

4. In the Per-App Settings screen that appears, tap the app you've just added, as shown in **Figure 4-19.**

**FIGURE 4-19**

5. On the screen that appears (see **Figure 4-20**), tap each option you'd like to customize, and then tap the name of the app in the upper-left corner to return to the list of options. Repeat this step until you're finished making customizations.

6. Tap Per-App Settings in the upper-left to return to the Per-App Settings screen.

7. If you want to customize additional apps, repeat Steps 3 to 6.

To delete a customization (don't worry, you're not deleting the app itself, just the Accessibility customizations you've made), tap Edit in the upper-right corner of the Per-App Settings screen, tap – in a red circle to the left of the customization you want to remove, and then tap the red Delete button that appears on the right.

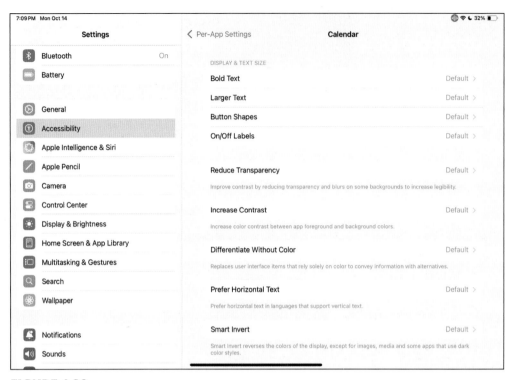

**FIGURE 4-20**

**IN THIS CHAPTER**

» Activate Siri

» Translate, get suggestions, and call contacts

» Create reminders and alerts

» Add events to your calendar

» Play music, get directions, and ask for facts

» Search the web

» Send and dictate messages

# Chapter 5

# Conversing with Siri

One of the most talked about (pun intended) features on your iPad is Siri, a personal assistant feature that responds to the commands you speak to your iPad. With Siri, you can ask for nearby restaurants, and a list appears. You can dictate your email messages rather than type them. You can open apps with a voice command. Calling your mother is as simple as saying, "Call Mom." Want to know the capital of Rhode Island? Just ask. Siri checks several online sources to answer questions ranging from the result of a mathematical equation to the next scheduled flight to Rome (in Italy or Georgia). You can have Siri search photos and videos and locate what you need by date, location, or album name. Ask Siri to remind you about an app you're working in, such as Safari, Mail, or Notes at a later time so you can pick up where you left off.

You can also have Siri perform tasks, such as returning calls and controlling the Music app. Siri can play music at your request and identify tagged songs (songs that contain embedded information that identifies them by categories such as artist or genre). You can also hail a ride with Uber or Lyft, watch live TV just by saying "Watch ESPN" (or, say, another app you might use, such as Netflix), find tagged photos, make payments with some third-party apps, and more. Siri can even tell you what tasks you can accomplish with your apps. And Siri's manners are impeccable!

Siri can offer you curated suggestions for Safari, Maps, and Podcasts. Siri also utilizes voice technology that allows it to sound more natural and smooth, particularly when speaking long phrases. Siri can also process requests entirely on your iPad. This means requests you make of Siri are performed much faster than in days past, which is a welcome change.

## SOMETHING COOL THIS WAY COMES

iPadOS 18 offers an overhaul to Siri, spearheaded by the introduction of Apple Intelligence, Apple's spin on generative artificial intelligence. Siri now has a greater understanding of personal context (Siri will be able to better understand what you mean when you ask something like, "When's my granddaughter's plane landing?"), can provide assistance with writing just about anything, and has built-in access to the latest incarnation of ChatGPT (a ChatGPT account is not required). Information you request will never leave the comfort of your iPad and Apple's servers. Some Apple Intelligence features are available now, but more will be released in future updates of iPadOS. Apple Intelligence is available only for iPad mini (A17 Pro), iPad Pro 11-inch (3rd and 4th generations) and 12.9-inch (5th and 6th generations), iPad Air (5th generation), or newer.

# Activate Siri

When you first go through the process of registering your iPad, you'll be prompted to begin making settings for your location, for using iCloud, and so on. At some point you'll see the option to activate Siri. As you begin to use your iPad, it will display a message reminding you about using Siri.

**TIP**

Siri requires internet access for some purposes, and cellular data charges could apply (if your iPad supports it) when Siri checks online sources if you're not connected to Wi-Fi. If you have an unlimited data plan from your cellular provider, these charges aren't something to worry about. (Available features may vary by area.)

If you didn't activate Siri during the registration process, you can use Settings to turn on Siri by following these steps:

1. Tap the Settings icon on the Home screen.

2. Tap Siri or Apple Intelligence & Siri (see **Figure 5-1**), depending on whether your iPad supports Apple Intelligence, and then tap Talk & Type to Siri.

3. In the Talk & Type to Siri options, activate either or both of the following features:

   - **Listen for "Siri" or "Hey Siri":** Activate Siri for hands-free use. When you first enable "Siri" or "Hey Siri," you'll be prompted to set up the feature. Just walk through the steps to enable it and continue.

     With this feature enabled, just say "Siri" or "Hey, Siri" and Siri opens, ready for a command. In addition, with streaming voice recognition, Siri displays in text what it's hearing as you speak, so you can verify that it has understood you correctly. This streaming feature makes the process of interacting with Siri faster.

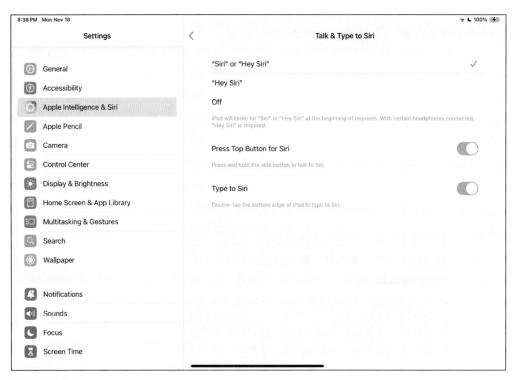

**FIGURE 5-1**

TIP

In the past, you had to say "Hey Siri," but now you can simply say "Siri" to invoke everyone's favorite digital assistant, if your iPad supports it. (If it doesn't, you won't see the option.) If you prefer things the way they used to be, you can opt for Siri to activate only when you attach the "Hey" to the front of its name; just go to Settings ⇨ Siri ⇨ Talk to Siri and tap "Hey Siri."

- **Press Home/Top Button for Siri:** Allows you to press the Home button or the top button (for iPads without a Home button) to activate Siri.

- **Type to Siri:** Double-tap the bottom edge of your iPad's screen to display the onscreen keyboard so you can type to Siri.

4. Tap Siri or Apple Intelligence & Siri in the left sidebar to return to the main Siri or Apple Intelligence & Siri page.

5. If you want to change the language Siri uses, tap Language and choose a different language in the list that appears.

**6.** To change the nationality or gender of Siri's voice from American to British or Australian (for example), or from female to male, tap Voice and make your selections.

Some nationalities have multiple voices you can select.

Give several nationalities and voices a shot. I've found that the Australian female voice (Voice 2) coupled with the English (United States) Language option was easier for me to understand.

**7.** Let Siri know about your contact information by tapping My Information and selecting yourself in your Contacts.

If you want to customize when Siri verbally responds to your requests, tap Siri Responses in the Siri or Apple Intelligence & Siri settings and choose from the selections. The Prefer Spoken Responses option causes Siri to verbally respond to your requests all the time — period. The Prefer Silent Responses option causes Siri to never verbally respond to your requests — period. Automatic allows Siri to determine on its own when it's appropriate to verbally respond. The Always Show Siri Captions switch displays whatever Siri says on your iPad's screen, while the Always Show Request switch displays the transcript of your entire exchange with Siri.

# Discover All That Siri Can Do

Siri allows you to interact by voice with many apps on your iPad.

No matter what kind of action you want to perform, first press and hold down the Home button or top button (depending on your iPad model) until Siri opens. Or, if you've enabled "Siri" or "Hey Siri," simply say the phrase.

You can pose questions or ask to do something like make a FaceTime call or add an event to your calendar, for example. Siri can also search the internet to provide information on just about any topic. In addition, you can use Siri to return a call, open and search the App Store, control Music playback, dictate text messages, and much more.

To see examples of what Siri can do for you, engage Siri and say, "What kind of questions can I ask you?" A dialog will appear onscreen telling you, "Here are some things you can try." Tap "Learn more about Siri" at the bottom of that dialog to visit www.apple.com/siri in Safari (or your default browser), as shown in **Figure 5-2.**

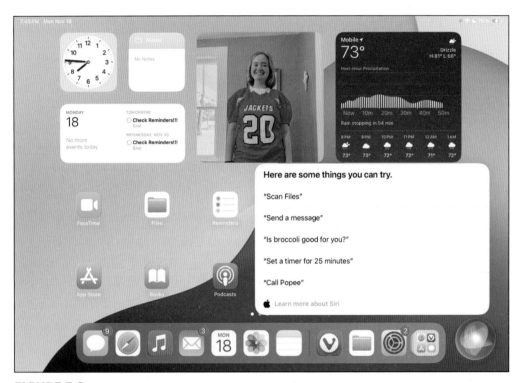

**FIGURE 5-2**

Siri learns your daily habits and will offer suggestions throughout the day when appropriate. For example, suppose that you usually stop by the local coffee shop around the same time each morning and use the shop's app to order a drink from your iPad. Siri will pick up on this activity and eventually begin asking if you'd like to order a drink when you're within proximity of the coffee shop.

If you buy a car with the Car Play feature, you can interact with your car using your voice and Siri.

**TIP**

Siri is very good at maintaining the context of questions. For example, if you ask something like "Where is the nearest Starbucks location?" and then follow it with "What's the phone number there?" Siri will automatically know you're asking for the phone number of the Starbucks location it finds. It's not always perfect, but this feature does make for a vastly improved Siri experience.

Siri knows what app you're using, though you don't have to have that app open to make a request involving it. However, if you're in the Messages app, you can make a statement like "Tell Matthew I'll be late," and Siri knows that you want to send a message. You can also ask Siri to remind you about what you're working on, and Siri will note what you're working on and which app you're working in, and remind you about it at a later time you specify.

TIP

If you want to dictate text in apps like Notes or Mail, use the dictation icon on the onscreen keyboard to do so. See the task "Use Dictation," later in this chapter, for more about this feature.

Siri is able to announce possibly time-sensitive notifications when you're wearing AirPods (second generation or newer). For example, if you're in the aforementioned coffee shop and it's getting close to time for a meeting, Siri will interrupt whatever you're listening to so that you're aware of the upcoming appointment.

Siri requires no preset structure for your questions; you can phrase things in several ways. For example, you might say, "Where am I?" to see a map of your current location, or you could say, "What is my current location?" or "What address is this?" and get the same results.

If you ask a question about, say, the weather, Siri responds both verbally and with text information (see **Figure 5-3**). Or Siri might open a form, as with email, or provide a graphic display for some items, such as maps. When a result appears, you can tap it to make a choice or open a related app.

**FIGURE 5-3**

**TIP**

Sometimes Siri's dialogs can get lost among the other items on your screen. To hide everything else and let Siri take center stage, go to Settings ➪ Accessibility ➪ Siri and toggle the Show Apps Behind Siri switch off (light gray; green is on).

Siri works with just about any app, including FaceTime, App Store, Music, Messages, Reminders, Calendar, Maps, Mail, Weather, Stocks, Clock, Contacts, Notes, social media apps (such as Facebook), and Safari or your default web browser (see **Figure 5-4**). In the following sections, I provide a quick guide to some of the most useful ways you can use Siri.

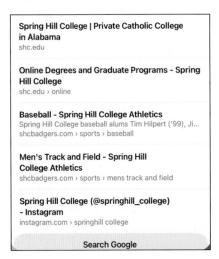

**FIGURE 5-4**

TIP

Siri supports many languages for translation, so you can finally show off those language lessons you took in high school. Languages supported for translation include Chinese, Dutch, English, French, German, Italian, Spanish, Arabic, Danish, Finnish, Hebrew, Japanese, and Korean. However, Siri can speak to you in more languages when providing the results of inquiries. Visit `www.apple.com/ios/feature-availability/#siri` for an up-to-date list.

# Get Suggestions

Siri anticipates your needs by making suggestions when you swipe down on any Home screen and tap in the search field at the top of the screen. Siri will list contacts you've communicated with recently, apps you've used, and nearby businesses, such as restaurants, gas stations, and coffee spots. If you tap an app in the suggestions, it will open and display the last viewed or listened to item.

Additionally, Siri lists news stories that may be of interest to you based on items you've viewed before.

# Call Contacts via FaceTime

First, make sure that the person you want to call is entered in your Contacts app and include that person's phone number in their record. If you want to call somebody by stating your relationship to them, such as "Call sister," be sure to enter that relationship in the Add Related Name field in your sister's contact record. Also make sure that the settings for Siri (refer to Figure 5-1) include your own contact name in the My Information field. (See Chapter 7 for more about creating contact records.)

Follow these steps to call a contact:

1. Engage Siri in one of the aforementioned ways.

2. Speak a command, such as "Make a FaceTime call to Cindy," or say "FaceTime Mom."

   If you have more than one contact who might match a spoken name, Siri responds with a list of possible matches.

3. Tap a match in the list or state the correct contact's name to proceed.

   The call is placed.

4. To end the call before it completes, press the Home or top button or tap the onscreen end button (red circle containing an X).

TIP

To cancel any spoken request, you have three options: Say "Cancel," tap the Siri button (swirling bands of light) on the Siri screen, or press the Home or top button (depending on your iPad model). If you're using a headset or Bluetooth device, tap the End button on the device.

# Create Reminders and Alerts

You can also use Siri with the Reminders app:

1. To create a reminder or alert, press and hold on the Home button or top button (depending on your iPad model) and then speak a command, such as "Remind me to call Dad on Thursday at 10 a.m." or "Wake me up tomorrow at 6:15 a.m."

   A preview of the reminder or alert is displayed (see **Figure 5-5**).

2. If you change your mind, tell Siri to "Cancel" or "Remove."

3. If you want a reminder ahead of the event that you created, activate Siri and speak a command, such as "Remind me tonight about the play on Thursday at 8 p.m."

   A second reminder is created, which you can confirm or cancel if you change your mind.

FIGURE 5-5

You can always edit or delete reminders and alerts using Siri or via the Reminders app.

# Add Events to Your Calendar

You can also set up events on your Calendar using Siri:

1. Press and hold the Home or top button and then speak a phrase, such as "Set up a meeting at 3 p.m. tomorrow."

   Siri sets up the appointment (see **Figure 5-6**).

2. If Siri asks you if you want to make changes, respond accordingly.

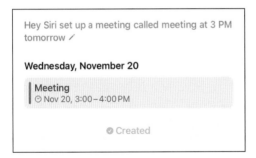

FIGURE 5-6

# Play Music

You can use Siri to play music from the Music app:

1. Engage Siri in one of the aforementioned ways.

2. To play music, speak a command, such as "Play music" or "Play Jazz radio station" to play a specific song, album, or radio station, as shown in **Figure 5-7.**

FIGURE 5-7

Apple has integrated Siri into Shazam, a music identifier app, to identify music. To use this integration:

1. When you're near an audio source playing music, press and hold down the Home button or top button to activate Siri.

2. Ask Siri a question, such as "What music is playing?" or "What's this song?"

   Siri listens for a bit. If Siri recognizes the song, you see the song name, artist, any other available information, and a link to purchase the music in the iTunes Store.

**TIP**

If you're listening to music or a podcast with earphones (plugged in or connected wirelessly) and you stop midstream, the next time you plug in or reconnect earphones, Siri recognizes that you might want to continue with the same item.

# Get Directions

You can use the Maps app and Siri to find your current location, get directions, find nearby businesses (such as restaurants or a bank), or get a map of another location. Be sure to turn on Location Services to allow Siri to know your current location (go to Settings and tap Privacy & Security ⇨ Location Services; make sure Location Services is on and that Siri, further down in these settings, is set to While Using the App and that the Precise Location switch is toggled on).

Here are some of the commands that you can try to get directions or a list of nearby businesses:

» **"Where am I?"** displays a map of your current location.

» **"Where is Battleship Memorial Park?"** displays a map of the city where that site is located, as shown in **Figure 5-8.**

» **"Find pizza restaurants."** displays a list of restaurants near your current location. Tap one to display a map of its location.

» **"Find PNC Bank."** displays a map with the location of the indicated business (or in some cases, several nearby locations, such as a bank branch and all ATMs).

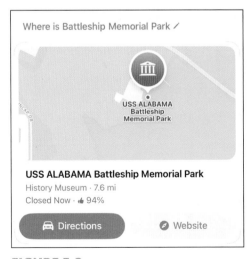

Where is Battleship Memorial Park ✎

USS ALABAMA
Battleship
Memorial Park

**USS ALABAMA Battleship Memorial Park**
History Museum · 7.6 mi
Closed Now · 👍 94%

🚗 Directions          🌐 Website

**FIGURE 5-8**

» **"Get directions to Neville Arena in Auburn."** loads a map with a route drawn and provides a narration of directions to the site from your current location.

# Ask for Facts

Siri uses numerous information sources to look up facts in response to questions. For example, you can ask, "What is the capital of Kansas?" or "What is the square root of 2,300?" or "How large is Mars?" Just press and hold on the Home button or top button and ask your question; Siri consults its resources and returns a set of relevant facts.

You can also get information about other things, such as the weather, stocks, or a scientific fact. Just say a phrase like one of these to get what you need:

» **"What is the weather?"** displays the weather report for your current location. If you want weather in another location, just specify the location in your question.

» **"What is the price of Apple stock?"** gets you the current price of the stock or the price of the stock when the stock market last closed.

» **"How hot is the sun?"** results in Siri telling you the temperature of the sun, in various unit conversions.

# Search the Web

Although Siri can use its resources to respond to specific requests such as "Who is the King of England?" more general requests for information will cause Siri to search further on the web. Siri can also search X (formerly Twitter) for comments related to your search.

For example, if you speak a phrase, such as "Find a website about birds" or "Find information about the World Series," Siri can respond in a couple of ways. The app can simply display a list of search results by using the default search engine specified in your settings for Safari. Or Siri can suggest, "If you like, I can search the web for such and such." In the first instance, just tap a result to go to that website. In the second, you can confirm that you want to search the web or cancel.

# Send Email, Messages, or Tweets

You can create an email or an instant message using Siri and existing contacts. For example, if you say "Email Fr. Phil Steele," a form opens that is already addressed to that stored contact. Siri asks for a subject and then a message. Speak your message contents and then say "Send" to speed your message on its way.

Siri also works with messaging apps, such as Messages. If you have the Messages app open and you say "Tell Keaton I'll call soon," Siri creates a message for you to approve and send.

# Use Dictation

Text entry isn't Siri's strongest attribute, but it's rapidly improving. Instead, you can use the Dictation feature. To activate the feature, tap the dictation key, which appears with a microphone symbol on the onscreen keyboard (see **Figure 5-9**), to speak text rather than type it.

To use dictation:

1. Go to any app where you enter text, such as Notes or Mail, and tap in the document or form.

   The onscreen keyboard appears.

2. Tap the dictation key on the keyboard and speak your text.

3. To end the dictation, tap the dictation key again.

**Dictation key**

FIGURE 5-9

**TIP**

When you finish speaking text, you can use the keyboard to make edits to the text Siri entered, although as voice recognition programs go, Dictation is pretty darn accurate. If a word sports a blue underline, which means there may be an error, you can tap to select the word and edit it.

# Translate Words and Phrases

One of Siri's coolest features is the capability to translate English into multiple languages (including Mandarin, French, German, Italian, and Spanish), with support for approximately 40 language pairs, according to Apple. That's great if you're on a road trip and don't speak the local language.

To try Siri's translation feature:

1. Engage Siri.

2. Say "translate" followed by your phrase and the language of your choice, as shown in **Figure 5-10.**

   Siri displays the translation on your screen and speaks it while also providing a phonetic translation to help with pronunciation.

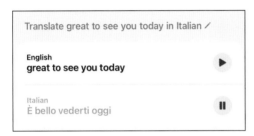

Tap the play icon to the right of the translation to hear Siri speak it again.

TIP

Chapter **6**

# Expanding Your iPad Horizons with Apps

S ome apps (short for *applications*), such as News and Music, come preinstalled on your iPad. But you can choose from a universe of other apps out there for your iPad — some for free (such as Google's Chrome web browser or Microsoft's Outlook email app) and some for a price (typically, ranging from 99 cents to about $10, though some can top out at much steeper prices).

Apps range from games to financial tools (such as loan calculators and budgeting assistants) to apps that help you when you're planning an exercise regimen or taking a trip. Still more apps are developed for use by private entities, such as hospitals, businesses, and government agencies.

In this chapter, I suggest some apps that you may want to check out; explain how to use the App Store feature of your iPad to find, purchase, and download apps; and detail how to organize your apps. You also find out a bit about having fun with games on your iPad.

# Search the App Store

Access the App Store by tapping the App Store icon on the Home screen. You can start by exploring the Today tab (which features various apps and articles), by Categories, or by the Top Charts. Or you can tap Search and find apps on your own. Tap an app to see more information about it.

If you've got the time, you can find lots of happy surprises by simply browsing the App Store, but if you're in a hurry or already know what you're looking for, a search is the best way to go.

To search the App Store:

1. Tap the App Store icon on the Home screen; by default, the first time you use App Store, it will open to the Today tab, as shown in **Figure 6-1.**

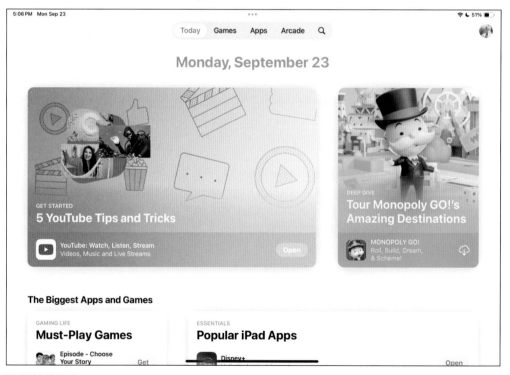

**FIGURE 6-1**

2. At this point, you have several options for finding apps:

- Scroll downward to view various featured apps and articles, such as What We're Playing, Games We Love, and Our Favorites.

- Tap a category to see more apps in it.

- Tap the Apps tab at the top of the screen to browse by the type of app you're looking for or search by categories, such as Entertainment or Utilities, as shown in **Figure 6-2.** To see the list of categories, tap Browse Categories; you may have to scroll a bit to get to that section.

- Tap the Games tab at the top of the screen to see the newest releases and bestselling games. Explore by paid apps, free apps, by categories, and even by special subjects such as Gorgeous Games and What We're Playing Right Now.

- Tap the search icon at the top of the screen, tap in the search field, enter a search term, and then tap the result you want to view.

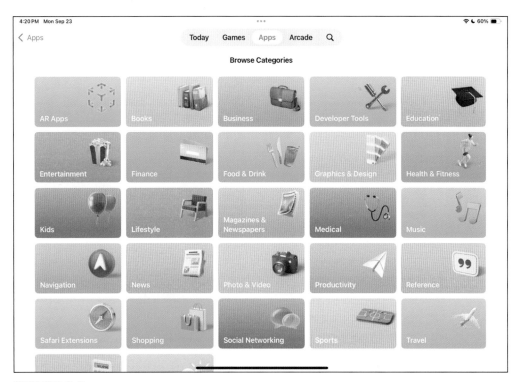

**FIGURE 6-2**

# Get Applications from the App Store

Buying or getting free apps requires that you have an Apple Account (you authenticate using your Apple ID), which I cover in Chapter 3. After you have an account, you can use the saved payment information there to buy apps or download free apps with a few simple steps:

1. With the App Store open, tap the Apps tab and then tap Top Free Apps, as shown in **Figure 6-3.**

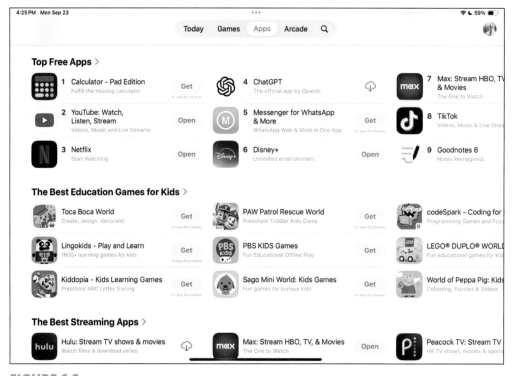

FIGURE 6-3

2. Tap the Get button (or the Price button, if it's a paid app) for an app that appeals to you or, if you'd like more information, simply tap the app's icon or name.

   If you already have the app and an update is available for it, the button will be labeled Update. If you've already downloaded the up-to-date version of the app, this button will say Open.

If you've previously downloaded the app but it's no longer on your iPad, or if you've downloaded the app on another device that's signed in to the same Apple Account, the icon looks like a cloud with a downward arrow. Tap to download the app again.

**TIP**

If you've opened an iCloud account, you can set it up so that anything you purchase on your iPad is automatically pushed to your other iPads and iPhones and your media libraries, and vice versa. See Chapter 3 for more about iCloud.

A sheet opens onscreen, listing the app and the Apple Account being used to get or purchase the app.

**3.** Tap the Install button at the bottom of the sheet, tap the Password field, and then enter the password.

Alternatively, you may simply need only to use Touch ID or Face ID (whichever your iPad model supports) to approve the download/purchase. The Get (or Price) button changes to the Installing button, which looks like a circle; the thick blue line on the circle represents the progress of the installation.

The app downloads, and you can find it on one of the Home screen pages. If you purchase an app that isn't free, your credit card or gift card balance is charged at this point for the purchase price.

**TIP**

Out of the box, only preinstalled apps are located on the first iPad Home screen page, with several more (such as Passwords and Translate) located on the second Home screen page. Apps that you download are placed on available Home screen pages, and you have to scroll to view and use them. This procedure is covered later in the chapter. See the next task for help in finding your newly downloaded apps.

# Organize Your Applications on Home Screen Pages

As explained in Chapter 2, your iPad has multiple Home screen pages. The first two contain preinstalled apps, and after those initial pages are full of app icons, other pages are created to contain any further apps you download or sync to your iPad. At the bottom of any iPad Home screen page (just above the dock), dots indicate the number of Home screen pages you have; a solid white dot specifies which Home screen page you're on now, as shown in **Figure 6-4.**

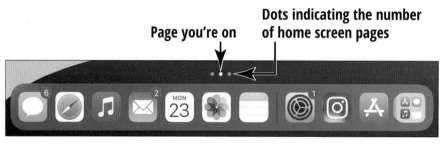

FIGURE 6-4

1. Swipe up from the very bottom of the screen or press the Home button to open the last displayed Home screen page.

2. Flick your finger from right to left to move to the next Home screen page. To move back, flick from left to right.

3. To reorganize apps on a Home screen page, press and hold on any app on that page to open a contextual menu; tap Edit Home Screen, as shown in **Figure 6-5.** Alternatively, press and hold the app icon just a bit longer to skip the menu, if you prefer.

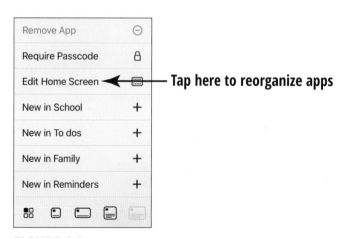

FIGURE 6-5

The app icons begin to jiggle (see **Figure 6-6**), and many (not all) apps will sport a delete icon, which looks like a light gray circle with a black minus sign (–) on it.

**A delete button**

FIGURE 6-6

4. To move an app to another location on the page, hold down on the app icon and drag it. Unlike previous iPadOS versions, iPadOS 18 allows you to place icons wherever you like on the screen.

TIP

While the apps are jiggling, you can move an app from one Home screen page to another by dragging the app to the left or right. You may have to pause at the edge of the screen before it will switch over.

5. Tap an empty area on the screen, tap the Done button in the upper-right corner of the screen, press the Home button, or swipe up from the bottom of the screen to stop all those icons from jiggling!

# Organize Apps in Folders

Your iPad lets you organize apps in folders so that you can find them more easily. The process is simple:

1. Press and hold on an app (continue to hold even if a menu pops up on the screen) until all apps start jiggling.

2. Drag one app on top of another app. This can be a tricky task, but trust me, it works.

   The two apps appear in a box with a placeholder name in a box above them (see **Figure 6-7**).

FIGURE 6-7

3. To change the name, tap in the field at the end of the placeholder name, and the keyboard appears.

4. Tap the Delete key to delete the placeholder name and type one of your own.

5. Tap Done on the keyboard and then tap anywhere outside the box to close it.

6. Tap Done or press the Home button to stop the icons from dancing around.

   You see your folder on the Home screen where you began this process.

Here's a neat trick that allows you to move multiple apps together at the same time (you'll probably want to place your iPad on a flat surface or support it in a case to pull this off more smoothly):

1. Press and hold the first app you'd like to move until the apps are jiggling.

2. Move the app just a bit so that it's no longer in its original place, but be sure to keep your finger on it.

3. With your free hand, tap the other app(s) you'd like to move along with the first app.

   As you tap additional apps, their icons "move under" or "attach themselves" to the first app.

4. After you've selected all your apps, move them to their new location; they'll all move together in a little app caravan.

# Delete Apps You No Longer Need

When you no longer need an app you've installed, it's time to get rid of it. Not only is it just good practice not to clutter your iPad with unused apps, it also frees valuable storage space. You can also remove most of the preinstalled apps that are native to iPadOS.

If you use iCloud to sync content across your iPads and iPhones, deleting an app on your iPad won't affect that app on other devices.

Follow these steps to delete an app:

1. Display the Home screen page that contains the app you want to delete.

If you remove an app that comes with iPadOS 18 and decide later that you need it again, you can find the app in the App Store and reinstall it. Some apps, such as Clock, will simply be removed from the Home screen, not deleted.

2. Press and hold the app until all the apps begin to jiggle.

3. Tap the delete icon, which is the light gray circle containing the black minus sign (–), for the app you want to delete.

   A confirmation like the one shown in **Figure 6-8** appears.

4. Tap Delete App to proceed and tap Delete again at the next prompt to complete the deletion.

If you want the app to remain in the App Library, tap the Remove from Home Screen button instead.

Don't worry about wiping out several apps at one time by deleting a folder. When you delete a folder, the apps that were contained in the folder are not deleted but placed back on a Home screen page where space is available. You can easily find the apps using the search feature.

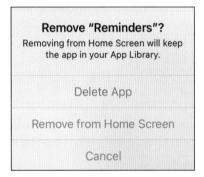

FIGURE 6-8

# Update Apps

App developers update their apps all the time, so you might want to check for those updates. The App Store icon on the Home screen displays the number of available updates in a red badge. To update apps, follow these steps:

1. Tap the App Store icon on the Home screen.

2. Tap your Apple Account icon (in the upper-right on the Apps screen, similar to the one shown in **Figure 6-9**).

Apple Account button

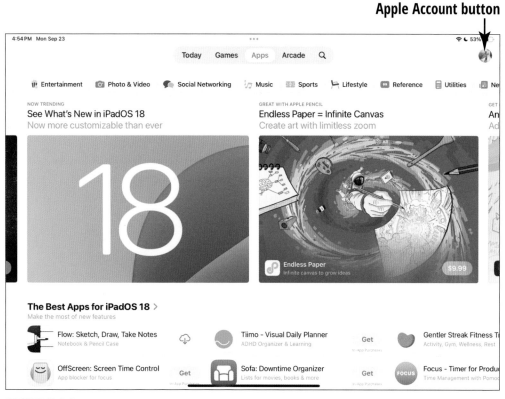

FIGURE 6-9

3. In the Account window that opens, scroll down to the Upcoming Automatic Updates section and tap the Update button for any item you want to update. To update all at one time, tap the Update All button to the left.

TIP

Note that if you have Family Sharing turned on, there will be a folder called Family Purchases that you can tap to display apps that are shared across your family's devices.

TIP

If you choose more than one app to update instead of downloading apps sequentially, several items will download simultaneously.

4. If you're asked to confirm that you want to update or to enter your Apple ID, do so and tap OK to proceed.

5. If you're asked to confirm that you are over a certain age or agree to terms and conditions, scroll down the terms dialog and, at the bottom, tap Agree.

The download progress is displayed.

Your iPad can update iPadOS automatically as updates become available. To enable this feature, go to Settings ➪ General ➪ Software Update ➪ Automatic Updates. Under the Automatically Install section, toggle the iPadOS Updates and Security Responses & System Files switches on (green) or off (white). Do the same for the iPadOS Updates switch in the Automatically Download section.

## GAMING WITH APPLE ARCADE

Apple Arcade is an Apple service that allows unlimited gaming for a monthly fee of $6.99, after a free one-month trial. A subscription grants access to a ton of top-flight games that you can play online or download for offline gaming. Up to six family members can use a single subscription, so Apple Arcade is a great way for families to interact and have fun. Games can be played on iPhone, iPad, Apple TV, and Macs. You can even continue a game across devices, jumping from one device to another! The games in Apple Arcade are state-of-the-art and created by the top developers in the business. Check out www.apple.com/apple-arcade/ to sign up.

Apple Arcade is also available as part of Apple One, which is a bundle of Apple services. If you subscribe to multiple Apple services (such as Apple TV+ or Apple Fitness+), you'll save money by combining your individual subscriptions into an Apple One bundle. Visit www.apple.com/apple-one/ to find out more about the various Apple One subscriptions.

Enjoy, gamers!

# Purchase and Download Games

Time to get your game on!

The iPad is super for playing games, with its bright screen, portable size, and ability to rotate the screen as you play and track your motions. You can download game apps from the App Store and play them on your device.

**TIP**

Although a few games have versions for both Mac and iPadOS users, the majority are either macOS-version only (macOS is the operating system used on Apple's Mac computers) or iPadOS-version only — something to be aware of when you buy games.

1. Open the App Store.
2. Tap the Games tab at the top of the screen.
3. Navigate the Games screen as follows:
   - Swipe from right to left to see featured apps in such categories as "What We're Playing" and "Happening Now."
   - Swipe down to find the Top Paid and Free games or to shop by categories (tap Browse Categories to view all the available categories).

4. Explore the list of games in the type you selected until you find something you like; tap the game to see its information screen (see **Figure 6-10** for an example).

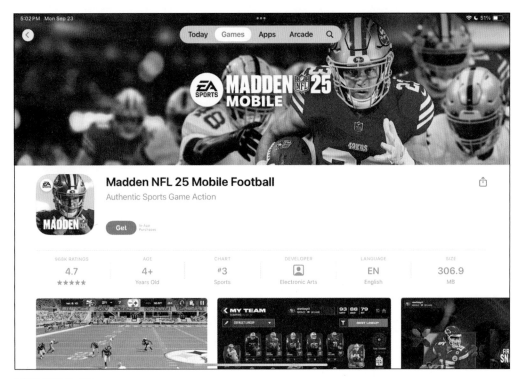

FIGURE 6-10

5. To buy a game, tap the button labeled with either the word *Get* or the price (such as $2.99).

6. When the dialog appears at the bottom of the screen, tap Purchase (if it's a Paid game) or Install (if it's a Free game), type your password in the Password field on the next screen, and then tap Sign In to download the game. Alternatively, use Touch ID or Face ID (for iPad models that support them) if it's enabled for iTunes and App Store purchases. The dialog will display "Pay with Touch ID," or you'll be prompted to initiate Face ID authentication (if your iPad supports it).

**TIP**

Beware using Touch ID or Face ID for iTunes and App Store purchases. I know it's simpler than entering a password, but it can also make it easier for others to make purchases. In case you're wondering how that could be so, when they were much smaller, my children tried holding my iPhone in front of my face while I was asleep in a clandestine attempt at purchasing the latest game craze with Face ID. Imagine the kids in your life trying to do the same to you, and I believe you'll see where I'm coming from.

7. The game downloads. Tap the Open button to go to the down-loaded game or find the games icon on your Home screen and tap to open it.

8. Have fun!

Chapter **7**

# Organizing Contacts

The Contacts app is the iPad equivalent of the dog-eared address book or Rolodex that used to sit by your phone. The Contacts app is simple to set up and use, and it has some powerful features beyond simply storing names, addresses, and phone numbers.

For example, you can pinpoint a contact's address in the iPad's Maps app. You can use your contacts to address email and Facebook messages, and X (formerly known as Twitter) tweets quickly. If you store a contact record that includes a website, you can use a link in Contacts to view that website instantly. In addition, of course, you can easily search for a contact by a variety of criteria, including how people are related to you, such as family or mutual friends, or by lists you create.

Onscreen context is a feature that allows you to make requests of Siri while viewing a specific contact. Siri will then carry out the request for the contact you're viewing, without the need to reference the person.

In this chapter, you discover the various features of Contacts, including how to save yourself spending time entering contact information by syncing contacts with such services as iCloud.

# Add a Contact

1. Tap the Contacts icon on one of your iPad's Home screen pages; it's on the second page by default.

   An alphabetical list of contacts appears, like the one shown in **Figure 7-1.**

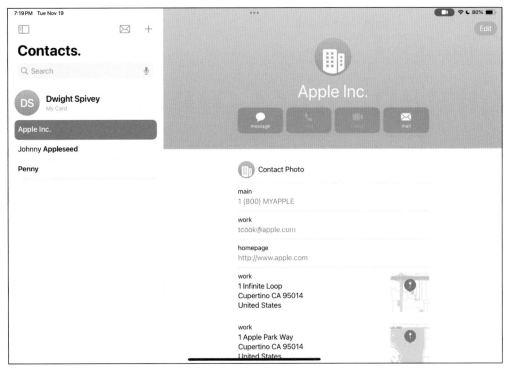

**FIGURE 7-1**

2. Tap the add icon (+) in the upper-right corner of the Contacts list. When a blank New Contact page opens (see **Figure 7-2**), tap in any field to display the onscreen keyboard (if it doesn't appear automatically, that is).

3. Enter any contact information you want.

   Only one of the First name, Last name, or Company fields is required, but feel free to add as much information as you like. (I highly encourage that you do so.)

TIP

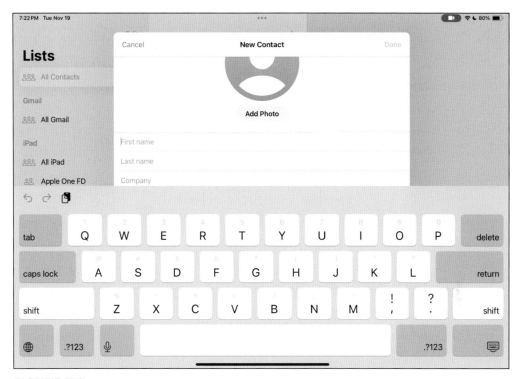

FIGURE 7-2

4. Swipe the contact's page to see more fields.

5. If you want to add information (such as a mailing or street address), tap the relevant add field, which opens additional entry fields.

6. To add an information field, such as Nickname or Suffix, tap the blue Add Field button toward the bottom of the page. In the Add Field dialog that appears (see **Figure 7-3**), choose a field to add, and then populate it with the relevant info.

**TIP** To view all the fields, flick up or down the screen.

**TIP** If your contact has a name that's difficult for you to pronounce, consider adding the Phonetic First Name, Phonetic Middle Name, or Phonetic Last Name field, or some combination thereof, to that person's record. Then you can spell the name phonetically to assist you with pronunciation. This also assists Siri with pronunciation of the name.

| Cancel | Add Field |
|---|---|
| Prefix | |
| Phonetic first name | |
| Pronunciation first name | |
| Middle name | |
| Phonetic middle name | |
| Phonetic last name | |
| Pronunciation last name | |
| Maiden name | |
| Suffix | |
| Nickname | |
| Job title | |
| Department | |
| Phonetic company name | |

**FIGURE 7-3**

**7.** Tap the Done button in the upper-right corner when you've finished making entries.

The new contact appears in your address book. You can tap it to see the details (see **Figure 7-4**).

**TIP**

You can choose a distinct ringtone or text tone for a new contact. Just tap the Ringtone field or Text Tone field in the New Contact form or when editing a contact. When that person calls either on the phone or via FaceTime, or texts you via SMS, MMS, RCS, or iMessage, you will quickly and easily recognize them from the tone that plays. For more information, see the upcoming "Set Individual Ringtones and Text Tones" section, which covers this feature in more depth.

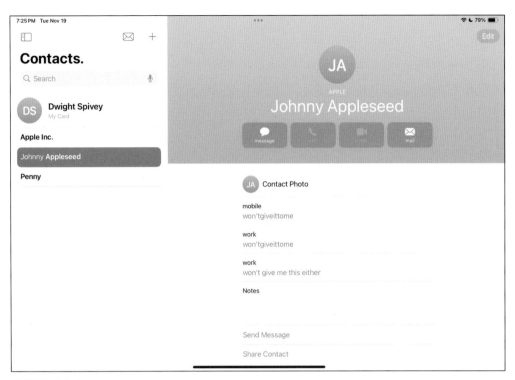

FIGURE 7-4

# Sync Contacts with iCloud

You can use your iCloud account to sync contacts from your iPad to iCloud to back them up. These also become available to your iCloud email account, if you set one up.

**TIP**

Mac users can also use iTunes or Finder (if your Mac is running macOS Catalina or newer) to sync contacts among all your Apple devices. Windows PC users can also use iTunes. See Chapter 3 for more about iTunes settings.

To sync contacts with iCloud:

1. On the Home screen, tap Settings, tap your Apple Account (at the top left of the screen; you may need to swipe to see it), and then tap iCloud.

2. In the iCloud settings screen, tap See All in the Saved to iCloud section.

3. In the Saved to iCloud screen, shown in **Figure 7-5,** make sure that the switch for Contacts is on (green) to sync contacts.

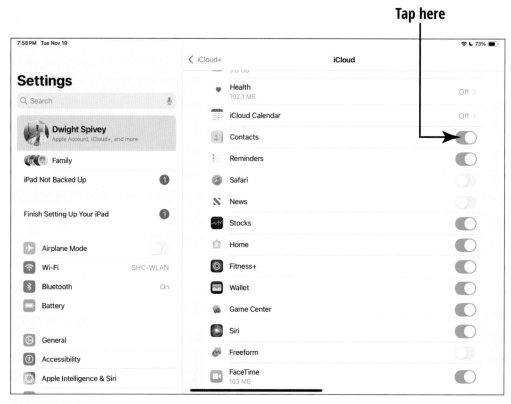

FIGURE 7-5

4. To choose which email account to sync with (if you have more than one account set up), scroll down the left sidebar and tap Apps, and then scroll down to the M section and tap Mail. Tap Mail Accounts, and then tap the email account you want to use.

5. In the following screen (see **Figure 7-6**), toggle the Contacts switch on to merge contacts from that account via iCloud.

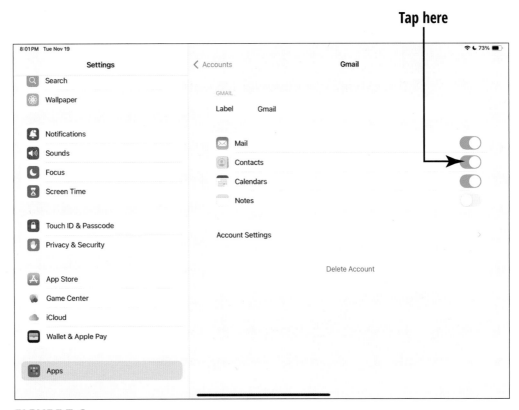

**FIGURE 7-6**

# Add Photos to Contacts

Adding a photo to a contact can be both functional and aesthetic.

Here's how to add a photo to a contact record:

1. With Contacts open, tap the + button to create a contact. Go ahead and enter the contact's name and other information as needed.

2. Tap Add Photo (or Edit if the contact already has a photo assigned) at the top of the page.

3. On the next screen (see **Figure 7-7**), select an option from those presented. Tap Camera to take the contact's photo on the spot, tap Photos to select a photo in your Photo Library (that's what I'm doing in this example), tap Memoji to select or create a memoji, or tap Monogram to use the contact's initials.

**FIGURE 7-7**

4. In the Move and Scale screen (see **Figure 7-8**) that appears, position the photo by dragging it with one finger. Pinch or unpinch your fingers on the iPad screen to contract or expand the photo, respectively.

5. Tap the Choose button in the lower right of the Move and Scale screen to use the photo for this contact. When prompted, you may also select a filter to use with the image.

6. Tap Next in the upper right to add the photo to the contact, as shown in **Figure 7-9**.

7. To finish, tap Done in the upper-right corner of the contact (refer to Figure 7-9).

**FIGURE 7-8**

**FIGURE 7-9**

# Designate Related People

You can quickly designate relationships in a contact record if those people are saved to Contacts. One great use for this feature is to then tell Siri to, for example, "Call sister" to call someone who is designated in your contact information as your sister.

**TIP**

There's a setting for Linked Contacts in the Contacts app when you're editing a contact's record. Using this setting isn't like adding a relation; rather, if you have records for the same person that have been imported into Contacts from different sources, such as Google or X, you can link them to show only a single contact.

1. Tap a contact and then tap Edit.

2. Scroll down the record and tap Add Related Name.

   The field labeled Mother now appears (see **Figure 7-10**).

FIGURE 7-10

3. Do one of the following:

   • If the contact you're looking for is indeed your mother, leave it as is. You're finished!

   • Otherwise, tap Mother and select the correct relationship from the list provided. I chose Sister for this example.

4. Tap the blue info icon to the right of the Related Name field, and your Contacts list appears. Tap the related person's name, and it appears in the field (see **Figure 7-11**).

5. If you would like to add additional names (such as a nickname), tap Add Related Name again and continue to add additional names as needed.

6. Tap Done to complete the edits.

After you add relations to a contact record, when you select the person in the Contacts main screen, all the related people for that contact are listed there.

**TIP**

# Set Individual Ringtones and Text Tones

If you want to hear a unique tone when you receive a phone or FaceTime call from a particular contact (such as your spouse, friend, or boss), you can set up this feature in Contacts. Then you'll know instantly when that person is calling.

To set up custom tones, follow these steps:

1. Tap + in the upper-right corner of the Contacts list to add a new contact, or select a contact in the list of contacts and tap Edit.

2. Tap the Ringtone field.

   A list of tones appears (see **Figure 7-12**).

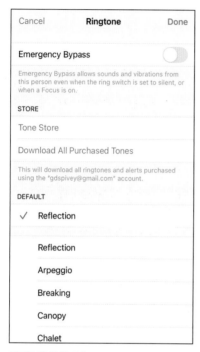

**FIGURE 7-12**

TIP

You can also set a custom text tone to be used when the person sends you a text message by tapping Text Tone instead of Ringtone.

3. Scroll up and down to see the full list of tones. Tap a tone, and a preview of the tone plays. When you hear one you like, tap Done in the upper right.

TIP

If your Apple devices are synced via iCloud, setting a unique ringtone for a contact on your iPad also sets it for use with FaceTime and Messages on your iPhone, Mac, and Apple Watch.

# Delete a Contact

When it's time to remove a name or two from your Contacts, it's easy to do:

1. With Contacts open, tap the contact you want to delete.

2. On the information page, tap Edit in the upper-right corner.

3. On the info page that appears, scroll down to the bottom of the record and then tap Delete Contact.

4. The confirmation pop-up message, shown in **Figure 7-13,** appears; tap the Delete Contact button to confirm the deletion.

**TIP**

Be careful: After you tap Delete Contact, there's no going back! Your contact is deleted from your iPad and any other device that syncs to your iPad by iCloud, Google, or other means. If you change your mind, simply tap Cancel in the upper left.

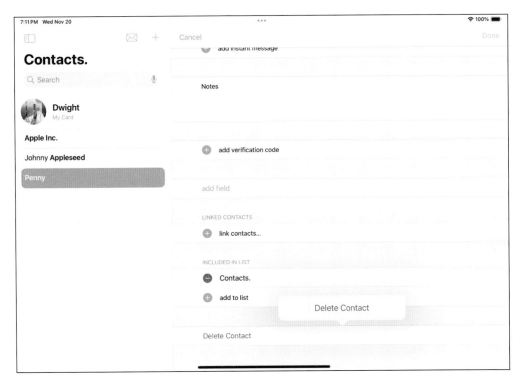

**FIGURE 7-13**

IN THIS CHAPTER

» Make, accept, and end
FaceTime calls

» Set up an iMessage account

» Create, send, and read
messages

» Send emojis and special effects

» Send audio, photos, videos,
maps, and group messages

» Find and install popular social
media apps

Chapter **8**

# Getting Social with Your iPad

Your iPad offers many ways to communicate with friends, family, and others. For example, FaceTime is an excellent video-calling app that lets you call people who have FaceTime on their devices by using either a phone number or an email address. You and your friend, colleague, or family member can see each other as you talk, which makes for a much more personal and engaging calling experience. You can even leave FaceTime messages, similar to voicemail.

Apple recently put a new face (user interface) on FaceTime and added some other tweaks and techs. Among my favorites are audio upgrades, which include spatial audio (helps make those you're speaking with sound like they're in the room) and voice isolation mode (isolates your voice from other noises around you). I also like portrait mode, which causes your iPad's cameras to focus on you while blurring everything behind you.

iMessage is a feature available through the preinstalled Messages app for instant messaging (IM). IM involves sending a text message to someone's iPad, Mac running macOS 10.9 or later, or iPhone (using the person's phone number or email address to carry on an instant conversation). You can even send audio, images, and videos via Messages, as well as message users with non-Apple devices. If you see a green speech bubble in your texts instead of a blue one, the person you're conversing with is most likely using a non-Apple device.

Social media apps keep us in close digital contact with others and for some have become as important a digital staple as email. In this chapter, you discover how to get and set up Facebook, X (formerly known as Twitter), and Instagram, some of the most popular social media apps.

Facebook is a platform for sharing posts about your life, with or without photos and video. X (Twitter) is for sharing information in quick bursts, with a 280-character limit. (If you need more, you must subscribe to an X Premium option.) Instagram is a photo-sharing app, allowing you to add captions to personalize your pictures.

In this chapter, I introduce you to FaceTime and the Messages app and review their simple controls. You also take a look at installing and customizing Facebook, X, and Instagram. In no time, you'll be socializing with all and sundry.

# What You Need to Use FaceTime

Here's a quick rundown of the type of device and the information you need for using FaceTime's various features:

>> You can use FaceTime to call people over a Wi-Fi connection to call people who have an iPhone 4 or later, an iPad 2 or a

third-generation iPad or later, any iPad mini or iPad Pro model, or a Mac (running macOS 10.6.6 or later). If you want to connect over a cellular connection, you must have an iPhone 4s or later or a third-generation cellular iPad or later.

» You can use a phone number or an email address to connect with anyone with an iPhone, an iPad, or a Mac and an iCloud account.

» The person you're contacting must have FaceTime enabled in the Settings app. It's enabled by default.

# An Overview of FaceTime

FaceTime works with the iPad's built-in cameras and microphones so that you can call other folks who have a device that supports FaceTime. You can use FaceTime to chat while sharing video images with another person. This preinstalled app is useful for seniors who want to keep up with distant family members and friends and see (as well as hear) the latest and greatest news.

You can make and receive calls with FaceTime by using a phone number or an email account and make calls to those with an Apple Account. When connected, you can show the person on the other end what's going on around you. Using the app is straightforward, although its features are limited (but getting better with each iteration). You can use your Apple Account to access FaceTime, so it works pretty much right away. See Chapter 3 for more about getting an Apple Account.

TIP

If you're having trouble using FaceTime, make sure that the FaceTime feature is turned on. To do so, tap Settings on the Home screen, tap Apps at the bottom of the left sidebar, tap FaceTime, and then tap the FaceTime switch to turn it on (green), if it isn't already. On the same screen, you can also select the phone number or email address or both that others can use to make FaceTime calls to you, as well as which one of those is displayed as your caller ID.

To view information for recent calls, open the FaceTime app and then tap the *i*-in-a-circle (information) icon on a recent call. Your iPad displays that person's information. You can tap the contact to call the person back.

Apple encrypts (digitally protects) all FaceTime calls, both one-on-one and group calls, with industry-leading technology to make sure that snoops are kept at bay.

TIP

# Make a FaceTime Call with Wi-Fi or Cellular

If you know the person you're calling has FaceTime available on their device, adding that person to your iPad's contacts is a good idea so that you can initiate FaceTime calls from within the Contacts app, if you like, or from the contacts list that you can access through the FaceTime app.

When you call somebody using an email address, the person must be signed in to their Apple Account and have verified that the address can be used for FaceTime calls. You can verify the address by tapping Settings, Apps, and then FaceTime ➪ You Can Be Reached by FaceTime At. FaceTime for Mac users must open the FaceTime app and select Preferences or Settings (depending on your version of macOS).

To make a FaceTime call:

1. Tap the FaceTime icon to launch the app.

   If you've made or received FaceTime calls already, you'll see a list of recent calls in the FaceTime menu on the left side of the screen. You can simply tap one of those to initiate a new call, or continue with these steps to learn how to start a new call from scratch.

2. Tap the green New FaceTime button in the upper-left corner to open the New FaceTime screen. Enter a contact's name (shown in **Figure 8-1, left**) by tapping the To field, or find a contact in your Contacts list by tapping the green plus (+) button to the right of the To field.

**FIGURE 8-1**

3. Tap one of the green buttons below the To field and Suggested section (but above the keyboard, shown in **Figure 8-1, right**) to choose a video call (large, green FaceTime button) or an audio call (small, green phone button).

    Video includes your voice and image; audio includes only your voice.

    **TIP**

    You see a video button if that contact's device supports FaceTime video, and an audio button if the contact's device supports FaceTime audio. (If you haven't saved this person in your contacts and you know the phone number to call or email, you can just enter that information in the Enter Name, Email, or Number field.)

    When the person accepts the call, you see a large screen that displays the recipient's image and a small screen, referred to as a picture-in-picture (PiP), containing your image superimposed. You can tap and drag your PiP to another location on the screen, if you prefer.

# Use a Memoji with FaceTime

Want to have a little fun during your call? Use memoji characters, which are digital illustrations that you can superimpose over your face, if your iPad supports Face ID. During your FaceTime call, tap the star (effects) icon (if you don't see it, just tap the screen), tap the memoji icon (smiling illustrated character), and then select a memoji character from the list. You can create your own memoji characters, as can the people you're speaking with (again, if their iPad, iPhone, or Mac supports Face ID).

**TIP**

iOS 6 and later versions allow you to use FaceTime over a Wi-Fi network or your iPad's cellular connection (only if your iPad supports cellular, of course). However, if you use FaceTime over a cellular connection, you may incur costly data usage fees. To avoid the extra cost, in Settings under Cellular, toggle the FaceTime switch off (white).

# Accept, Enjoy, and End a FaceTime Call

If you're on the receiving end of a FaceTime call, accepting the call is about as easy as it gets.

**TIP**

If you'd rather not be available for calls, you can go to Control Center and turn on Do Not Disturb. This stops incoming calls or notifications other than for the people you've designated as exceptions. After you turn on Do Not Disturb, you can use the feature's settings to schedule when it's active, allow calls from certain people, or allow a second call from the same person in a three-minute interval to go through.

To accept, enjoy, and end a FaceTime call, follow these steps:

1. When the call comes in, drag the Slide to Answer slider to take the call (see **Figure 8-2**).

2. Chat away with your friend, swapping video images.

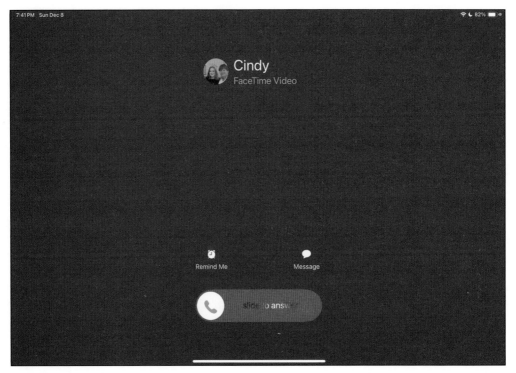

FIGURE 8-2

3. To end the call, tap the red End button in the call controls window, as shown in **Figure 8-3.**

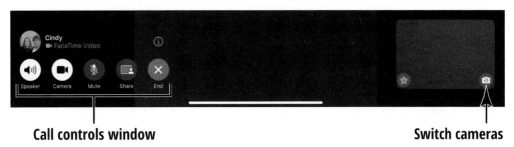

**Call controls window**          **Switch cameras**

FIGURE 8-3

TIP

To mute sound during a call, tap the mute button (microphone with a line through it) in the call controls window. Tap the button again to unmute your iPad.

FaceTime allows group calls for up to 32 people! You can have a family reunion without leaving your front porch. To add more folks to a current call:

1. Tap the screen to open the call controls window in the lower-left corner (refer to Figure 8-3) if it's not already open.

2. Tap the call controls window to expand it.

3. Tap the Add People button.

4. Tap the To field, enter or find a contact, tap a contact to add them to the To field, and finally, tap the green Add Person to FaceTime button to place them in the call.

## Switch Views

When you're on a FaceTime call, you might want to use the iPad's rear-facing camera to show the person you're talking to what's going on around you.

1. To switch from the front-facing camera that's displaying your image to the back-facing camera that captures whatever you're looking at, tap the switch cameras icon (refer to Figure 8-3) in your tile (the window with your image in it).

2. To switch back to the front camera displaying your image, tap the switch cameras icon again.

## Set Up an iMessage Account

iMessage is a service available through the preinstalled Messages app that allows you to send an instant message (IM) to and receive an IM from others who are using an iPad, iPhone, or a suitably configured Mac. iMessage is a way of sending instant messages through a Wi-Fi network, but you can send messages through your cellular connection without having iMessage activated, assuming that your iPad supports cellular data.

Assuming that the person wants to participate in a live conversation, the chat begins immediately, allowing a back-and-forth dialogue in real time.

1. To set up Messages, tap Settings on the Home screen and then tap Apps.

2. Tap Messages.

   The settings shown in **Figure 8-4** appear.

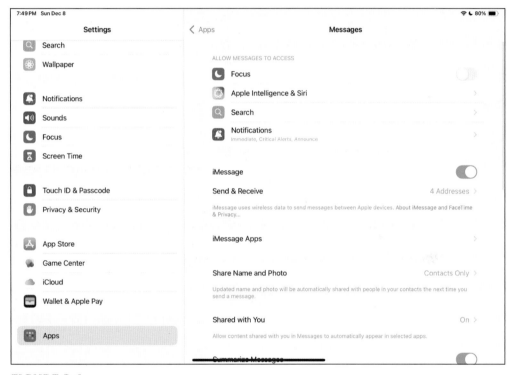

FIGURE 8-4

3. If iMessage isn't enabled (it is by default), tap the switch to toggle it on (green).

TIP

Be sure that the phone number or email account (or both) associated with your iPad under the Send & Receive setting is correct. (This should be set up automatically based on your Apple Account settings.) If it isn't correct, tap the Send & Receive field, add an email or phone, and then tap Messages to return to the previous screen.

4. To allow a notice to be sent to the sender when you've read a message, tap the switch on for Send Read Receipts.

You can also choose to show a subject field in your messages.

5. To leave Settings, press the Home button or swipe up from the bottom of the screen (depending on your iPad model).

To enable or disable email accounts used by Messages, tap Send & Receive and then tap an email address to enable it (check mark appears to the left) or disable it (no check mark appears to the left).

# Use Messages to Address, Create, and Send Messages

Now you're ready to use Messages:

1. From the Home screen, tap the Messages icon (in the dock by default).

2. Tap the compose icon (paper and pencil) in the top-right corner of the Messages list (on the left of the screen) to begin a conversation.

3. In the form that appears (see **Figure 8-5**), begin to address your message in one of the following ways:

- Start to type a name in the To field, and a list of matching contacts appears.

- Tap the dictation key (microphone) on the onscreen keyboard and speak the address, and then select the contact from the list that appears.

- Tap + on the right side of the address field, and the contacts list is displayed.

4. Tap a contact in the list displayed in Step 3.

If the contact has both an email address and a phone number, the Info dialog appears, allowing you to tap one to use to address the message.

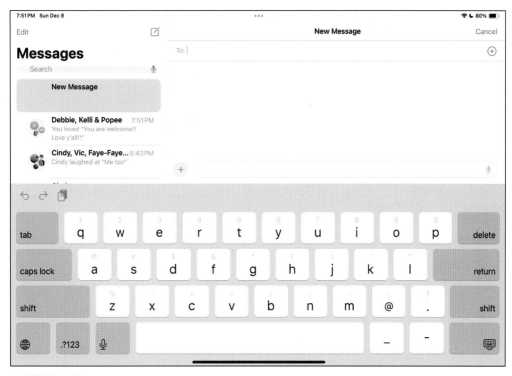

**FIGURE 8-5**

5. To create a message, simply tap in the message field above the keyboard and type or dictate your message.

6. To send the message, tap the send icon (blue circle with a white arrow).

   When the recipient responds, the conversation is displayed on the screen.

7. Tap in the message field again to respond to the last message.

**TIP**

You can address a message to more than one person by simply choosing more recipients in Step 3.

**TIP**

iPadOS 18 lets you send messages at a later date and time! Tap + to the left of the message, and then tap Send Later in the list of options that appears. A blue bar with a preset date and time appears above your message; tap it to select a different date and time, if you want. Finally, tap the send icon to send the message at your preferred date and time.

# Read Messages

When you receive a message, it's as easy to read as email — easier, actually!

1. Tap Messages on the Home screen.

   When the app opens, you see a list of your previous text conversations.

2. Tap a conversation to see the message string, including all attachments, as shown in **Figure 8-6.**

FIGURE 8-6

3. To view all attachments to a conversation, tap the recipient's name at the top of the message and then scroll down.

   You'll find attachments and links you've shared with that individual or group.

**TIP** iPadOS 18 includes the option to mark a conversation as read or unread. In the Messages panel, swipe a conversation you've already read from left to right, and then tap the blue button to mark it as unread. (A blue dot to the left indicates the message is unread.) Do the same with an unread message to mark it as read.

# Clear a Conversation

When you've finished chatting, you might want to delete a conversation to remove the clutter before you start a new chat.

1. With Messages open and your conversations displayed, swipe to the left on the conversation you want to delete.

2. Tap the delete icon (trash can) next to the conversation you want to get rid of, as shown in **Figure 8-7.**

FIGURE 8-7

To delete multiple conversations at once, tap Edit in the upper left of the Messages list, tap Select Messages, and then tap the circle to the immediate left of each conversation you want to delete. Then tap the Delete button in the lower right.

TIP

Tap the hide alerts icon (bell with a slash) to keep from being alerted to new messages in the conversation. To reactivate alerts for the conversation, swipe left again, and then tap the show alerts icon.

# Send Emojis with Your Text

*Emojis* are small pictures that can help convey a feeling or an idea. For example, smiley faces and sad faces show emotions, and a thumbs-up emoji conveys approval. To send an emoji in place of text:

**1.** From within a conversation, tap the emoji key (smiley face) on the onscreen keyboard.

If you can't see the keyboard, tap in the Message field to display it.

**2.** When the emojis appear (see **Figure 8-8**), swipe left and right to find the right emoji for the moment and tap to select it.

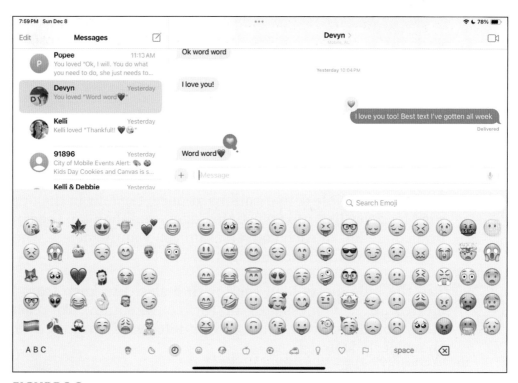

**FIGURE 8-8**

You can add as many as you like to the conversation.

**TIP**

You can type a message and then tap the emoji key to make Messages highlight each word that has an associated emoji. Then tap a highlighted word to insert the emoji or choose from available emojis.

# Use Messages Apps and Tools

Messages apps and tools allow you to add items that spice up your messages with information from other apps installed on your iPad, as well as drawings and other images from the web.

Tap the + button to the left of the iMessage field in your conversation. A list of Messages apps and tools appears on the screen, as shown in **Figure 8-9**. Tap an item to see what it offers your messaging; tap More at the bottom of the list (or swipe up on the screen) to see even more apps and tools.

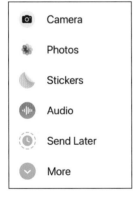

Camera

Photos

Stickers

Audio

Send Later

More

**FIGURE 8-9**

Messages apps and tools include

» **The App Store:** Tap the App Store icon to find tons of stickers, games, and apps for your messages.

» **Digital Touch:** Send special effects in Messages. These can include sending a heartbeat, sketching a quick picture, or sending a kiss. I explain how to use Digital Touch in a message shortly.

» **Other apps you've installed:** These may appear if they have the capability to add functions and information to your messages. For example, use ESPN to send the latest scores, YouTube to send a link to a video, an AccuWeather app icon to let your friend know the weather forecast, or the Fandango app to send movie information.

Digital Touch is one of the most personal ways to send special effects to others. Here's a close look:

1. To send a Digital Touch in a message, open a conversation, tap + to view Messages apps and tools, tap More, and then tap the Digital Touch icon to open the Digital Touch window, as shown in **Figure 8-10.**

FIGURE 8-10

2. Tap the information icon (*i* in a gray circle) in the lower right to see a list of gestures and what they do.

3. Perform a gesture in the Digital Touch window and send it to your recipient.

# Send and Receive Audio

When you're creating a message, you can also create an audio message:

1. With Messages open, tap the new message icon (paper and pencil).
2. Enter an addressee's name in the To field.
3. Tap the + button to view Messages apps and tools, and then tap the audio icon.
4. Immediately begin speaking your message; you'll see the red waveform as you proceed.
5. When you've finished recording, tap the red stop button to the right of the waveform.
6. To send your message, tap the send icon (upward-pointing blue arrow).

   The message appears as an audio track in the recipient's Messages inbox. To play the track, the recipient taps the play icon or, if using an iPhone, holds it up to an ear.

# Send a Photo or Video

When you're creating a message, you can also send a picture or create a short video message.

1. With Messages open, tap the new message icon (paper and pencil) and add a recipient to the message.
2. Tap the + button to view the Messages apps and tools list, tap the Camera app, and then take a picture.

   After you take the picture, the tools shown in **Figure 8-11** appear.
3. Work with the picture before sending it along to your recipient:
   - Tap Retake to take a different picture.
   - Tap Effects to add items such as memoji or customized text or to apply filters.

FIGURE 8-11

- Tap Edit to edit the picture.
- Tap Markup to add notes or other text to your picture.
- Tap Done to place the picture in your message but not send it yet.
- Tap the send icon (upward-pointing arrow in the blue circle) to send the picture immediately.

# Send a Map of Your Location

When responding to a message, you can also send a map showing your current location:

1. Tap a conversation, and then tap the name of the recipient in the upper center of the screen.

2. In the conversation details dialog that pops up, tap Share My Location.

3. In the screen shown in **Figure 8-12,** tap For 1 Hour, Until End of Day, or Indefinitely.

   A map showing your location appears above your conversation until you stop sharing.

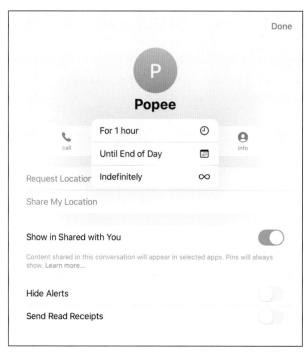

FIGURE 8-12

# Understand Group Messaging

If you want to start a conversation with a group of people, you can use group messaging. Group messaging is great for keeping several people in a conversational loop.

Group messaging functionality includes the following features:

» When you participate in a group message, the participants appear in the information screen for the message (see **Figure 8-13**). Access the information screen by tapping the icons for your contacts at the top of the message thread. You can drop people whom you don't want to include any longer and leave the conversation yourself when you want to by simply opening the information screen and then tapping Leave This Conversation.

» When you turn on Hide Alerts in the information screen of a message, you won't get notifications of messages from this group, but you can still read the group's messages at a later time (this also works for individual messages).

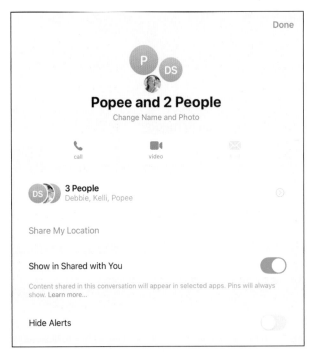

**FIGURE 8-13**

Taking you further into the workings of group messages is beyond the scope of this book, but if you're intrigued, go to https://support. apple.com/en-us/118236 for more information.

# Find and Install Social Media Apps

To begin using social media apps, you first need to find and install them on your iPad. I focus on Facebook, X (Twitter), and Instagram in this chapter because they're currently three of the most popular social media apps, and frankly, I don't have the space here to discuss more.

## SOME SOCIAL MEDIA DOS AND DON'TS

Social media has its pros and cons. While you can connect with old friends, swap stories, and share vacation pics, you might also be preyed upon by cyber thugs and other ne'er-do-wells prowling the internet. This short list (by no means exhaustive) of dos and don'ts will help keep you safe on social media:

- Do connect with family and friends, but keep your social media circle close. Branching out too far can lead to mischief by some who don't know you.

- Do use strong and unique passwords for your accounts. This safeguard makes it tougher for someone to access your account and potentially post things in your name that you wouldn't condone.

- Do set up privacy controls for each social media account you use. You may want some people to see everything you post but prevent others from seeing personal information.

- Don't share your social security number, credit card numbers, banking accounts, or any other financial information — period!

- Don't type in ALL CAPS. It's the internet equivalent of yelling and may start a social media dust-up.

- Don't accept a friend request from someone you're already friends with on a social media platform. If you're already friends with them on the platform, it's a good indication that something fishy is going on. Send a private message to the friend or get in contact some other way to confirm that they've sent the friend request.

- Don't believe everything you read! If something sounds too crazy to be true, it probably is. Research the topic by using multiple trustworthy and varied sources before commenting on it in social media environs.

- Don't advertise that you're on vacation. Wait until you return to post pictures of your dream trip. Otherwise, someone might take advantage of the opportunity to pay your home an unannounced and unwanted visit.

Twitter changed its iconic name to a simple stark X. I'm still trying to process the logic of that decision.

To find and install the apps using the App Store, follow these steps:

1. Open the App Store.

2. Tap the Search icon at the top of the screen.

3. Tap the search field and enter Facebook, X, Instagram, or any other social media app you might be interested in.

4. To download and install the app, tap the button labeled Get or with the price (such as $2.99). Note that Facebook, X, and Instagram are free to install and use.

If you've had the app installed before but have since deleted it, you will instead see a cloud with a downward-pointing arrow (as shown to the right of the Facebook logo in **Figure 8-14**). Tap that to begin the download. If the app is already installed, you'll see an Open button; just tap it to open the app.

5. When the dialog appears on the screen, tap Purchase (if it's a paid app) or Install (if it's free), type your Apple Account password in the Password field on the next screen, and then tap Sign In to download the app. Alternatively, use Touch ID if you have it enabled for iTunes and App Store purchases; the dialog will display "Pay with Touch ID" if you do. Some iPad models use Face ID instead of Touch ID. When you're prompted to pay (with Face ID enabled), double-click the top button and glance at your iPad to initiate payment.

The app will download and install on one of your Home screens.

The deluge of false news on social media has taken its toll on society, and social media developers are taking steps to combat the misuse of their platforms.

FIGURE 8-14

# Create a Facebook Account

You can create a Facebook account from within the app.

**TIP**

If you already have a Facebook account, you can simply use that account information to log in.

To create an account in the Facebook app, follow these steps:

1. Launch the newly downloaded Facebook app.

2. Tap the Sign Up for Facebook option at the bottom of the screen, as shown in **Figure 8-15** (you almost need a magnifying glass to see it).

3. Tap Get Started and walk through the steps to complete the registration of your account.

   When finished, you'll be logged into your account in the Facebook app.

Phone number or email

Password

Log in

Sign up for Facebook          Need Help?

**FIGURE 8-15**

You may create a Facebook account also by visiting its website at www.facebook.com.

TIP

# Create an X Account

To create an account in the X app, follow these steps:

1. Open the X app by tapping its icon.

2. Tap the Create Account button near the bottom of the screen, as shown in **Figure 8-16.**

If you already have an X account, tap the tiny Log In text at the very bottom of the screen to log in.

TIP

3. Answer the questions.

When you're done, the app logs you into your new account.

7:14 PM  Sun Dec 8                                    •••                                    89%

X

**See what's happening in the world right now.**

G  Continue with Google

 Continue with Apple

or

Create account

By signing up, you agree to our Terms, Privacy Policy, and Cookie Use.

Have an account already? Log in

**FIGURE 8-16**

As with Facebook, you can create an account also on the X website at www.x.com.

TIP

# Create an Instagram Account

To create an account in the Instagram app:

1. Open the Instagram app by tapping its icon.

2. Tap the Create New Account button, shown in **Figure 8-17,** to walk through the steps of creating a new Instagram account.

If you already have an Instagram account, tap the Log In button to access it.

TIP

3. Answer the questions that the app asks to help you create your account.

When completed, the app logs you into your new account.

**FIGURE 8-17**

**TIP**

You can create an account also on the Instagram website at www. instagram.com.

## IN THIS CHAPTER

» Connect to the internet

» Navigate web pages and tabs

» Organize your searches with tab groups

» View history and search the web

» Use bookmarks

» Download files

» Translate web pages

Chapter **9**

# Browsing with Safari

You can get on the internet with your iPad by using its Wi-Fi or cellular capabilities. After you're online, Safari, the built-in browser (software that helps you navigate the internet's contents), is your ticket to a wide world of information, entertainment, education, and more. Safari will look familiar to you if you've used a web browser on a PC or Mac computer, though the way you move around by using the iPad touchscreen may be new to you. If you've never used Safari, don't worry because I take you by the hand and show you all the basics of making it work for you.

In this chapter, you see how to go online with your iPad, navigate among web pages, and use iCloud tabs to share your browsing experience between devices. Along the way, you place a bookmark for a favorite site, create a tab group, and then learn how to share said tab group, one of Safari's newer features. You can also view your browsing history, save online images to the Photos app, search the web, or email or tweet a link to a friend. Finally, you explore how to translate web pages so that you can read what's going on around the world, even if you may not speak the language.

# Connect to the Internet

How you connect to the internet depends on which types of connections are available:

>> You can connect to the internet via a Wi-Fi network. You can set up this type of network in your home using your computer and some equipment from your internet provider. You can also connect over public Wi-Fi networks, referred to as hotspots.

TIP

You might be surprised to discover the number of hotspots in your town or city. Look for internet cafes, coffee shops, hotels, libraries, and transportation centers (such as airports or bus stations). Many of these businesses display signs alerting you to their free Wi-Fi.

>> You can use the paid data network provided by AT&T, Sprint, T-Mobile, Verizon, or almost any other cellular provider to connect from just about anywhere you can get coverage through a cellular network. Of course, you have to have an iPad model that supports cellular connections to hop on the internet this way.

To enable cellular data (if your iPad supports it), tap Settings and then tap Cellular. Tap to toggle the Cellular Data switch on (green).

TIP

Browsing the internet using a cellular connection can eat up your data plan allotment quickly if your plan doesn't include unlimited data access. If you think you'll often use the internet with your iPad away from a Wi-Fi connection, double-check your data allotment with your cellular provider or consider getting an unlimited data plan.

To connect to a Wi-Fi network, you have to complete a few steps:

1. Tap Settings on the Home screen and then tap Wi-Fi.

2. Be sure that the Wi-Fi toggle switch is set on (green) and choose a network to connect to by tapping it.

TIP

Network names should appear automatically when you're in range of them. When you're in range of a public hotspot, if access to several nearby networks is available, you may see a message asking you to tap a network name to select it. After you select a network, you may see a message asking for your password. Ask the owner of the hotspot (for example, a hotel desk clerk or business owner) for this password or enter your own network password if you're connecting to your home network.

TIP

Free public Wi-Fi networks usually don't require passwords, or the password is posted prominently for all to see. (If you can't find the password, don't be shy about asking someone.)

3. Tap the Join button when prompted.

You're connected! Your iPad will now recognize the network and connect again in the future without you having to repeatedly enter the password.

TIP

After you connect to public Wi-Fi, someone else can possibly track your online activities because these networks are unsecured. When connected to a public hotspot, don't access financial accounts, make online purchases, or send emails containing sensitive information. It's best to avoid using a public unsecured network.

# Explore Safari

Safari is your iPad's default web browsing app.

TIP

This is not the Safari of old. Safari changed a lot with iPadOS 15 — and the changes continue in iPadOS 18. So even if you're familiar with previous versions of iPadOS, it's worthwhile to peruse this chapter.

TIP

You can change your iPad's default browser from Safari to another you've downloaded. Go to Settings, tap Apps at the bottom of the settings list on the left, find and tap the name of the browser you want to use, tap Default Browser App, and then tap the name of the browser you want to use as default. If you don't see the Default Browser App option in Safari, Safari is already set as the default.

Here's how to get around in Safari:

1. After you're connected to a network, tap Safari in the dock at the bottom of the Home screen.

   Safari opens, possibly displaying the Apple iPad homepage the first time you go online (see **Figure 9-1**).

2. Hold down two fingers (thumb and forefinger may be easiest) together on the screen and spread them apart to expand the view (also known as zooming in). Hold down your fingers on the screen about an inch or so apart and quickly bring them together to zoom back out.

   You can also double-tap the screen with a single finger to restore the default view size. (If you tap a link, though, your gesture will just open that link.)

TIP

   Using your fingers on the screen to enlarge or reduce the size of a web page allows you to view what's displayed at various sizes, giving you more flexibility than the double-tap method.

3. Put your finger on the screen and flick (or swipe, as some call it) upward to scroll down on the page.

4. To return to the top of the web page, put your finger on the screen and drag downward, or tap the status bar at the very top of the screen twice.

TIP

When you zoom in, you'll have more control by using two fingers to drag from left to right or from top to bottom on the screen. When you zoom out, one finger works fine for making these gestures.

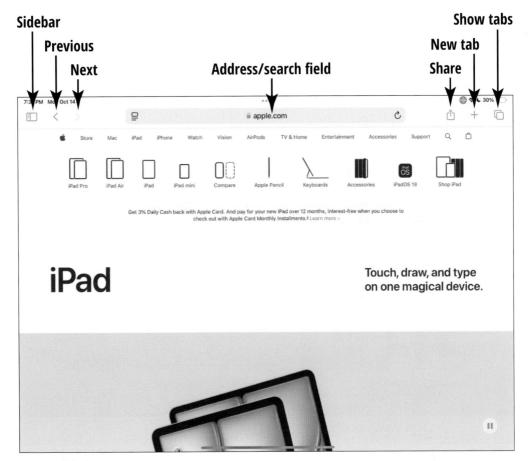

**Sidebar**
**Previous**
**Next**
**Address/search field**
**Show tabs**
**New tab**
**Share**

FIGURE 9-1

# Navigate Web Pages

Web pages are chock-full of information and gateways to other web resources. To navigate the landscape of web pages in Safari:

1. Tap in the Address field at the very top of the screen to display the onscreen keyboard (see **Figure 9-2**).

2. Enter a web address; for example, you can go to www.dummies.com.

3. Tap the Go key on the keyboard.

**FIGURE 9-2**

The website appears.

- If a page doesn't display properly, tap the reload icon (circular arrow) at the right end of the address field.

- If Safari is loading a web page and you change your mind about viewing the page, you can stop loading the page by tapping the X (cancel) that appears at the right end of the address field during this process.

4. Tap the previous icon (<) in the upper-left corner to go to the last page you displayed.

5. Tap the next icon (>) in the upper-left corner to go forward to the page you just backed up from.

6. To follow a link to another web page (links are typically indicated by colored text or graphics), tap the link with your finger.

**TIP**

To preview the destination of the link before you tap it, just touch and hold down on the link. A menu appears next to a preview of the site, as shown in **Figure 9-3.** Choose an option from the menu to proceed, or tap anywhere outside the menu to close it and the preview window.

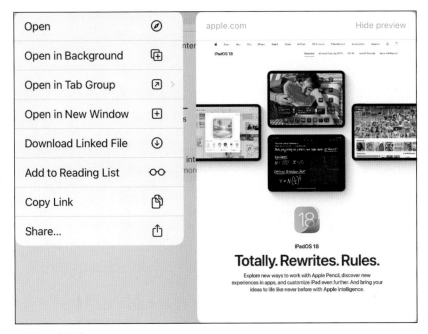

FIGURE 9-3

# Use Tabbed Browsing

Tabbed browsing is a feature that allows you to have several websites open at one time so that you can move easily among those sites.

1. With Safari open and a web page already displaying, tap the show tabs icon in the upper-right corner (labeled in Figure 9-1).

   The Tab view appears.

2. To add a new tab (meaning that you're opening a new web page), tap the new tab icon (+) in the upper right of the screen (see **Figure 9-4**).

A page appears with an address field and your favorite or currently open sites.

**Tap to open a new tab**

FIGURE 9-4

TIP

You can get to the same new page by simply tapping in the address field from any site.

3. Tap in the address field and use the onscreen keyboard to enter the web address for the website you want to open. Tap the Go key.

The website opens on the page.

TIP

Repeat Steps 1 to 3 to open as many new web pages as you'd like.

4. You can now switch among open sites by tapping outside the keyboard to close it and tapping the show tabs icon and scrolling among recent sites. Find the one you want and then tap it.

TIP

You can easily rearrange sites in the tabs window. Just tap and hold down on the tab you want to move and then drag it to the right or left in the list until it's in the spot you'd like it to be (the other sites in the window politely move to make room). To drop it in the new location, simply remove your finger from the screen.

5. To delete a tab, tap the show tabs icon, scroll to locate the tab (if necessary), and then tap the close icon (X) in the upper-right corner of the tab. (The X it may be difficult to see on some sites, but trust me, it's there.) Tap the Done button in the upper-right corner to close the Tabs view.

# Organize with Tab Groups

The tab groups feature enables you to keep similar tabs together so that they're easier to organize and find. This feature is especially helpful if you're someone who likes a million tabs open at one time; tab groups keep you from having to swipe until your fingers bleed to find the site tab you're looking for. Another function in iPadOS 18 is the capability to share tab groups. Anyone participating in the shared tab group can add or delete tabs in the group; others in the group see the changes instantly.

1. With Safari open, tap the sidebar icon in the upper-left corner (refer to Figure 9-1).

2. In the sidebar, tap *x* Tabs, where *x* represents the number of open tabs.

    **Figure 9-5** shows that I have two open tabs in Safari.

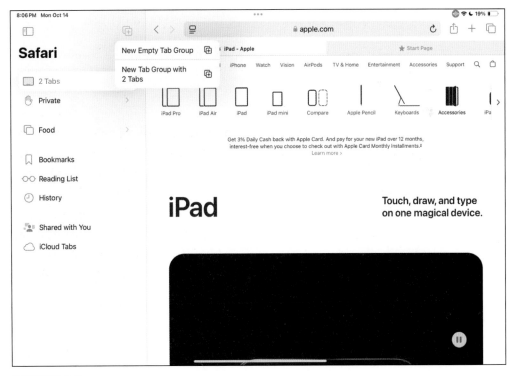

FIGURE 9-5

3. In the sidebar, do any of the following:

- Tap a group to open it (such as my group, Food, in Figure 9-5).

- To create a new group, tap the tab groups icon in the upper right of the sidebar; then tap New Empty Tab Group (refer to Figure 9-5). When prompted, give it a descriptive name (like Food in **Figure 9-6**). Tap Save to finish.

**New Tab Group**

Enter a name for this Tab Group. This Tab Group will sync across all your devices.

Food

Cancel    Save

FIGURE 9-6

- To create a tab group from the tabs you currently have open, tap New Tab Group with *x* Tabs (refer to Figure 9-5). Again, give the new group a descriptive name to help you stay organized, and then tap Save.

4. To move a tab to a tab group:

a. Tap the show tabs icon in the upper right of the Safari window (labeled in Figure 9-1).

b. Press and hold down on the tab for the site you want to move until a menu opens.

c. Tap the Move Tab option.

d. Tap the name of the group you want to move the site to (see **Figure 9-7**) and it will join that tab group (see **Figure 9-8**).

**FIGURE 9-7**

5. To share a tab group:

   a. In the sidebar, touch and hold down on the tab group name until a menu appears, and then tap Share.

   b. Tap the name of the person you want to share the group with from the list of suggested contacts that appears, or tap the Messages icon to select other recipients.

   c. Tap the blue arrow icon to send the link to your shared tab group to the folks you want to share it with.

      After your friends click the link, effectively accepting your invitation to the group, they can participate in your shared tab group.

**FIGURE 9-8**

# View Browsing History

As you move around the web, your browser keeps a record of your browsing history. This record can be handy when you want to visit a site that you viewed previously but whose address you've now forgotten, or if you accidentally close a site and want to quickly reopen it.

To view your browsing history:

1. With Safari open, tap the sidebar icon in the upper-left corner, and then tap History in the sidebar.

**TIP**

You might prefer a shortcut to view your History list. Tap and hold down on the < (previous) icon in the upper left on any screen, and your browsing history for the current tab appears. You can also tap and hold down on the > (next) icon to look at sites you backtracked from.

2. In the History list that appears (see **Figure 9-9**), tap a site to navigate to it.

3. Tap the Safari button in the upper-left corner to leave History and return to the sidebar, or tap the sidebar icon to close the sidebar.

FIGURE 9-9

To clear the history, tap the Clear button in the bottom of the History list (refer to Figure 9-9), and on the screen that appears, tap an option: The Last Hour, Today, Today and Yesterday, or All History. This button is useful when you don't want your spouse or grandchildren to see where you've been browsing for anniversary, birthday, or holiday gifts!

# Search the Web

If you don't know the address of the site you want to visit (or you want to research a topic or find other information online), get acquainted with Safari's search feature on your iPad. By default, Safari uses the Google search engine.

To search the web:

1. With Safari open, tap in the address field (refer to Figure 9-1).

   The onscreen keyboard appears.

**TIP**

   To change your default search engine from Google to Yahoo!, Bing, DuckDuckGo, or Ecosia, go to the Home screen and tap Settings, tap Apps, tap Safari, and then tap Search Engine. Tap Yahoo!, Bing, DuckDuckGo, or Ecosia, and your default search engine changes.

2. Enter a search term.

   With recent versions of Safari, the search term can be a topic or a web address because of what's called the unified smart search field. You can tap one of the suggested sites or complete your entry and tap the Go key (see **Figure 9-10**) on your keyboard.

3. In the search results that are displayed, tap a link to visit that site.

# Add and Use Bookmarks

Bookmarks are a way to save favorite pages so that you can easily visit them again.

To add and use bookmarks:

1. With a page open that you want to bookmark, tap the share icon (box with an upward-pointing arrow) in the upper right of the screen.

**FIGURE 9-10**

**TIP**

If you want to sync your bookmarks on your iPad browser, open the Settings app on your iPad and make sure that iCloud is set to sync with Safari. To do so, go to Settings ⇨ Apple ID ⇨ iCloud, tap Show All in the Saved to iCloud section, and make sure the Safari switch is set on (green).

2. On the menu that appears (see **Figure 9-11**), tap Add Bookmark. (You may need to swipe up the window to see it.)

3. In the Add Bookmark dialog, shown in **Figure 9-12,** edit the name of the bookmark if you want by tapping the name of the site and using the onscreen keyboard to edit its name.

4. Tap the Save button in the upper-right corner of the Add Bookmark dialog.

   The item is saved to your Favorites by default, but you can select a different location by tapping Favorites and then tapping the preferred location.

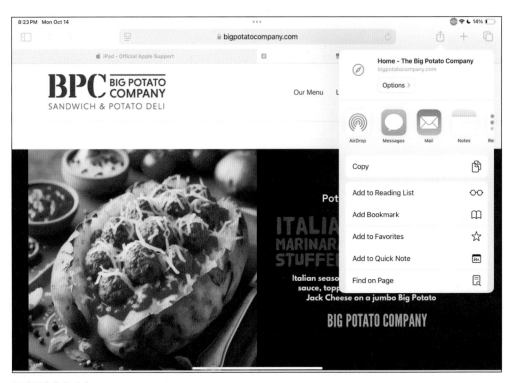

FIGURE 9-11

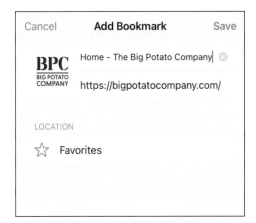

FIGURE 9-12

5. To go to the bookmark, tap the sidebar icon in the upper left, and then tap Bookmarks in the sidebar.

6. In the Bookmarks list that appears, find and tap the bookmarked site that you want to visit.

(Use the search field in the Bookmarks list if you need to.) In **Figure 9-13,** I've searched for and found the site I bookmarked back in Step 3 (it's found under Favorites, which is a subsection of the Bookmarks list).

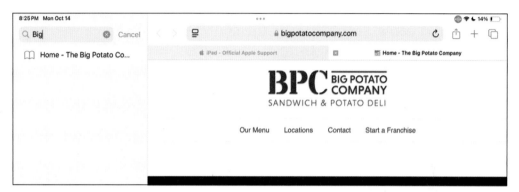

FIGURE 9-13

TIP

When you tap Bookmarks and the Bookmarks list opens, you can tap Edit in the lower right of the Bookmarks list and then use the New Folder option (in the lower left) to create folders to organize your bookmarks or folders. When you next add a bookmark, you can then choose, from the dialog that appears, any folder to which you want to add the new bookmark.

TIP

You can reorder your bookmarks easily. Tap Bookmarks to open the Bookmarks list and tap the Edit button (lower right of the list). Find the bookmark you'd like to rearrange, press and hold down on the three parallel lines (called a *handle*) to the right of the bookmark, and then drag the bookmark up and down the list, releasing it after you get to the place you'd like it to reside. You can also delete bookmarks from the same screen by tapping the red circle to the left of a bookmark and then tapping the red Delete button that appears to the right. Tap Done at the bottom of the Bookmarks list when you're finished.

# Save Links and Web Pages to Safari Reading List

The Safari Reading List provides a way to save content that you want to read at a later time so that you can easily call up that content again. You can essentially save the content rather than a web page address, which allows you to read the content even when you're offline. You can scroll from one item to the next easily.

To save content to the Reading List, follow these steps:

1. Displaying a site that you want to add to your Reading List, tap the share icon.

2. On the menu that appears (refer to Figure 9-11), tap Add to Reading List (you may need to swipe to see it).

   The site is added to your Reading List.

3. To view your Reading List, tap the sidebar icon in the upper-left corner and then tap Reading List in the sidebar.

**TIP**

If you want to see both the Reading List material you've read and the material you haven't read, tap the Show Unread button in the bottom-left corner of the Reading List. To see all reading material, tap the Show All button.

4. In the Reading List that appears (see **Figure 9-14**), tap the content that you want to revisit and resume reading.

**TIP**

To delete an item, make sure the Reading List is displayed, and swipe from right to left on an item. A red Delete button appears to the right. Tap this button to delete the item from the Reading List. To save an item for offline (when you're not connected to the internet) reading, tap the Save Offline button when you swipe. You can also swipe the item from left to right to mark it as read or unread.

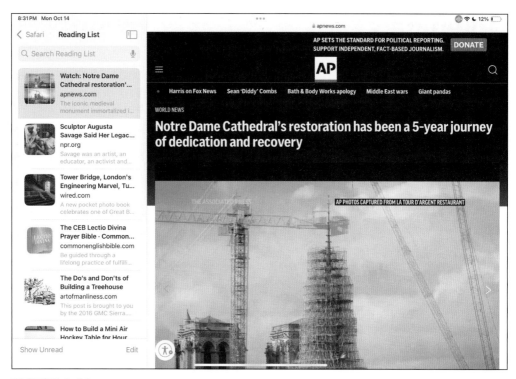

FIGURE 9-14

# Enable Private Browsing

Apple has provided some privacy settings for Safari that you should consider using.

Private browsing automatically stops Safari from using autofill to save information used to complete certain entries as you type, and erases some browsing history information. This feature can keep your online activities more private. To enable private browsing:

1. Tap the sidebar icon in the upper-left corner.

2. Tap Private in the sidebar; you're now in private browsing mode.

3. Tap the *x* Tabs button (where *x* is the number of tabs you have open) or a tab group in the sidebar to exit private browsing.

# Download Files

Download Manager for Safari helps you efficiently download files from websites and store them to a location of your choosing. You can store downloaded files on your iPad or in iCloud.

**TIP**

Set the default download location for files you download in Safari. Go to Settings ➪ Apps ➪ Safari ➪ Downloads and tap the location you want to use.

1. Open a site in Safari that contains a file you'd like to download.

2. Tap and hold down on the link for the file until a menu like the one in **Figure 9-15** appears.

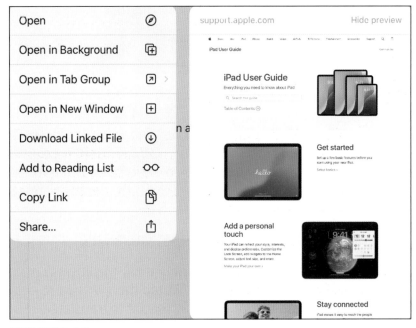

**FIGURE 9-15**

3. Tap Download Linked File to download the file to your iPad, iCloud, or another destination.

4. Tap the Download Manager icon (a circle with a downward-pointing arrow), which appears to the right of the address field at the top of the screen (see **Figure 9-16**), to see the progress of the download.

5. When the download is finished, tap it in the Downloads menu (refer to Figure 9-16) to open it, or tap the magnifying glass button to see where the file is stored.

FIGURE 9-16

# Translate Web Pages

Don't understand the language of the website you're viewing? Safari's web page translation feature to the rescue! Visit a compatible web page, and Safari can translate it into several languages (with more sure to come): English, Spanish, Brazilian Portuguese, Simplified Chinese, German, Russian, and French.

1. Open a site in Safari that's in a language you'd like to translate.

2. Tap the options icon (a box on top of two parallel lines) on the left side of the URL field (see **Figure 9-17**), tap the Translate Website button, and then tap the language you want to translate the page to.

   The page is translated into the language you selected. If you don't see the Translate Website button, Safari is unable to translate the site.

**Tap to translate**

**FIGURE 9-17**

**IN THIS CHAPTER**

» **Add an email account**

» **Read, reply to, or forward email**

» **Create, format, and send emails**

» **Search email**

» **Mark or flag email**

» **Create events with email contents**

» **Delete and organize email**

» **Create a VIP list**

Chapter **10**

# Working with Email in Mail

Staying in touch with others by email is a great way to use your iPad. You can access an existing account using the handy Mail app supplied with your iPad or sign in to your email account using the Safari browser. In this chapter, you take a look at using Mail, which includes adding an existing email account. Then you can use Mail to write, format, retrieve, and forward messages from that account.

Mail offers the capability to mark the messages you've read, delete messages, and organize your messages in a set of folders, as well as use a handy search feature. You can also create a VIP list so that you're notified when that special person sends you an email. In this chapter, you familiarize yourself with the Mail app and its various features.

# Add an Email Account

You can add one or more email accounts, including the email account associated with your iCloud account, using iPad Settings. If you have an iCloud, Microsoft Exchange (often used for business accounts), Gmail, Yahoo!, AOL, or Outlook.com account (including Microsoft accounts from Live, Hotmail, and so on), your iPad pretty much automates the setup.

If you have an iCloud account and have signed in to it already, your iCloud email account will already be set up for you in Mail.

If this is the first time you're adding an account and you need to add only one, save yourself a few taps: Just open Mail and begin from Step 4 in the following steps.

Follow these steps to set up your iPad to retrieve messages from your email account at one of these popular providers:

1. Tap the Settings icon on the Home screen.

2. In Settings, tap Apps, Mail, and then Mail Accounts.

   The screen shown in **Figure 10-1** appears.

3. Tap Add Account, found in the Accounts section.

   The options shown in **Figure 10-2** appear.

4. Tap iCloud, Microsoft Exchange, Google, Yahoo!, AOL, or Outlook.com. Enter your account information in the form that appears and follow any instructions to complete the process.

   (Each service is slightly different, but none are complicated.) If you have a different email service than these, skip to the next section, "Manually Set Up an Email Account."

   Your iPad takes a moment to verify the account information.

5. On the next screen (shown in **Figure 10-3**), you can tap any switch to have services from that account synced with your iPad.

6. When you're done, tap Save in the upper-right corner.

   The account is saved, and you can now open it using Mail.

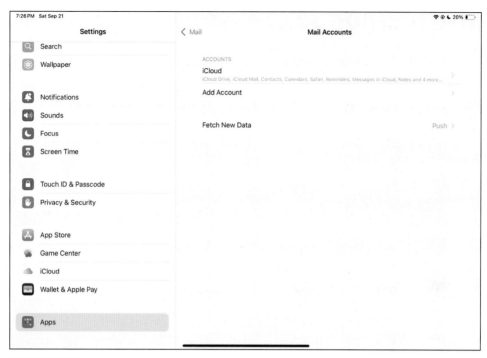

**FIGURE 10-1**

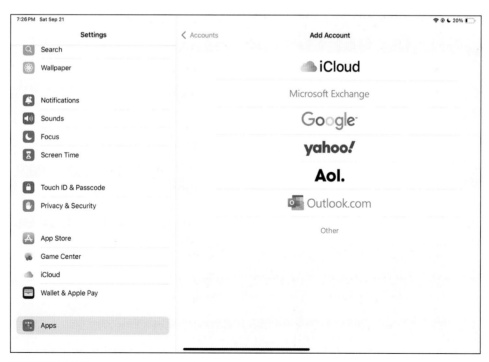

**FIGURE 10-2**

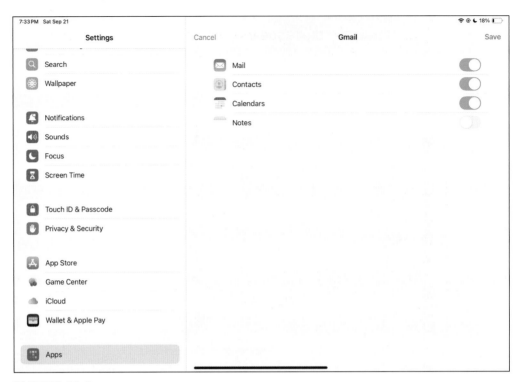

Search                        Mail

Wallpaper                     Contacts

                              Calendars

Notifications                 Notes

Sounds

Focus

Screen Time

Touch ID & Passcode

Privacy & Security

App Store

Game Center

iCloud

Wallet & Apple Pay

Apps

**FIGURE 10-3**

# Manually Set Up an Email Account

You can also set up many email accounts, such as those available through EarthLink or a cable provider's service, by obtaining the host name from the provider.

**TIP**

If this is the first time you're adding an account, just open Mail and begin from Step 3 in the following steps.

To set up an existing account with a provider other than iCloud (Apple), Microsoft Exchange, Gmail (Google), Yahoo!, AOL, or Outlook.com, you enter the account settings yourself:

1. Tap the Settings icon on the Home screen.

2. In Settings, tap Apps, Mail, Mail Accounts, and then tap the Add Account button (refer to Figure 10-1).

3. On the screen that appears (refer to Figure 10-2), tap Other.

4. On the screen shown in **Figure 10-4,** tap Add Mail Account.

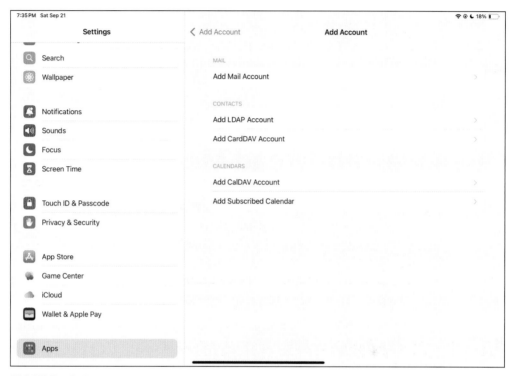

FIGURE 10-4

5. In the form that appears, enter your name, your account's email address and password, and a description. Then tap Next.

Your iPad takes a moment to verify your account.

TIP

Your iPad will probably add the outgoing mail server (SMTP) information for you. If it doesn't, you may have to enter it yourself. If you have a less mainstream email service, you may have to enter the mail server protocol (POP3 or IMAP — ask your provider for this information) and your password.

6. On the next screen, tap either IMAP or POP, enter the appropriate information in the required fields, and then tap Save to return to the Accounts screen.

   You can now access the account through your iPad's Mail app.

TIP

If you turn on Calendars in the Mail settings, any information you've put in your calendar in that email account is brought over to the Calendar app on your iPad (discussed in more detail in Chapter 16).

# Open Mail and Read Messages

Now for the exciting part: opening and reading your email! It's kind of like checking your mailbox, but you won't get wet if it's raining or eaten up by mosquitoes in the middle of summer.

1. Tap the Mail app icon (a blue square containing an envelope) located on the dock at the bottom of the Home screen.

   A red circle, called a badge, may appear on the icon, indicating the number of unread emails in your inbox.

2. In the Mail app (see **Figure 10-5**), tap an Inbox on the left to see your emails. If you have more than one account listed, tap the inbox whose contents you want to display.

3. Tap a message to read it.

   It opens on the right side (see **Figure 10-6**).

TIP

You can preview an email before you open it. Simply press lightly and hold down on an email in the inbox to open a preview of the message. From the preview, you can elect to perform several functions, such as open in new window, reply, forward, mark as read or unread, block sender, archive, and send to trash. If you want to view the entire message, release the hold and tap the preview.

4. If you need to scroll to see the entire message, just place your finger on the screen and flick upward to scroll down.

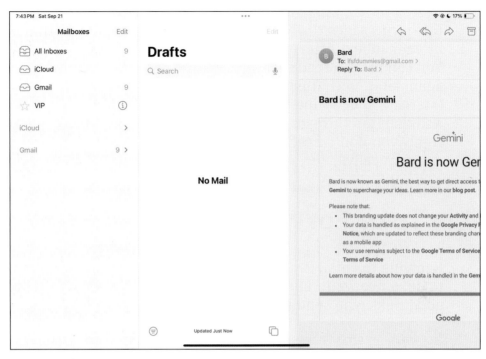

FIGURE 10-5

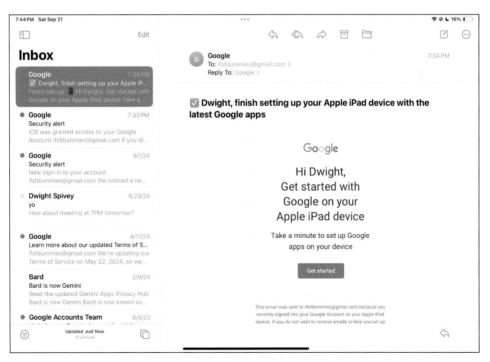

FIGURE 10-6

Email messages that you haven't read are marked with a blue circle in your inbox. After you read a message, the blue circle disappears. You can mark a read message as unread to help remind you to read it again later. With the inbox displayed, swipe to the right on a message (starting your swipe just a little in from the left edge of the screen) and then tap Unread. If you swipe quickly (like *quickly* quickly) to the right, you don't need to tap; the message will be marked as unread automatically.

# Reply To or Forward Email

Replying to email is just like replying to snail mail; it's the nice thing to do. Since we're all nice people, let's find out how to reply to those good folks who send us messages.

**1.** With an email message open, tap the reply/forward icon in the lower-right corner, which looks like a left-pointing arrow (refer to Figure 10-6). Then tap Reply, Reply All (available if there are multiple recipients), or Forward in the menu that appears (see **Figure 10-7**).

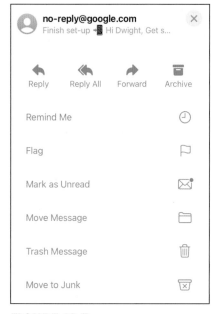

**FIGURE 10-7**

2. In the new email message that appears, tap in the To field and enter another addressee if you like (you have to do this if you're forwarding), as shown in **Figure 10-8.** Next, tap in the message body and enter a message (see **Figure 10-9**).

**FIGURE 10-8**

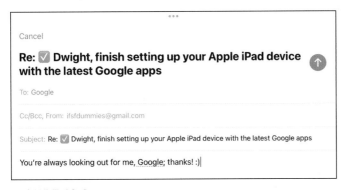

**FIGURE 10-9**

TIP

If you want to move an email address from the To field to the Cc or Bcc field, press and hold down on the address and drag it to the other field.

3. Tap the send icon (a blue circle with an upward-pointing arrow) in the upper-right corner and the email goes on its way.

If you tap Forward to send the message to someone else and the original message had an attachment, you're offered the option of including or omitting the attachment.

**TIP**

Some people send messages that sound legitimate but are not. These messages can harm you if you're not careful. If you see an email from a source you're unfamiliar with, investigate further before sending them any personal information. And never ever send financial information via email; no legitimate party would ask you to.

# Create and Send a New Message

It's time to reach out to everyone to plan for the family reunion, or maybe you need to provide vacation information to a friend who's accompanying you. "How to create and send that new email?" you ask? Well, here's how:

1. With Mail open, tap the compose icon (a page with a pencil) in the upper-right corner. A blank email appears (see **Figure 10-10**).

**FIGURE 10-10**

2. Enter a recipient's address in the To field by tapping in the field and typing the address.

    If you have addresses in Contacts, you can tap the plus sign (+) on the right side of the To field and choose an addressee from the Contacts list that appears.

3. If you want to send a copy of the message to other people, tap the Cc/Bcc field. When the Cc and Bcc fields open, enter addresses in either or both.

   Use the Bcc field to specify recipients of blind carbon copies, which means that no other recipients are aware that that person received this reply (being sneaky, are we?).

4. In the Subject field, enter the subject of the message.

5. Tap in the message body and type your message.

6. If you want to check a fact or copy and paste some part of another message into your draft message, tap anywhere outside the email message to minimize it (you can see it in a small window near the bottom of the screen) and display your Inbox and other folders. Locate the message you want to check or copy from, and when you're ready to return to your draft, tap the minimized window of your draft email near the bottom of the screen.

7. When you've finished creating your message, tap the send icon.

You can also schedule your email to send later. Instead of tapping the send icon, hold down on the send icon until a menu appears. Select Send Now, Send 9:00 PM Tonight, Send 8:00 AM Tomorrow, Send 8:00 AM the next business day, or Send Later (customize the date and time to send your email).

TIP

Oops! Did you forget to mention something or accidentally send the email to the wrong recipient? Well, if you're quick about it, iPadOS 18 lets you undo your action. Immediately after you send an email, you'll see an Undo Send button at the bottom left of the screen. Tap that button within ten seconds to open the draft of your previous email message, and then tap the Cancel button in the upper-left corner to save the email to your Drafts folder. Remember: You have only ten seconds after tapping the send icon to undo it!

# Format Email

You can apply some basic formatting to email text. You can use bold, underline, and italic formats, and indent text using the Quote Level feature.

To format an email:

**1.** Press and hold on the text in the message you're creating and choose Select or Select All to select a single word or all the words in the email; next you see the pop-up menu shown in **Figure 10-11.**

Cancel            **Draft**

To:

Cc/Bcc, From: ifsfdummies@gmail.com

| Cut | Copy | Paste | Add Link | AutoFill | Format | Find Selection | › |

Fall is finally here! ⭐ 🍂 Looking forward to some cooler, weather down here. How are things in your neck of the woods?

Sent from my iPad

**FIGURE 10-11**

**TIP**

When you make a selection, blue handles appear that you can drag to add adjacent words to your selection. If the toolbar disappears after you select the text, just tap one of the selection handles and the toolbar will reappear.

**2.** To apply bold, italic, or underline formatting, tap Format.

**TIP**

To see more tools (such as adding documents or inserting drawings), tap the arrow to the far right of the toolbar.

**3.** In the toolbar that appears (see **Figure 10-12**), tap Bold, Italic, or Underline to apply formatting.

FIGURE 10-12

4. To change the indent level, press and hold at the beginning of a line and then tap Quote Level in the toolbar that appears. (You might have to tap an arrow on the right or left of the toolbar to see it.)

5. Tap Increase to indent the text or Decrease to move indented text farther toward the left margin.

TIP

To use the Quote Level feature, make sure that it's on. From the Home screen, tap Settings ⇨ Apps ⇨ Mail ⇨ Increase Quote Level and then toggle (tap) the Increase Quote Level switch to turn it on (green).

Mail in iPadOS 18 allows you to go beyond the basics, though. It includes much-improved text formatting and font support, freeing you to create some really great-looking emails. However, it doesn't stop there: The format bar (which appears above the keyboard, shown in **Figure 10-13**) allows you to easily jazz up your email with a variety of options.

Here's a quick look at the options in the format bar, from left to right (refer to Figure 10-13):

» **Undo/redo:** Tap to undo or redo your previous action.

» **Desktop-class text formatting:** Tap the Aa icon to see a bevy of formatting options (shown in **Figure 10-14**), such as

• Choose bold, italic, underline, and strikethrough.

**FIGURE 10-13**

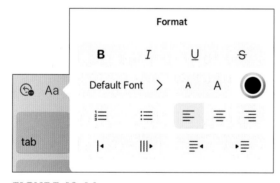

**FIGURE 10-14**

- Change the font by tapping Default Font and browsing a surprisingly extensive list of fonts.

- Decrease or increase the text size by tapping the small *A* or the large *A,* respectively.

- Tap the color wheel to select a color for your text.

- Insert numbered or bulleted lists.

- Select left, center, or right justification.

- Increase or decrease the quote level.

- Indent or outdent paragraphs.

» **Camera:** Tap to insert a new photo or video directly from the Camera app, or to insert a photo or video from the Photo Library. You can also scan a paper document and add it to your email, as well as scan a paper document or image for text, which is then inserted automatically into your email.

» **Attachment:** Tap to add an attachment to the email from the Files app. (See Chapter 3 for more info about Files.)

» **Insert drawing:** Tap to create a new drawing and insert it into your email.

## ALTERNATIVE EMAIL APPS

You can choose from lots of great email apps for your iPhone if Mail isn't what you're used to (or you don't like it). Here are a few of the better options: Gmail (the official app for Google Mail), Outlook (Microsoft's official app for Outlook), Edison Mail, Airmail, Spark, and Yahoo! Mail (Yahoo!'s official app).

iPadOS 18 enables you to replace Mail with a third-party email app as your default. Just go to Settings ⇨ Apps, scroll down until you see the name of your favorite email app, and tap it. Then tap the Default Mail App option, and on the Default Mail App screen that appears, tap the app you want to set as default.

# Search Email

What do you do if you want to find all messages from a certain person or containing a certain word? You can use Mail's handy search feature to find these emails.

To search email:

1. With Mail open, tap an account to display its inbox.

2. In the inbox, tap in the search field to make the onscreen keyboard appear.

   If you don't see the search field, just swipe down on the inbox's email list and it should appear at the top.

**TIP**

   You can also use the iPad-wide search feature covered in Chapter 2 to search for terms in the To, From, or Subject lines of email messages.

3. Tap the All Mailboxes tab to view messages that contain the search term in any mailbox, or tap the Current Mailbox tab to see only matches in the current mailbox.

   (These options may vary slightly depending on which email service you use.)

4. Enter a search term or name, as shown in **Figure 10-15.** If multiple types of information are found, such as People or Subjects, tap the one you're looking for.

   Matching emails are listed in the results.

**FIGURE 10-15**

# Mark Email as Unread or Flag for Follow-Up

You can use a simple swipe to access tools that either mark an email as unread after you've read it (placing a blue dot to the left of the message) or flag an email (which by default places an orange flag to the right of it, although you can choose an alternate color). If the email is both marked as unread and is flagged, a blue dot and an orange flag will appear on the message. These methods help you to remember to reread an email that you've already read or to follow up on a message at a later time.

**To mark email as unread or to flag it for follow-up:**

1. With Mail open and an inbox displayed, swipe to the left on an email in the sidebar to display three options: More, Flag, and Trash or Archive.

   Whether Trash or Archive appears depends on the settings for each account.

2. Tap More.

   On the menu shown in **Figure 10-16,** you're given several options, including Flag and Mark as Read or Mark as Unread (depending on the current state of the email).

   You can also get to the Mark as Read/Unread command by swiping to the right on a message displayed in your inbox.

TIP

3. To mark a message as read or unread, tap the appropriate command.

   You return to your inbox.

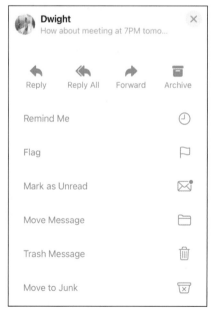

FIGURE 10-16

4. To assign a flag to the email, swipe to the left on an email and tap Flag and choose a color for the flag (again, the default is orange). To remove the flag, just tap More and then tap Unflag.

   You can get to the Flag command also by swiping to the left on an email in the sidebar and then tapping Flag. An orange flag appears to the right of the email. Perform the same action to unflag it, if you like.

**TIP**
On the menu shown in Figure 10-16, you can also select the Mute or Notify Me commands (which you may need to scroll to see), among a few other options. Mute allows you to mute a thread of emails that just won't stop bugging you. Notify Me causes Mail to notify you when someone replies to this email thread.

# Create an Event from Email Contents

A neat feature in Mail is the ability to create a Calendar event from an email. To test this out:

1. Create an email to yourself, mentioning a reservation on a specific airline on a specific date and time.

   You could instead mention another type of reservation, such as for dinner, or mention a phone number.

2. Send the message to yourself and then open Mail.

3. In your inbox, open the email.

   The pertinent information is displayed in underlined text.

4. Tap the underlined text, and the menu shown in **Figure 10-17** appears.

5. Tap Create Event to display the New Event form from Calendar.

6. Enter additional information about the event and then tap Add.

**TIP**
Siri may also detect an event in your email. If so, you see a notification at the top of the email that Siri did indeed find an event. Tap the small Add button to quickly create the event with little to no muss or fuss.

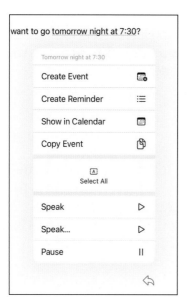

FIGURE 10-17

# Delete Email

When you no longer want an email cluttering your inbox, you can delete it.

1. With the inbox displayed, tap the Select button (found just to the left of the center screen).

   Circular check buttons are displayed to the left of each message (see **Figure 10-18**).

2. Tap the circle next to the message that you want to delete.

   A message marked for deletion shows a check mark in the circular check button and is highlighted in blue.

   You can tap multiple items if you have several emails to delete.

3. Tap the Trash or Archive button at the bottom of the inbox list.

   The selected messages are moved to the Trash or Archive folder.

What's the difference between Trash and Archive? Basically, email sent to a Trash folder typically is deleted forever after a certain

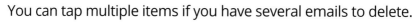

amount of time (usually 30 days); email sent to an Archive folder is removed from the inbox but kept indefinitely for future use.

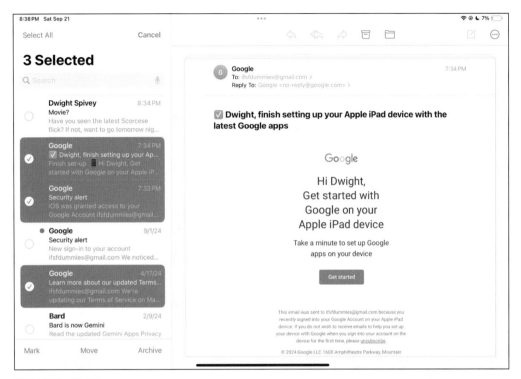

You can delete an open email also by tapping the Reply button in the bottom-right corner of the screen and then tapping the Trash Message or Archive Message option, or by swiping left on a message displayed in an inbox and tapping the Trash or Archive button that appears.

# Organize Email

You can move messages into any of several predefined folders in Mail, or you can create your own folder. (The predefined folders vary depending on your email provider and the folders you've created on your provider's server.)

1. After displaying the folder containing the message you want to move (for example, the Inbox folder), tap the Select button.

   Circular buttons are displayed to the left of each message (refer to Figure 10-18).

2. Tap the circle next to the message you want to move. Select multiple messages if you like.

3. Tap Move at the bottom of the inbox list.

4. In the Mailboxes list that appears on the left (see **Figure 10-19**), tap the folder where you want to store the message.

   The message is moved.

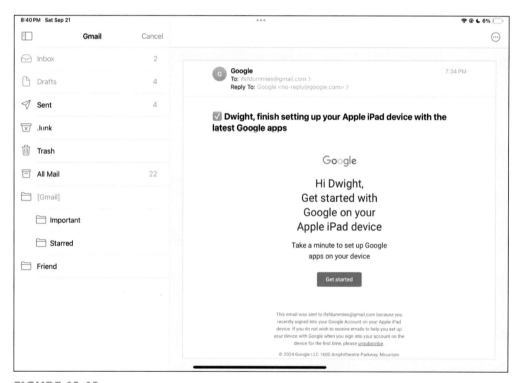

**FIGURE 10-19**

# Create a VIP List

A VIP list is a way to create a list of senders that you deem more important than others. When any of these senders sends you an email, you'll be notified of it through the Notifications feature of iPadOS.

1. In the main list of Mailboxes, tap the info icon (the circled *i*) next to the VIP option (refer to Figure 10-5).

2. Tap Add VIP (see **Figure 10-20**), and your Contacts list appears.

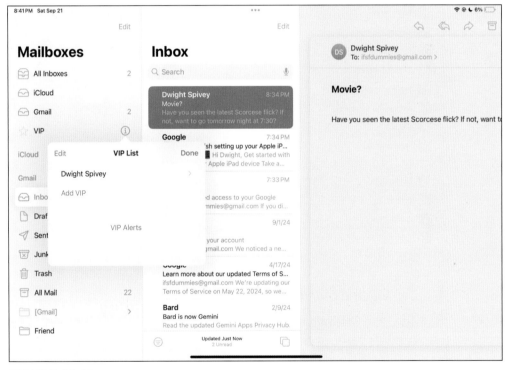

FIGURE 10-20

3. Tap a contact to make that person a VIP.

4. To make settings for whether VIP mail is flagged in Notification Center, swipe up from the bottom of the screen (if your iPad uses FaceID or TouchID) or press the Home button, and then tap Settings.

5. Tap Notifications and then tap Mail. In the settings that appear, shown in **Figure 10-21,** tap Customize Notifications at the bottom of the list.

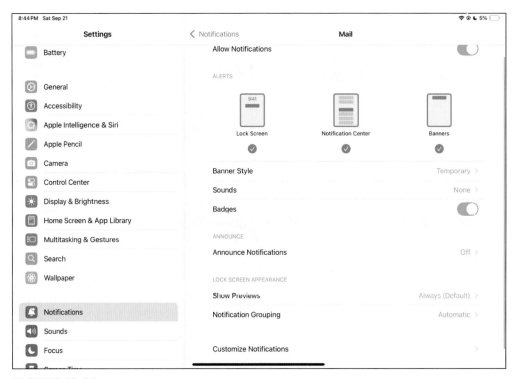

6. Tap VIP and then toggle the Alerts switch on (green).

7. To close Settings, swipe up from the bottom of the screen (on iPad models without a Home button) or press the Home button.

   New mail from your VIPs should now appear in Notification Center. And, depending on the settings you chose, new mail may cause a sound to play, a badge icon to appear on your lock screen, or a gold star icon to appear to the left of the message in the inbox in Mail. Definitely VIP treatment.

# 3

# Enjoying Media

**IN THIS PART . . .**

Shopping for movies, music, and more

Finding, buying, and reading books

Listening to audio and watching video

Taking and sharing photos

Shooting and sharing videos

IN THIS CHAPTER

» Explore music in the iTunes Store

» Buy selections

» Find movies and shows in the Apple TV app

» Use Apple Pay, Wallet, and Family Sharing

Chapter **11**

# Shopping the iTunes Store and Apple TV

The iTunes Store app lets you easily shop for music, and the Apple TV app is your place for finding movies and TV shows. As Chapter 12 explains, you can also get electronic books and audiobooks via Apple's Books app.

In this chapter, you learn how to find content in the iTunes Store and Apple TV app. You can download the content directly to your iPad, or you can download the content to another device and then sync it to your iPad. With the Family Sharing feature, as many as six people in a family can share purchases using the same credit card. Finally, you discover a few options for buying content from other online stores and using Apple Pay to make real-world purchases using a stored payment method.

TIP

Chapter 3 tells you how to find Apple support for opening an iTunes account (Apple ID) and how to sign in to iTunes. You might need to read Chapter 3 before digging into this chapter.

# Explore the iTunes Store

Visiting the iTunes Store from your iPad is easy with the iTunes Store app.

If you're in search of other kinds of content, check out the Podcasts app (discussed in Chapter 13), which you use to find and download podcasts to your iPad.

To check out the iTunes Store, follow these steps:

1. Go to your Home screen and tap the iTunes Store icon.

   The icon might be on the second Home screen page.

2. Tap Music (if it isn't already selected) in the row of tabs at the top of the screen. Swipe up and down the screen, and you'll find several categories of selections, such as New Music, Pre-Orders, and Recent Releases (these category change from time to time).

3. Flick your finger up to scroll through the featured selections, or tap See All to see more selections in any category, as shown in **Figure 11-1.**

The navigation techniques in these steps work essentially the same in any of the content categories (the buttons at the bottom of the screen): Music, Top Charts, and Purchased. You might also see Movies and TV Shows, but they redirect you to the Apple TV app.

4. Tap Top Charts at the top of the screen. Doing so displays lists of bestselling songs, albums, and music videos in the iTunes Store.

5. Tap any listed item to see more detail about it, as shown in **Figure 11-2,** and hear a brief preview when you tap the title of a song. Tap anywhere on the screen outside the information window to close it.

You can also find ringtones for your iPad and iPhone in the iTunes Store. Tap the Genres button at the upper-left corner of the screen, and then locate and tap Tones. Search through Tones just as you would the Music section of the iTunes Store. You'll find tons of fun tones taken from your favorite songs, movies, and television shows.

**Tap to see all in a category**

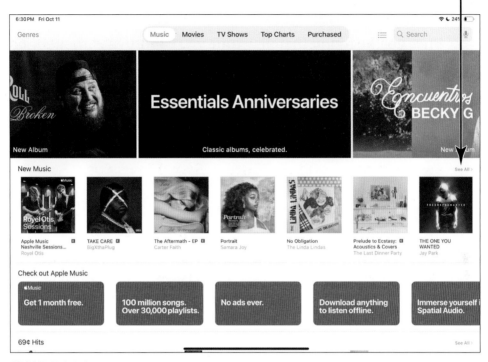

FIGURE 11-1

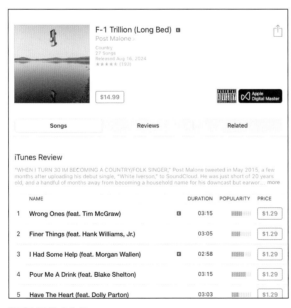

FIGURE 11-2

# Buy a Selection

Once you've found that new tune you can't live without or have redis-covered those older tracks that bring back so many memories, you may decide to purchase them for your collection:

1. When you find an item that you want to buy, tap the button that shows either the price (if the selection available for purchase; refer to **Figure 11-3**) or Get (if the selection available for free).

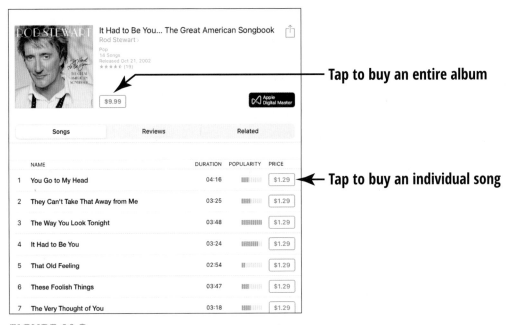

Tap to buy an entire album

Tap to buy an individual song

**FIGURE 11-3**

**TIP**

When buying music, you can open the description page for an album and tap the album price, or buy individual songs rather than the entire album. Tap the price for a song and then proceed to purchase it.

2. When the dialog appears on the screen, tap Purchase, type your password in the Password field on the next screen, and then tap Sign In to buy the item. Alternatively, use Touch ID or Face ID (depending on your iPad model) if you have it enabled for iTunes and App Store purchases.

The item begins downloading, and the cost, if any, is automatically charged to your account.

3. When the download finishes, tap OK in the Purchase Complete message, and you can then listen to the content using the Music app.

If you have a cellular-capable iPad and aren't near a Wi-Fi hotspot, downloading over your cellular network might be your only option. Tap Settings and then tap Cellular. Scroll down to the Cellular Data section, find iTunes Store, and set the switch on (green). Go through the list of apps while you're there and enable or disable apps as you see the need, especially if you allow others to use your iPad and are concerned that they may consume large quantities of cellular data.

Music files can be large, usually several megabytes per track. You could incur hefty data charges with your cellular provider if you run over your allotted data.

# Rent or Buy Movies and TV Shows

You can rent movies or buy movies or TV shows in the Apple TV app. If you rent a movie, you have 30 days from the time you rent the item to begin watching it. After you've begun to watch it, you have 48 hours to watch it on the same device, as many times as you like. If you buy the content, it's yours forever to watch as many times as you want.

I never buy a movie or show I've not yet seen. Who wants to plunk that kind of money down on something you may end up not liking?

As mentioned, music files are sometimes large, but movie and show files are always much, much larger. I recommend down-loading movie and show files only via Wi-Fi, if possible. Plus, they'll typically download much more quickly than when using cellular data (assuming you have a cellular-capable iPad).

## To rent or buy movies:

1. With the Apple TV app open, tap the Store button in the left sidebar, as shown in **Figure 11-4.** (Tap the sidebar icon in the upper-left corner if the sidebar isn't visible.)

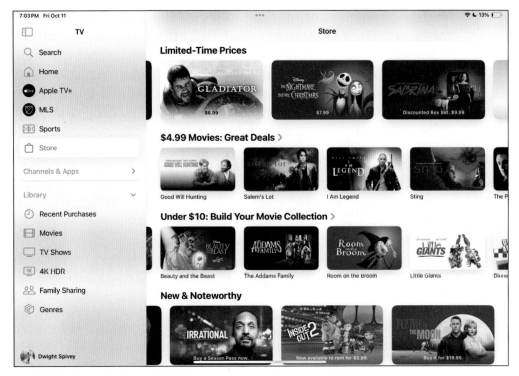

**FIGURE 11-4**

2. Locate the movie or show you want to rent or buy and tap it.

3. In the detailed description of the movie or show that appears, tap the Rent button (if it's available for rental) or the Buy button; see **Figure 11-5.**

4. When the dialog appears, tap Rent or Purchase, type your password in the Password field on the next screen, and then tap Sign In to rent or buy the item. Alternatively, use Touch ID or Face ID (depending on your iPad model) if you have it enabled for iTunes Store and App Store purchases.

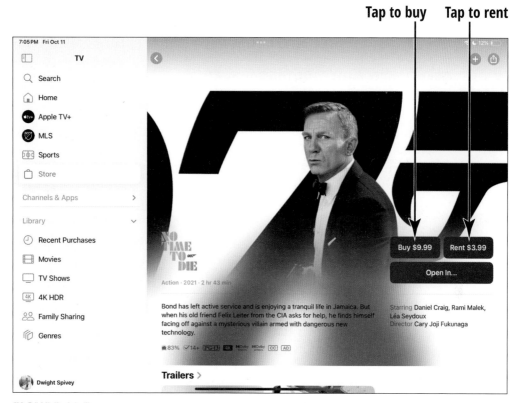

**Tap to buy**   **Tap to rent**

FIGURE 11-5

After you've been authenticated, the movie or show begins to download to your iPad immediately, and your account is charged the rental fee or purchase amount.

5. After the download is complete, you can use the Apple TV app to watch it.

See Chapter 15 to read about how the Apple TV app works.

# Use Apple Pay and Wallet

Apple is the creator of Apple Pay, an increasingly popular method of paying for items by using your iPad (or other Apple devices). Fancying itself as a mobile wallet, this service uses the Touch ID feature in your iPad's Home button, or the Face ID feature if your iPad doesn't have a Home button, to identify you and any credit cards you've stored in the iTunes Store to make payments via a feature called Wallet.

Your credit card information isn't stored on your phone or iPad, and Apple doesn't know a thing about your purchases. In addition, Apple considers Apple Pay safer than paying with a credit card at the store because the store cashier doesn't even have to know your name.

You can store more than just credit cards in Apple Wallet. Apple Wallet supports debit cards, ID cards, electronic tickets (for movies, as one example), transit fare cards, and more.

To set up Apple Pay, go to Settings and tap Wallet & Apple Pay. Add information about a credit card. You can also change settings, set your default card, and add and delete cards from the Wallet app itself.

For more information on Apple Pay, check out www.apple.com/apple-pay. To learn how to use your iPad with Apple Pay for purchases on websites or in apps, visit www.apple.com/wallet.

# Set Up Family Sharing

Family Sharing is a feature that allows as many as six people in your family to share whatever anyone in the group has purchased from the iTunes, Apple TV, Apple Books, and App Stores even though you don't share Apple IDs. Your family must all use the same credit card to purchase items (tied to whichever Apple ID is managing the family), but you can approve purchases by children under 13 years of age. (The age may vary depending on the country or region.) You can also share calendars, photos, and any Apple services (Apple TV+, Apple Music, and so on) that you're subscribed to.

Start by turning on Family Sharing:

1. Tap Settings and then tap the Apple ID.
2. Tap Family Sharing.

3. Tap Set Up Your Family, and then follow the onscreen directions to complete the setup and invite family members to join.

   An invitation is sent to the person's email. When the invitation is accepted, the person is added to your family.

The payment method for the family is displayed under Purchase Sharing in this screen. All those involved in a family have to use a single payment method for family purchases.

There's also a link called Create a Child Account. When you tap this link and enter information to create the ID, the child's account is automatically added to your family account and retains the child status until the child turns 13. If a child accesses the iTunes Store, Apple TV app, Apple Books store, or the App Store to buy something, a prompt appears to ask permission. You get an Ask to Buy notification in the Messages app and via email. You can then accept or decline the purchase, giving you control over your child's spending.

IN THIS CHAPTER

» Discover e-reading

» Find books

» Navigate and search a book

» Make it easier to read your
   e-books

# Chapter **12**

# Reading Books

A traditional e-reader is a device that's used primarily to read the electronic version of books, magazines, and newspapers. Apple has touted the iPad as a great e-reader, and although it isn't a traditional e-reader device like the Kindle Paperwhite, you don't want to miss this cool functionality.

Apple's free app that turns your iPad into an e-reader is Apple Books. This app also enables you to buy and download e-books and audiobooks from the Apple Book Store (offering millions of books and growing by the day). You can also use one of several other free e-reader apps — for example, Kindle or Nook. Then you can download books to your iPad from a variety of online sources, such as Amazon and Google, so that you can read to your heart's content.

In this chapter, you discover the options available for reading material and how to buy books. You also learn how to navigate a book or periodical and adjust the brightness and type. If you've used the Books app in prior iPadOS versions, you'll find that book navigation and customization settings have changed a bit. But no worries — I cover them all in the upcoming pages.

# Find Books with Apple Books

The Apple Books app isn't much to look at unless it's populated with books for you to peruse and enjoy. As always, Apple has already thought this through and provided its Book Store for you to explore.

When you buy a book online, or get one of many free publications, it downloads to your iPad in a few seconds (or minutes, depending on your internet connection speed and the size of the files) using a Wi-Fi or cellular connection. To shop using the Books app:

1. Tap the Apple Books icon to open the app.

   The icon looks like a white book against an orange background; it's also simply labeled Books.

2. Tap the Book Store tab at the top of the screen.

   In the Book Store, shown in **Figure 12-1,** featured titles and suggestions (based on your past reading habits and searches) are shown.

3. You can do any of the following to find a book:

   - Swipe left or right to see and read articles and suggestions for the latest books in various categories, such as Just Announced, as shown in **Figure 12-2,** and Featured Collection.

   - Scroll down on the Book Store's main page to see links to popular categories of books, as shown in **Figure 12-3.** Tap a category to view those selections.

   - Scroll down to Top Charts to view both Paid and Free books listed on top bestseller lists. Tap the Paid or Free button in Top Charts to focus on books that are the latest hits in those charts.

   - Swipe further down to the very bottom of the page to find a list of genres. Tap All Genres to see everything the Book Store has to offer.

   - On the main screen of the Book Store, tap Sections at the top right of the Book Store screen to open the Book Store Sections menu, shown in **Figure 12-4.** From here, you can easily scroll up and down the screen to browse Book Store sections and genres. Touch anywhere else on the screen to close the Book Store Sections menu.

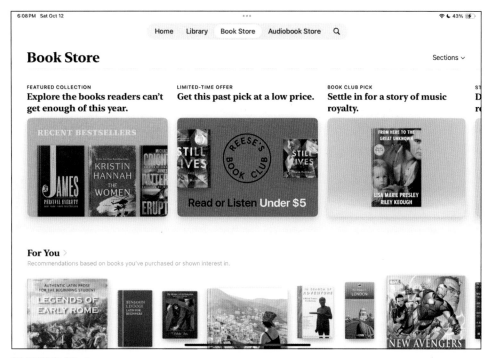

**FIGURE 12-1**

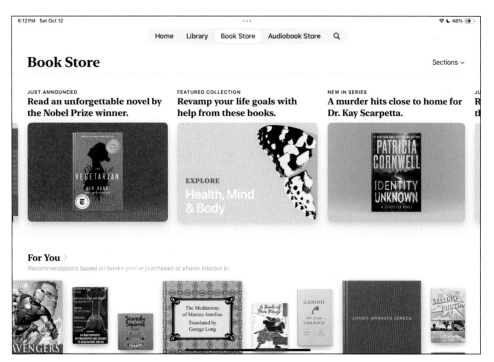

**FIGURE 12-2**

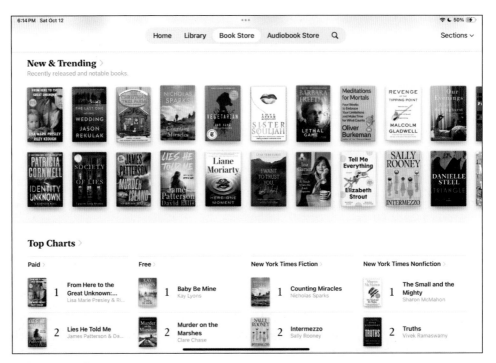

**FIGURE 12-3**

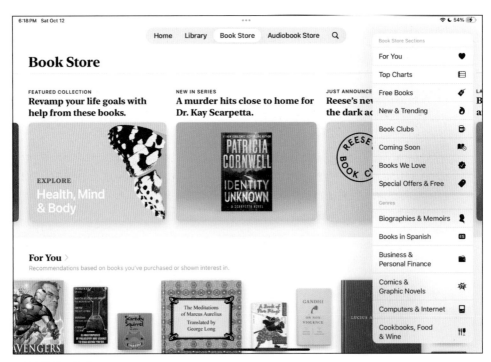

**FIGURE 12-4**

- Tap a suggested selection or featured book to read more information about it.

- Tap the search icon (magnifying glass) at the top of the screen, tap in the search field that appears, and then type a search word or phrase using the onscreen keyboard.

# Explore Other E-Book Sources

Beyond using Apple Books, the iPad is capable of using other e-reader apps to read book content from other bookstores. You first have to download another e-reader application, such as Amazon's Kindle or the Barnes & Noble Nook reader, from the App Store. (See Chapter 6 for how to download apps.) You can also download a non-vendor-specific app such as Bluefire Reader, which handles ePub and PDF formats, as well as the format that most public libraries use (protected PDF). Then use the app's features to search for, purchase, and download content.

Amazon's Kindle e-reader application is shown in **Figure 12-5.** To use the Kindle e-reader:

1. After downloading the free app from the App Store, open the app and enter the email address (username) and password associated with your Amazon account.

   Any content you've already bought from the Amazon.com Kindle Store from your computer or Kindle Fire tablet is archived online and appears on your Kindle home page on the iPad for you to read anytime you like.

2. Tap the Library tab at the bottom of the screen and tap All near the top middle of the screen to see all content you own. Tap the Downloaded tab (next to All near the top middle of the screen) to see titles stored on your iPad rather than in Amazon's Cloud library.

**FIGURE 12-5**

3. To enhance your reading experience, you can change the background to a sepia tone or change the font.

4. To delete a book from this reader, press and hold the title with your finger, and the Remove Download button appears in a menu; simply tap the button to remove the book from your iPad.

**TIP**

E-books are everywhere! You can get content from a variety of other sources, such as Project Gutenberg, Google Play, and some publishers such as Baen. Download the content using your computer, if you like, and then just add the items to Apple Books in Finder or iTunes and sync them to your iPad. You can also open items from a web link or email, and they're copied to Apple Books for you. Another option is to set up iCloud so that books are pushed across your Apple devices, or you can place them in an online storage service (such as Dropbox or Google Drive) and access them from there.

**TIP**

E-books come in different formats, and Apple Books won't work with formats other than ePub or PDF. (For example, it can't use such formats as Kindle's Mobi and AZW.)

# Buy Books

If you've set up an Apple Account, you can buy books at the Apple Book Store using the Apple Books app. (See Chapter 3 for more info.)

1. Open the Apple Books app, tap Book Store, and begin looking for a book.

2. When you find a book in the Book Store, you can buy it by tapping it and then tapping the Buy|*price* button (as shown in **Figure 12-6**) or the Get button (if it's free).

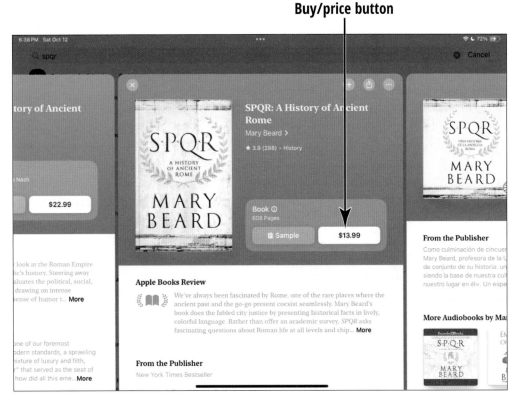

**FIGURE 12-6**

TIP

Many books let you download samples before you buy. You get to read several pages of the book to see whether it appeals to you, and previewing doesn't cost you a dime, kind of like when you browse the shelves in a bricks-and-mortar bookstore! Look for the Sample button when you view book details. (The button usually appears next to the price of the book.)

TIP

If you'd like to keep this book in mind for a future purchase, tap + above the title of the book. Your want-to-read list is on the Home tab at the top of the screen.

3. When the dialog appears on the screen, tap Purchase, type your password in the Password field on the next screen, and then tap Sign In to buy the book. Alternatively, use Touch ID or Face ID if you have it enabled for iTunes and App Store purchases (and if your iPad supports it, of course).

The book begins downloading, and the cost, if any, is automatically charged to your account.

4. When the download finishes, tap OK in the Purchase Complete message, and then find your new purchase by tapping the Library tab at the top of the screen.

TIP

Books that you've downloaded to your computer can be accessed from any Apple device through iCloud. Content can also be synced with your iPad by using the Lightning-to-USB, Lightning-to-USB-C, or USB-C cable (depending on the types of connection ports on your iPad and computer) and your iTunes account, or by using the wireless iTunes Wi-Fi Sync setting on the General Settings screen. See Chapter 3 for more about syncing.

## Navigate a Book

Getting around in Apple Books is half the fun!

1. Open Apple Books and tap the Library tab at the top of the screen.

2. Tap a book to open it.

The book opens to its title page or the last spot you read in Apple Books on any compatible device, as shown in **Figure 12-7.**

**Menu icon**

FIGURE 12-7

3. Take any of these actions to navigate the book:

   - **Go to the book's table of contents:** Tap the menu icon at the bottom right of the page (labeled in Figure 12-7), tap the Contents button/slider (shown in **Figure 12-8**), and then tap the name of a chapter to go to it.

TIP

     If you don't see the menu icon, simply tap the screen once to display it.

   - **Turn to the next page:** Tap the right margin, or place your finger anywhere along the right edge of the page and flick to the left.

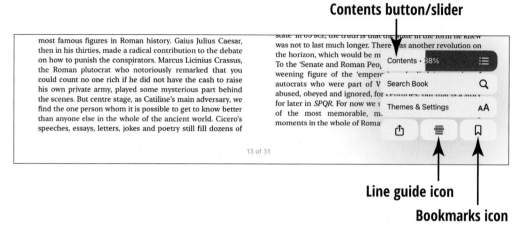

**Contents button/slider**

**Line guide icon**

**Bookmarks icon**

FIGURE 12-8

- **Turn to the preceding page:** Tap the left margin, or place your finger anywhere on the left edge of a page and flick to the right.

- **Move to another page in the book:** Touch and hold down on the Contents button/slider, drag to the right or left until you find the page number you want to move to, and then remove your finger from the Contents button/slider.

- **Highlight the line you're currently reading:** Tap the line guide icon (refer to Figure 12-8) and note that one line is highlighted and the rest are dimmed. Tap above or below the highlighted line to move to the previous or next line, respectively. Tap the line guide settings icon that's now in the lower-left corner to adjust the background dimming or to turn off the line guide.

- **Bookmark a page:** Tap the menu icon at the bottom right of the page (refer to Figure 12-7), and then tap the bookmark icon in the lower right (refer to Figure 12-8). The bookmark icon turns red when the page is bookmarked. You can view a list of bookmarks by tapping the menu icon and then tapping the Bookmarks & Highlights button (if you don't see it, you don't have any bookmarks or highlights). Then just tap a bookmark from the list to be whisked away to the bookmarked page.

TIP

Tap the Search Book button to search the current book for keywords or by page number, and then tap the result you want when listed.

TIP

Return to the library to view another book at any time by tapping the X icon in the upper-right corner of the screen (if you don't see it, just tap the screen to make it appear). You can also simply swipe down from near the top of the screen to close the current book.

# Customize Your Reading Experience

You've always been able to customize the look and feel of your books in the Apple Books app, but iPadOS 18 has turned up the ability to customize a notch or two. Let's check out how you can make your reading experience suit your needs and taste in the revised Apple Books app.

## Select and customize themes

The Books app comes with six predefined themes: Original, Quiet, Paper, Bold, Calm, and Focus. Each provides a combination of fonts and background colors curated for a particular reading experience (as their names skillfully suggest). Feel free to select one of these predefined themes, or customize them to your liking.

1. With a book open, tap the menu icon in the lower right of the screen (refer to Figure 12-7).

2. Tap the Themes & Settings button (refer to Figure 12-8).

3. Tap to select one of the predefined themes, shown in **Figure 12-9.**

TIP

Original is the default theme. After you select a different one, the new theme is applied to all your books until you change it.

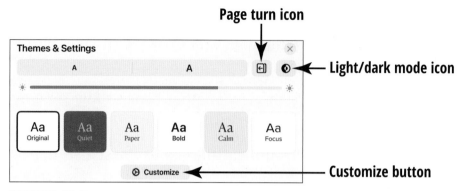

**Page turn icon**

**Light/dark mode icon**

**Customize button**

FIGURE 12-9

4. Further customize your book's appearance, if you like (refer to Figure 12-9 to locate the following items):

- Tap the small A to decrease the font size, or tap the larger A to increase it.

- Tap the page turn icon to select the animation you'd like to see when turning pages in your book. (I prefer the good old-fashioned curl animation, myself, but you should give them all a try.) You can also use the Scroll option to enable or disable the vertical scroll bar, which allows you to vertically scroll through the text of your book as opposed to swiping right or left to turn pages. To view the vertical scroll bar when enabled, tap the menu icon in the lower right; the scroll bar will appear to the right of the other buttons.

- Tap the light/dark mode icon to switch between the two modes, or to allow the Books app to match your surroundings or the default settings for your iPad.

## Modify your book's font

If the type on your screen is difficult for you to make out, you might want to choose a different font and perhaps use bold text for readability:

1. With a book open, tap the menu icon in the lower right, and then tap the Themes & Settings button.

2. In the Themes & Settings sheet, tap Customize (refer to Figure 12-9).

3. In the Customize Theme sheet, shown in **Figure 12-10,** do one or both of the following:

- Tap Font, and then tap a font name to select it. The font changes on the book page.

- Tap the Bold Text switch to enable or disable bold text.

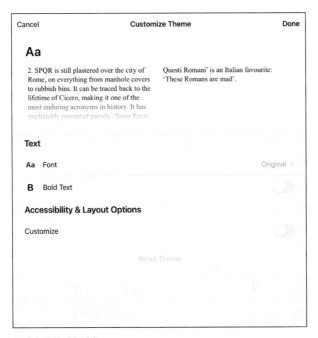

**FIGURE 12-10**

4. Tap the Done button in the upper-right corner to save your changes and return to the Themes & Settings sheet, or tap the Cancel button in the upper-left corner to discard your changes.

## Adjust Accessibility & Layout options

Several features in Apple Books allow you to further enhance your reading experience. They can be found in the Accessibility & Layout area of the Customize Theme sheet:

1. With a book open, tap the menu icon in the lower right, and then tap the Themes & Settings button.

2. In the Themes & Settings sheet, tap Customize (refer to Figure 12-9).

3. In the Customize Theme sheet, tap the Customize switch on in the Accessibility & Layout Options area to enable these features (refer to Figure 12-10).

4. In the Accessibility & Layout Options section, shown in **Figure 12-11,** do one, some, or all of the following:

   - Adjust the line spacing, character spacing, word spacing, and margins by dragging their respective sliders right or left.

   - Tap to enable or disable the Justify Text switch, which, if enabled, automatically adjusts the spacing of characters and words so that the text fills the width of the screen.

   - Tap the Columns pop-up button to adjust how you view columns in your books.

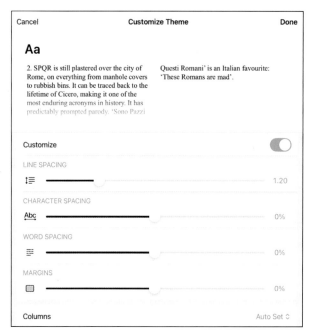

**FIGURE 12-11**

5. Tap the Done button in the upper-right corner to save your changes and return to the Themes & Settings sheet, or tap the Cancel button in the upper-left corner to leave everything the way you found it.

**TIP**

Don't like any of the changes you've made and want to start from scratch? Easily done, dear reader! Tap the menu icon in the lower-right side of your book, tap the Themes & Settings button, and tap Customize. Then swipe to the bottom of the options (if you need to), tap the Reset Theme button (refer to Figure 12-10), and then tap the Reset button when prompted for verification. Done!

IN THIS CHAPTER

» View the library and create playlists

» Search for music

» Play and shuffle music

» Listen with earbuds

» Check out spatial audio

» Use AirPlay

» Play music with the Radio feature

» Find, subscribe to, and play podcasts

# Chapter **13**

# Enjoying Music and Podcasts

PadOS 18 includes an app called Music that allows you to take advantage of your iPad's amazing little sound system to play your favorite music or other audio files.

In this chapter, you get acquainted with the Music app and its features that allow you to sort and find music and control playback. You also get an overview of AirPlay for accessing and playing your music over a home network or over any connected device (this also works also with videos and photos). Finally, I introduce you to podcasts to enhance your listening pleasure.

# View the Music Library

The library in Music contains the music or other audio files that you've placed on your iPad, either by purchasing them through the iTunes Store or copying them from your computer. Let's see how to work with those files on your iPad:

**1.** Tap the Music app, located in the dock on the Home screen, and the Music app opens, as shown in **Figure 13-1.**

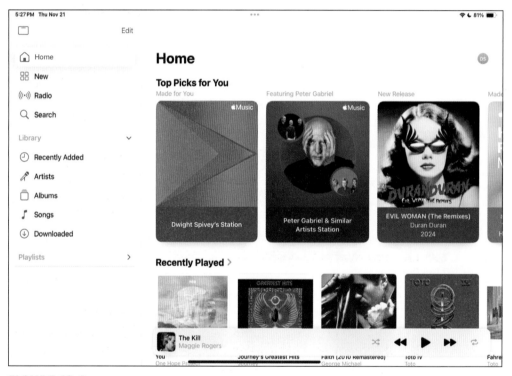

FIGURE 13-1

TIP

The figures in this chapter show the Music app in landscape mode. If you prefer portrait mode, you can access the sidebar mentioned in these steps by tapping the sidebar icon (a box divided in two sections) in the upper-left corner of the screen.

2. Tap Library in the sidebar on the left and then tap a category (see **Figure 13-2**) to view music by Recently Added, Artists, Albums, Songs, and other categories.

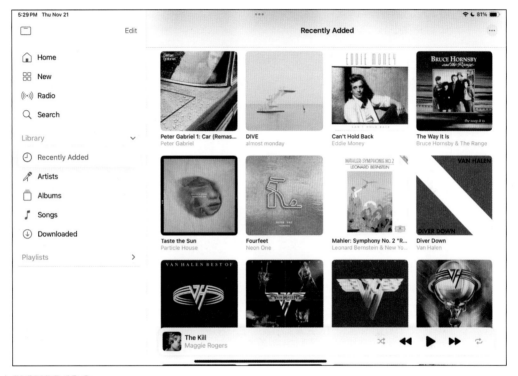

**FIGURE 13-2**

3. With the Library list expanded (tap the small arrow to the right of Library), tap Edit in the upper-right corner of the sidebar to edit the list of categories, as shown in **Figure 13-3.** Tap the check box to the left of categories that you'd like to sort your Music Library by; deselect those you don't want to use.

   You can also drag the categories into your preferred order by using the handles (three stacked lines) on the right side of the categories.

4. Tap Done in the upper-right corner of the sidebar when you're finished.

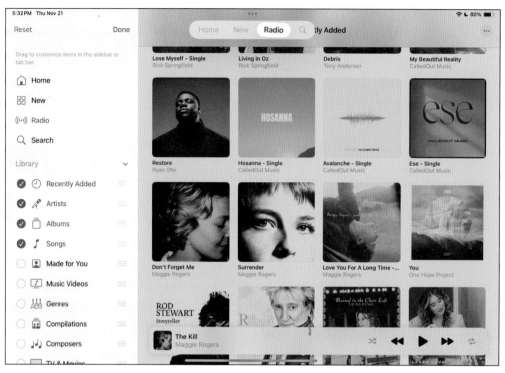

**FIGURE 13-3**

TIP

Apple offers a service called iTunes Match (visit `https://support.apple.com/en-us/108935` for more information). You pay $24.99 per year for the capability to match the music you've bought from other providers (and stored in the music library on your computer) to what's in Apple's Music Library. If there's a match (and there usually is), that content is added to your music library on iCloud. Then, using iCloud, you can sync the content among all your Apple devices. Is this service worth $24.99 a year? That's entirely up to you, my friend. However, for a few bucks more, you can have the benefits of iTunes Match plus access to millions of songs across all your Apple devices by using another Apple service: Apple Music (to which I'm admittedly partial and heavily invested). There's more about Apple Music later in this chapter, but for more info about subscribing and what a full-blown Apple Music subscription offers, check out `www.apple.com/apple-music`.

# Create Playlists

You can create your own playlists to put tracks from various sources into collections of your choosing:

1. Tap Playlists in the sidebar on the left of the screen.

2. Tap New Playlist; you may need to swipe to the bottom of the Playlists section to find it. In the dialog that appears (see **Figure 13-4**), tap Playlist Title and enter a title (see what Apple did there?) for the playlist.

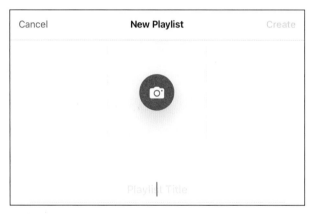

FIGURE 13-4

3. Tap the Create button in the upper right and you'll be taken to your new playlist. To curate your playlist, tap Add Music. Then search for music by artist, title, or lyrics; or browse for songs by tapping Artists, Albums, Songs, and so on.

4. In the list of selections that appears (see **Figure 13-5**), tap the plus sign to the right of each item you want to include (for individual songs, entire albums, or artists). Tap the arrow in the left corner of the window to go back and search for other items, if you like. Continue until you've selected all the songs you want to add to the playlist.

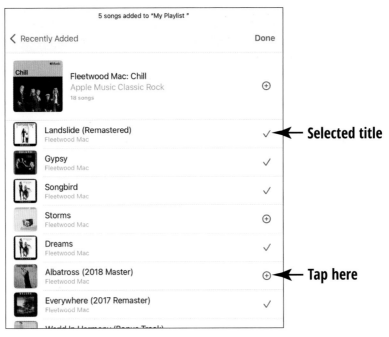

5 songs added to "My Playlist"

‹ Recently Added        Done

Fleetwood Mac: Chill
Apple Music Classic Rock
18 songs ⊕

Landslide (Remastered)
Fleetwood Mac ✓ ← **Selected title**

Gypsy
Fleetwood Mac ✓

Songbird
Fleetwood Mac ✓

Storms
Fleetwood Mac ⊕

Dreams
Fleetwood Mac ✓

Albatross (2018 Master)
Fleetwood Mac ⊕ ← **Tap here**

Everywhere (2017 Remaster)
Fleetwood Mac ✓

**FIGURE 13-5**

5. To finish adding tracks to the playlist, tap the Done button to return to the Playlists screen.

Your playlist appears under Playlists in the sidebar, and you can now play it by tapping its name and then tapping a track to play it.

# Search for Music

You can search for an item in your Music Library by using the search feature:

1. With the Music app open, tap Search in the sidebar on the left. When the Search screen appears, tap the search field at the top of the screen. Tap Apple Music to search the Apple Music library, or tap the Library tab to search for songs stored on your iPad.

You can search for items in Apple Music, but you must be subscribed to the service to play selections from it.

2. Enter a search term in the search field.

   As you type, you see results, which narrow as you continue to type, as shown in **Figure 13-6.**

**FIGURE 13-6**

3. Tap an item in the results to view or play it.

In the search field, you can enter an artist's name, a lyricist's or a composer's name, a word from the item's title, or even lyrics to find what you're looking for.

To search for and play a song in your music libraries from your Home screen (without opening the Music app), use the iPad-wise search feature. From the first Home screen, swipe down on the screen anywhere outside the dock and enter the name of the song in the search field. A list of search results appears. Tap the play icon and rock on!

# Play Music

Now that you know how to find your music (which will be more and more handy as your library grows), let's have some real fun by playing it!

TIP

You can use Siri to play music hands free. Just press and hold on the Home button (if your iPad has one) or the Top button (if your iPad doesn't have a Home button), and when Siri engages, say something like "Play 'Man in the Mirror'" or "Play 'I Walk the Line.'"

To play music on your iPad, follow these steps:

1. Locate the music that you want by using the methods described in previous tasks in this chapter.

2. Tap the item you want to play.

   If you're displaying the Songs category, you don't have to tap an album to open a song; you need only to tap the song to play it. If you're using any other categories, you have to tap items, such as albums (or multiple songs from one artist), to find the song you want to hear.

TIP

   Home Sharing is a feature of iTunes and the Music app that enables you to share music among up to five devices that have Home Sharing turned on. After Home Sharing is set up via iTunes or the Sharing pane in System Preferences or System Settings (Mac users only), any of your devices can stream music and videos to other devices, and you can even click and drag content between devices using iTunes or the Music app. For more about Home Sharing, visit https://support.apple.com/en-us/108958.

3. Tap the item you want to play from the list that appears, and it will begin to play, as shown in **Figure 13-7.**

   You can tell that the song is playing (assuming you can't hear it, of course) because the number to the left of its title turns into red audio equalizer bars and the name of the song appears at the bottom of the screen.

4. Tap the currently playing song title at the bottom of the screen to open it, displaying the playback controls. Use the previous and next icons near the bottom of the screen shown in **Figure 13-8** to navigate the audio file that's playing:

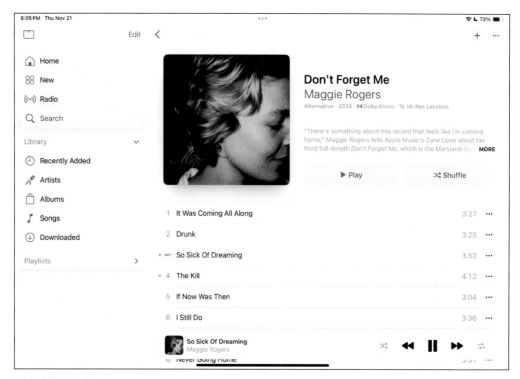

**FIGURE 13-7**

- The previous icon takes you back to the beginning of the item that's playing if you tap it, rewinds the song if you press and hold it, or takes you back to the start of the previous item if you tap it again.

- The next icon takes you to the next item if you tap it, or fast-forwards the song if you press and hold on it.

**TIP**

Rewinding songs with the previous icon or fast-forwarding songs with the next icon requires a bit of patience because they tend to jump around a bit in the process. I prefer dragging the playhead left or right. You can also touch anywhere on the track position bar to jump to a particular section of a song.

Drag the volume slider at the bottom of the screen (or the volume buttons on the side of your iPad) to increase or decrease the volume.

5. Tap the pause icon to pause playback. Tap the play icon, which replaces the pause icon, to resume playing.

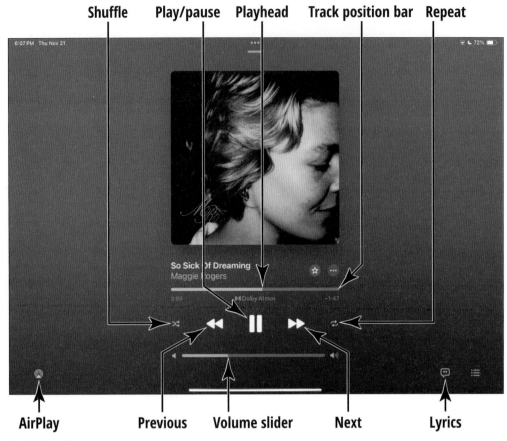

**Shuffle**    **Play/pause**    **Playhead**    **Track position bar**    **Repeat**

So Sick Of Dreaming
Maggie Rogers

2:05            Dolby Atmos            -1:47

**AirPlay**        **Previous**    **Volume slider**        **Next**        **Lyrics**

FIGURE 13-8

**TIP**

You can use music controls also for music playing from the lock screen.

6. Tap and drag the playhead in the track position bar near the middle of the screen (below the song title), which indicates the current playback location. Drag the line to the left or right to "scrub" to another location in the song.

7. If you like to sing along but sometimes flub the words, tap the lyrics icon in the lower right (a speech box with a quotation mark in it).

With most songs from the Apple Music library, the lyrics will scroll up the screen in sync with the song, as shown in **Figure 13-9.** You can swipe through the lyrics, or if you tap a lyric, Music will jump to that point in the song.

**Mic**

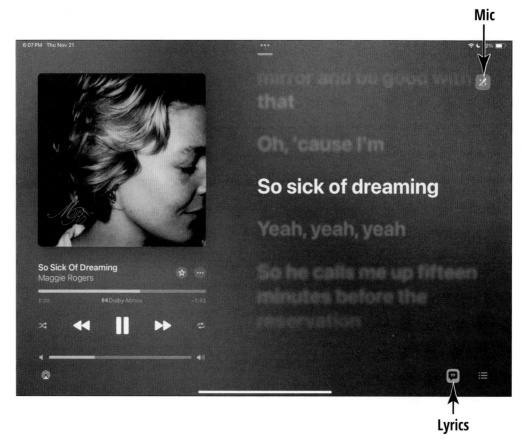

**Lyrics**

**FIGURE 13-9**

Another nifty thing you can do (if the song you're listening to is in the Apple Music library) is to lower the volume of the main singer so that your melodious voice can take over. You can activate this feature, called Apple Music Sing, by tapping the mic icon on the lyrics screen. For more on these features, visit `https://support.apple.com/en-us/105076`.

**TIP**

If you have an Apple Music subscription, you can see lyrics for almost any song (assuming it has lyrics). But what if you don't have an Apple Music subscription? You can add lyrics to songs if you have a Mac or PC! Using the Music app on your Mac or iTunes on a Windows-based PC, click the more icon (three dots) next to the name of a song and select Get Info from the list. Click the Lyrics tab, select the Custom Lyrics check box, add your lyrics, and then click

OK. Next, copy the song to your iPad, and the lyrics will appear when the song is played and you tap the lyrics icon.

8. If you don't like what's playing, make another selection by dragging down from the top of the playback controls screen to view other selections in the album that's playing and make a new choice.

**TIP**

Family Sharing allows up to six members of your family to share purchased content even if they don't share the same iTunes account. You can set up Family Sharing under iCloud in Settings. See Chapter 11 for more about Family Sharing.

# Shuffle Music

If you want to play a random selection of the music in an album on your iPad, you can use the shuffle feature:

1. Tap the name of the currently playing song at the bottom of the screen.

2. Tap the shuffle icon, which looks like two lines crossing to form an *X* and is located to the left of the previous icon. Your content plays in random order.

3. To play the songs over again continuously, tap the repeat icon, which looks like two arrows circling one another and is located to the right of the next icon.

# Listen with Your Earbuds

If you've set the volume slider as high as it goes but you're still having trouble hearing the music, consider using earbuds. These cut out extraneous noises and improve the sound quality of what you're listening to.

Some iPad models have 3.5mm headphone jacks; you can use 3.5mm stereo earbuds for them, inserting them into the headphone jack. If your iPad has a Lightning connector, you can use earbuds that have a Lightning connector, or you can use a Lightning-to-3.5mm adaptor with standard 3.5mm headphones. If your iPad has a USB-C connector, you can use earbuds that have a USB-C connector, or you can use a USB-C-to-3.5mm adaptor with standard 3.5mm headphones.

You might also look into purchasing Bluetooth earbuds, which allow you to listen wirelessly. (I think this is your best bet.) For a top-of-the-line wireless experience, try out Apple's AirPods, AirPods Pro, or AirPods Max (go to `www.apple.com/airpods` for more info). They're a little pricey but get rave reviews, and for very good reason.

Bluetooth is a tried-and-true technology, but even so, its connections and range can be flaky. To minimize the chances of a sub-par (and possibly infuriatingly frustrating) listening experience, remember that "you get what you pay for" is often accurate. As mentioned, Apple's AirPods line can be pricey. An alternative Apple product, Beats by Dr. Dre (`www.beatsbydre.com`), offers a wider range of earbuds and headphones, including some that aren't as expensive (but are still quite good).

# Listen with Spatial Audio

Spatial audio is a technology (part of Dolby Atmos) that helps listeners feel as if they're sitting in the middle of the band, orchestra, or what-have-you. The difference between spatial audio and standard stereo can be eye-popping when you first hear it.

**TIP** For more on Dolby Atmos, such as how to tell if audio files are in the format or whether your device can even play the format, visit `https://support.apple.com/en-us/109354`.

To enable Dolby Atmos for audio files that support the format:

1. Open the Settings app on your iPad and tap Apps at the very bottom of the left sidebar.

2. Find and tap Music.

3. Tap Dolby Atmos, and then tap Automatic or Always On to have audio files that support Dolby Atmos play in that format.

**To enable Spatial Audio while using AirPods Pro or AirPods Max:**

1. Swipe down from the top-right corner of your iPad's screen to open Control Center.

2. Tap and hold on the volume slider until the screen shown in **Figure 13-10** opens.

3. If the audio file that's currently playing supports Dolby Atmos and spatial audio, the Spatial Audio button will appear in the lower right (refer to Figure 13-10).

**FIGURE 13-10**

4. To enable or disable spatial audio, tap the Spatial Audio button. Then you can tap the Off button to disable spatial audio, or tap Fixed or Head Tracked to enable it in one of these two modes.

If the button is blue, spatial audio is enabled; if it's gray, spatial audio is not enabled.

# Use AirPlay

The AirPlay streaming technology is built into the iPad, Macs, PCs running iTunes for Windows, and iPhone. Streaming technology allows you to send media files from one device that supports AirPlay to be played on another. For example, you can send a movie you've purchased on your iPad or a slideshow of your photos to your Apple TV, and then control the TV playback from your iPad. You can also send music to compatible speakers, such as Apple's HomePod. (Go to www.apple.com/homepod for more information.) Check out Apple's Remote app in the Control Center, which you can use to control your Apple TV from your iPad.

To stream music via AirPlay on your iPad with another AirPlay-enabled device on your network or in close proximity, tap the AirPlay icon (triangle with sound waves) in the lower-left corner of the playback control screen while listening to a song. Then select the AirPlay device to stream the content to, or choose your iPad to move the playback back to it.

If you get a bit antsy watching a long movie, one of the beauties of AirPlay is that you can still use your iPad to check email, browse photos or the internet, or check your calendar while the media file is playing on the other device.

# Play Music with Radio

You can access Radio by tapping the Radio icon in the left sidebar of the Music screen, as shown in **Figure 13-11**.

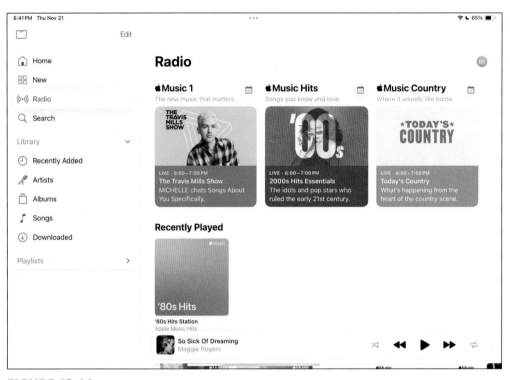

**FIGURE 13-11**

Swipe up and down and from left to right and you'll find lots of music specials and offers. Swipe further down to see Radio's offerings by categories, such as Local Broadcasters, International Broadcasters, and Genre (see **Figure 13-12**).

At one time, the Radio feature was free in the Music app, but now it's tied extensively into Apple's Music service, which is subscription based. The Radio app offers much more when you have an Apple Music subscription, but it can still be used without one for broadcast radio stations and Apple's flagship radio station, Beats 1. However, if you want to listen to most digital stations in Radio, you'll have to become a member of Apple Music.

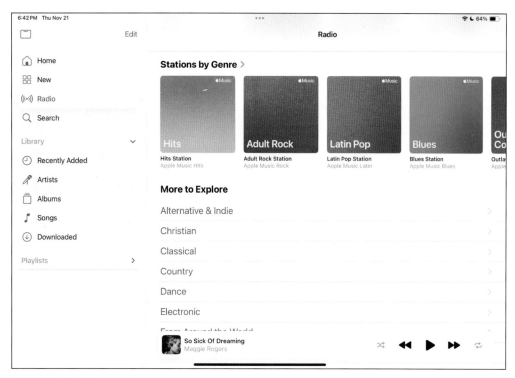

FIGURE 13-12

# Find and Subscribe to Podcasts

A *podcast* is sort of like a radio show with the glorious difference that you can listen to it at any time. The Podcasts app is the vehicle by which you find and listen to podcasts on your iPad.

To search Apple's massive library of podcasts and subscribe to them (which is free, with a few "premium" exceptions), just follow these steps:

1. Tap the Podcasts icon to open the app.

2. Discover podcasts in one of the following ways:

   - Tap Browse in the left sidebar (tap the sidebar icon in the upper-left corner if you don't see the sidebar). You see podcasts that are featured by the good folks at Apple, as shown in **Figure 13-13.**

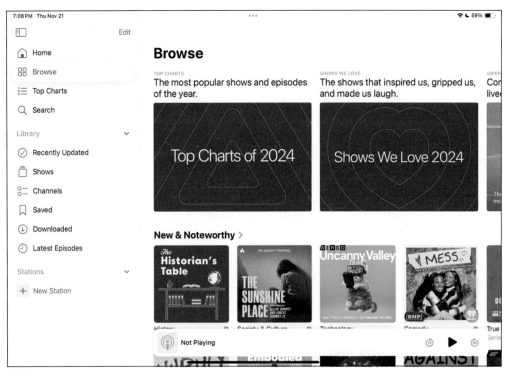

FIGURE 13-13

- Tap Browse in the left sidebar and swipe down to Top Shows or Top Episodes. Tap the arrow next to the title of a category and you'll be greeted with lists of the most popular podcasts. Tap Top Charts in the left sidebar and then tap All Categories in the upper-right corner to sift through the podcasts based on the category (such as Arts, Health & Fitness, Music, and much more).

- Tap Search in the left sidebar and then tap the search field at the top of the screen. When the keyboard appears, type the name or subject of a podcast to see a list of results.

3. When you find a podcast that intrigues you, tap its name to see its information page, which will be similar to the one in **Figure 13-14.**

4. Tap the + Follow button in the upper-right corner.

   The podcast now appears in the Library section of the app, and the newest episode is downloaded to your iPad.

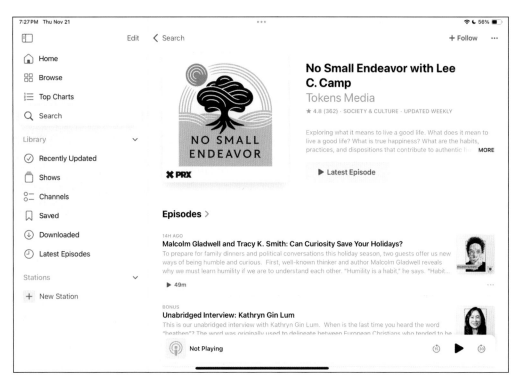

FIGURE 13-14

5. Tap Shows (under Library) in the left sidebar, and then tap the name of the podcast you subscribed to and view its information screen.

6. Tap the more button in the upper right (a circle with three dots) and then tap the settings icon (a gear) to see the settings for the podcast.

   From here (see **Figure 13-15**), you can customize how the podcast downloads and organizes episodes.

7. Tap Done in the upper-right corner when you're finished with the Settings options.

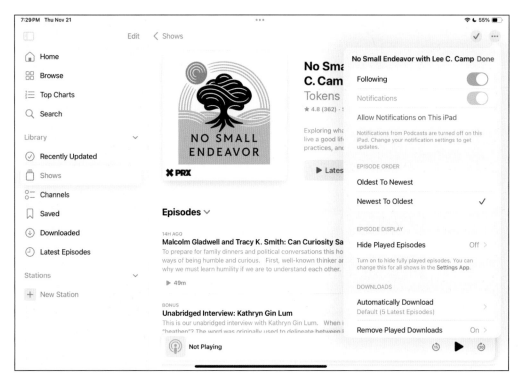

**FIGURE 13-15**

# Play Podcasts

Playing podcasts is a breeze and works very much like playing audio files in the Music app.

**1.** Open the Podcasts app and tap Shows (under Library) in the left sidebar.

**2.** Tap the name of the podcast you'd like to listen to.

**3.** Tap the episode you want to play.

The episode begins playing; you can see the currently playing episode in the bottom-right area of the screen.

**4.** Tap the currently playing episode in the lower right of the screen to open the playback controls, shown in **Figure 13-16.**

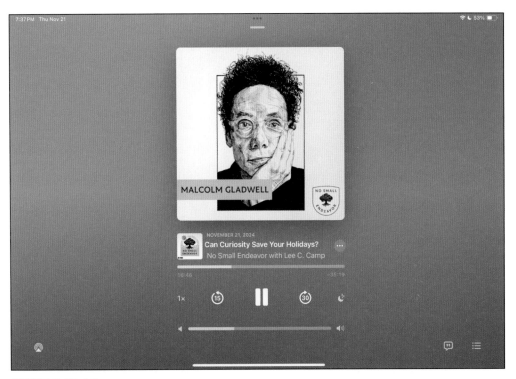

**FIGURE 13-16**

5. Drag the playhead line under the image to scrub to a different part of the episode, or tap the rewind or fast-forward icons to the left and right of the pause/play icon, respectively.

6. Adjust the playback speed by tapping the 1x icon in the lower left of the playback controls.

   Each tap increases or decreases playback speed.

7. Adjust the volume by dragging the volume slider near the bottom of the screen or by using the volume buttons on the side of your iPad.

**TIP**

Tap the Latest Episodes button in the left sidebar to see a list of the newest episodes that have been automatically downloaded to your iPad.

» Take pictures with your iPad

» View albums and single photos

» Edit and organize photos

» View photos by time and place

» Share and delete photos

» Print photos

Chapter **14**

# Taking and Sharing Photos

With its high-resolution camera modules and gorgeous screen, the iPad is a natural for taking and viewing photos. It supports JPEG and HEIF (High Efficiency Image Format) photos. You can shoot your photos by using the iPad cameras with built-in square or panorama mode. With recent iPad models, you can edit your images using smart adjustment filters. You can also sync photos from your computer, save images that you find online to your iPad, or receive them by email, MMS, RCS, or iMessage.

The photo-sharing feature lets you share groups of photos with people using iCloud on an iPad or iPhone, or on a Mac or Windows computer with iCloud access. Your iCloud photo library makes all this storage and sharing easy.

When you have taken or downloaded photos to play with, the Photos app lets you organize them and view them in albums, one by one, or in a slideshow. You can view photos also by the years in which they were taken, with images divided into collections by the location or time you took them. With iPadOS 18, videos and live photos will play as you browse through Photos, making it a more dynamic and inter-esting experience. You can also AirDrop, email, message, or tweet a photo to a friend, print it, share it via AirPlay, or post it to Facebook. Finally, you can create time-lapse videos with the Camera app, allowing you to record a sequence in time, such as a flower opening as the sun warms it or your grandchild stirring from sleep. You can read about all these features in this chapter.

# Take Pictures with the iPad Cameras

The cameras in the iPad are top-notch, so you'll be pleased with the results no matter which iPad model you have!

1. Tap the Camera app icon on the Home screen to open the app.

To go to the camera from the lock screen, swipe down from the right corner of the screen and tap the Camera app icon in Control Center. Or simply swipe from right to left on the lock screen.

2. If the camera type on the lower-right side of the screen (see **Figure 14-1**) is set to Video or something other than Photo, swipe to choose Photo (the still camera).

3. Make adjustments to the camera settings (discussed shortly), tap on the screen where you want the camera to focus (such as a person's face), and then tap the shutter button, which is the large white circle. You'll hear a camera shutter click as your iPad captures the image.

4. You can capture an image also by pressing the volume up or volume down button.

The iPad's front- and rear-facing cameras allow you to capture photos and video (see Chapter 15 for more about the video features) and share them with family and friends. Newer models offer incredible cameras with such features as

» Autofocus

» Automatic image stabilization to avoid fuzzy moving targets

Timer   Live photos

Switch camera   Shutter

**FIGURE 14-1**

» True Tone Flash (with certain models), a sensor that tells the iPad when a flash is needed

The following are adjustments you can make after you've opened the Camera app:

» You can set the Pano (for panorama) and Square options using the camera type control below the shutter button. These controls let you create square images like those you see on Instagram. With Pano selected, tap to begin to take a picture and pan across the view, and then tap Done to capture the panoramic display.

» If your iPad supports it, tap the flash icon (lightning bolt) when using the rear camera and then select a flash option:

- On, if your lighting is dim enough to require a flash

- Off, if you don't want your iPad to use a flash

- Flash Auto, if you want to let your iPad decide for you

» To use the High Dynamic Range (HDR) feature (if your iPad supports it), tap the HDR button to enable it. (If it's disabled, the button will appear with a line through it.) This feature captures several images, using a range of exposure settings, and combines the best ones into one image, sometimes providing a more finely detailed picture. If you don't see the HDR button, that means HDR is already enabled. For more on HDR, visit `https://support.apple.com/guide/ipad/adjust-hdr-camera-settings-ipadb9253d98/18.0/ipados/18.0`.

The file size of HDR pictures can be very large, meaning they'll take up more of your iPad's memory than standard pictures.

» If you want a time delay before the camera snaps the picture, tap the timer icon, and then tap 3s, 5s, or 10s for a 3-, 5-, or 10-second delay, respectively.

» To take a live photo, tap the live icon (concentric circles). As opposed to freezing a single moment in time, the live photos feature lets you capture 3-second moving images, which can create some truly beautiful photos. Be sure to hold your iPad still for at least 3 seconds so that you don't move too soon and cause part of your live photo to show the movement of your iPad as you get into position for the picture.

» Move the camera around until you find a pleasing image. You can do a couple of things at this point to help you take your photo:

- Tap the area of the screen where you want the camera to autofocus.

Tapping the screen also helps the camera determine the proper exposure settings for your subject. So don't skip this small step when taking pictures.

- Place two fingers apart from each other on the screen and then pinch them together (still pressing down on the screen) to display a digital zoom control (if it isn't displayed already). Drag the circle in the zoom bar on the left to zoom in or out on the image.

  On other models, hold down on the small circle on the left side that displays the current zoom level (such as 1x) to display the zoom arc, and rotate it to zoom in or out.

» Tap the shutter button. You've just taken a picture, and it's stored in the Photos app automatically.

» Tap the switch camera icon above the shutter button to switch between the front camera and rear camera. You can then take selfies (pictures of yourself), so go ahead and tap the shutter button to take another picture.

» To view the last photo taken, tap the thumbnail of the latest image directly beneath the shutter button; the Photos app opens and displays the photo.

» While viewing the image in Photos, tap the share icon (the box with an upward-pointing arrow, located near the upper-right corner of the screen) to display a menu that allows you to AirDrop (explained later in the chapter), email, or instant message the photo, assign it to a contact, use it as iPad wallpaper, tweet it, post it to Facebook, share it via iCloud Photo Sharing or other apps you have installed, or print it (see **Figure 14-2**). You can tap images to select more than one.

» To delete a displayed image, tap the trash icon at the bottom of the screen. Tap Delete Photo in the confirmation dialog that appears.

TIP

You can use the iCloud Photo Sharing feature to automatically sync your photos across various devices. Turn on iCloud Photo Sharing by tapping Settings on the Home screen, tapping Apps in the left sidebar, tapping Photos, and then toggling the iCloud Photos switch on (green).

**FIGURE 14-2**

# View Your Photos

iPadOS 18 introduces big changes to the way you organize and view photos and videos, but have no fear — getting the hang of these changes is easy. The Photos app organizes your pictures into collections and albums. The top portion of the app, called the *carousel*, displays all your photos. Swipe the carousel to view various collections, which can change daily. Tap the Customize & Reorder button at the bottom of the carousel to select what you want to see in both the carousel and in the collections and albums. As you swipe down in Photos, you'll see all your collections and albums, such as People & Pets, Memories, and Trips. Just keep swiping (shout out to Dory) up and down, left to right, and you'll find a treasure trove of all your favorite memories.

To view your photos:

1. Tap the Photos app icon on the Home screen.

2. Swipe down on the Photos carousel to see your library, where you can peruse every picture you've ever taken. To exit the library and return to the default screen, tap X in the lower right.

   Tap the Years, Months, or All button to narrow or expand your options, or tap the search field at the top to look for specific photos by events, places, names, and so on. Tap the options icon (two arrows facing opposite directions) in the lower left to change sorting and filter settings.

3. Swipe down to find collections and albums, as I'm doing in **Figure 14-3.** Then tap > to the right of each collection or album name to view its contents. To return to the previous screen, tap X in the upper right or Back in the upper left, depending on what you're viewing.

   If you don't see the X or Back, just tap your screen and it should pop up.

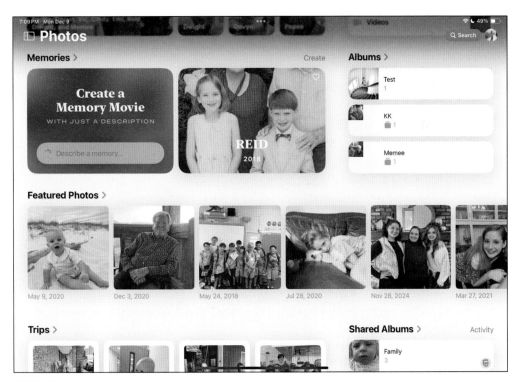

**FIGURE 14-3**

You can view photos individually by opening them from a collection or an album:

1. Tap the Photos app icon on the Home screen.

2. Find the collection or album that contains the photo you'd like to view, and then tap the photo.

   The picture expands, as shown in **Figure 14-4.**

FIGURE 14-4

3. To look at individual photos in the collection or album, flick your finger to the left or right to scroll.

4. To return to the previous screen, tap X in the upper-right corner.

 You can place a photo on a person's information record in Contacts. For more about how to do this, see Chapter 7.

TIP

# Edit Photos

The Photos app isn't Photoshop, but it does provide some tools for editing photos.

1. Tap the Photos app icon to open the app.

2. Using methods previously described in this chapter, locate and display a photo you want to edit.

3. Tap the edit icon (three stacked lines) in the toolbar at the bottom of the screen.

   The Adjust screen appears with various tools. The one shown in **Figure 14-5** is for a photo shot in portrait mode.

**Filters**

**Adjustments**

**Auto-enhance**

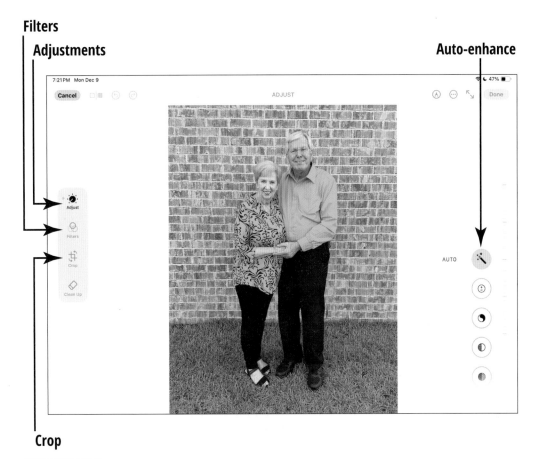

**Crop**

FIGURE 14-5

CHAPTER 14 **Taking and Sharing Photos** 295

4. At this point, you can take several possible actions with these tools:

- *Auto-enhance:* The icon for this feature looks like a magic wand, and it pretty much works like one. Tap the Adjust icon, and then tap the wand to apply automatic adjustments to your photo's exposure, saturation, contrast, and more.

- *Enhancements:* Tap the Adjust icon, and then swipe the items on the right side of the screen to see enhancement options such as Exposure, Brightness, and Saturation. You can use a slew of other tools to tweak contrast, color intensity, shadows, and more.

- *Filters:* Apply any of nine filters (such as Vivid, Mono, or Noir) to change the look of your image. These effects adjust the brightness of your image or apply a black-and-white tone to your color photos. Tap the Filters icon and scroll to view available filters. Tap one and then tap Done to apply the effect to your image.

TIP

If you want to revert to the original image and remove previously applied filters, use the Original filter.

- *Crop:* To crop the photo to a portion of its original area, tap the Crop icon. You can then tap any corner of the image and drag to remove areas of the photo. Tap Crop and then Save to apply your changes.

TIP

Each editing feature has a Cancel icon. If you don't like the changes you've made, tap Cancel to stop making changes before you save the image.

5. If you're pleased with your edits, tap the Done button. A copy of the edited photo is saved.

# Organize Photos

You'll probably want to organize your photos to make it simpler to find what you're looking for. Follow these steps:

1. If you want to create your own album, open the Library as described previously.

2. Tap the Select button in the top-right corner and then tap individual photos to select them.

Small check marks appear on the selected photos, as shown in **Figure 14-6.**

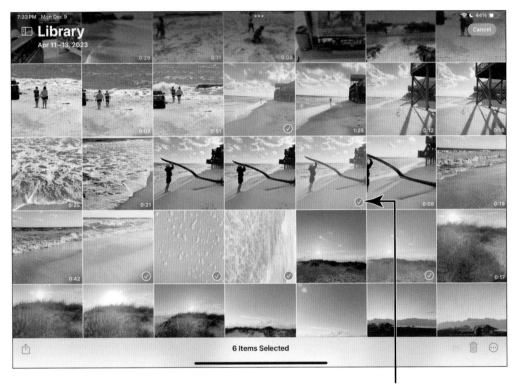

Check marks indicate selected items

FIGURE 14-6

3. Tap the share icon (box with an upward-pointing arrow) at the bottom left, tap Add to Album, and then tap + (new album).

TIP

If you've already created albums, you can choose to add the photo to an existing album at this point. Instead of tapping + to add a new album, tap the album that you want to add the photo to.

4. Enter a name for a new album and then tap Save.

## GOT DUPLICATES?

Pesky photo duplicates can cause you to run out of storage much more quickly than necessary. Thankfully, iPadOS 18 gives you a way to find duplicate photos without having to browse through your entire collection. In the Photos app sidebar, tap Duplicates in the Utilities section; if the sidebar isn't open, just scroll down until you see the Utilities section. You'll see a list of all duplicate photos, each set sporting a Merge button to the right; tap the Merge button to get rid of one copy. You can elect to go through your list individually, or you can knock out all duplicates in one fell swoop by tapping the Select button in the upper right, tapping the Select All button in the upper right, and then tapping the Merge button that appears at the bottom of the screen. Your iPad will thank you for freeing up so much space!

**TIP** Want to share or delete several photos at once? When you've selected photos in Step 2, choose several other share options or tap the trash can icon (delete).

# Share Photos via Mail, Social Media, or Other Apps

You can easily share photos stored on your iPad by sending them as email attachments or as a text message, by posting them to Facebook, by sharing them via iCloud photo sharing or Flickr, or by sending a tweet on X (Twitter).

1. Tap the Photos app icon on the Home screen.

2. Locate and tap the photo you want to share, and then tap the share icon (box with an arrow jumping out of it).

When the share sheet shown in **Figure 14-7** appears, you can tap additional photos to select them.

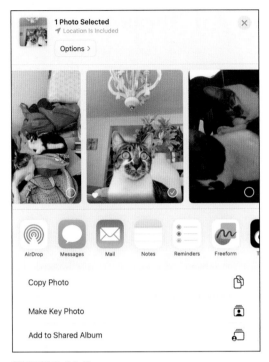

**1 Photo Selected**
◀ Location Is Included

Options >

AirDrop    Messages    Mail    Notes    Reminders    Freeform    T

Copy Photo

Make Key Photo

Add to Shared Album

**FIGURE 14-7**

3. Tap AirDrop, Messages, Mail, Facebook, X (formerly Twitter), Flickr, or any other option you'd like to use.

4. In the message form that appears, make any necessary modifications in the To, Cc/Bcc, and Subject fields and then type a message for email or enter your Facebook posting or X tweet.

5. Tap the Send button or Post button, and the message and photo are sent or posted.

**TIP**

You can also copy and paste a photo into documents, such as those created in the Pages word-processor app. To do this, tap a photo in Photos and then tap the share icon. Tap the Copy command. In the destination app, press and hold down on the screen and tap Paste.

# Share a Photo Using AirDrop

AirDrop provides a way to share content, such as photos, with others who are nearby and who have an AirDrop-enabled device (iPhones, iPads, and more recent Macs that can run OS X 10.10 or later).

Follow the steps in the previous task to locate a photo you want to share. Then:

1. Tap the share icon.

   If an AirDrop-enabled device is in your immediate vicinity (within 30 feet or so), you see the device listed below the selected image.

2. Tap the device name to send your photo to the other device.

**TIP** Other Apple devices (iPhones or iPads) must have AirDrop enabled to use this feature. To enable AirDrop, open Control Center and tap AirDrop. Choose Contacts Only or Everyone to specify the people you can use AirDrop with.

# Share Photos Using iCloud Photo Sharing

iCloud Photo Sharing allows you to automatically share photos using your iCloud account:

1. Open the Photos app.

2. Select a photo or photos you would like to share, and tap the share icon.

3. In the share sheet that opens, tap Add to Shared Album.

4. Enter a comment if you like (see **Figure 14-8**), tap Shared Album and choose the album you want to use, and then tap Post.

   The photos are posted to your shared album.

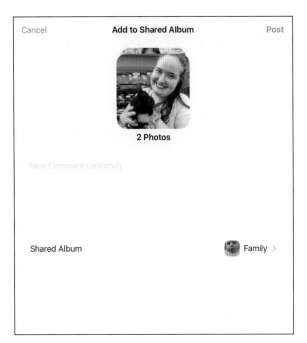

| Cancel | **Add to Shared Album** | Post |

2 Photos

New Comment (optional)

Shared Album                                    Family  >

**FIGURE 14-8**

# Print Photos

If you have a printer that's compatible with Apple's AirPrint technology, you can print photos from your iPad. Do the following:

1. With Photos open, tap the photo you want to print.

2. Tap the share icon. On the share sheet that appears, scroll to near the bottom of the list of options and then tap Print.

3. In the Options dialog that appears (see **Figure 14-9**), tap an available printer in the list, or tap the Printer button to display the list and then select a printer.

4. In the Copies field, tap the plus or minus symbol to set the number of copies to print.

5. On the Paper Size menu, select a paper size.

6. Tap the Print button in the upper right, and your photo is sent to the printer.

FIGURE 14-9

# Delete Photos

You might find that it's time to get rid of some of those old photos of the family reunion or the latest community center project. If the photos weren't transferred from your computer but instead were taken, downloaded, or captured as screenshots on the iPad, you can delete them.

1. Tap the Photos app icon on the Home screen.

2. Locate and tap a photo that you want to delete, and then tap the trash icon. In the confirmation dialog that appears, tap the Delete Photo button to finish the deletion.

If you delete a photo in iCloud Photo Sharing, it's deleted on all devices that you shared it with.

If you'd like to recover a photo you've deleted, open Photos, scroll to the Utilities section, and tap Recently Deleted. Tap the photo you want to retrieve, tap the Recover button, and then tap the Recover Photo button when prompted. Be aware that photos stay in the Recently Deleted album for only 30 days from the date they were originally deleted. After that, they're gone for good. The photos in Recently Deleted display the number of days remaining before they're permanently deleted.

Chapter **15**

# Creating and Watching Videos

ll current and recent iPad models sport front and rear video cameras that you can use to capture your own videos. And you can edit videos in the same way you edit photos — by applying adjustments and filters as well as cropping. You can also download the iMovie app for iPad (a more limited version of the longtime mainstay on Mac computers) and do an editing deep dive by adding titles, music, transitions, and much more.

Using the TV app (formerly known as Videos), you can watch downloaded movies or TV shows, media you've synced from iCloud or your Mac or PC, and even media provided from other content providers, such as cable and streaming video services. The TV app aims to be your one-stop shop for your viewing pleasure.

In this chapter, I explain all about shooting and watching video content from a variety of sources. For practice, you might want to refer to Chapter 11 first to find out how to purchase or download one of many available TV shows or movies from Apple.

# Capture Your Own Videos with the Built-In Cameras

The camera lenses on newer iPads have perks for photographers, including large apertures and highly accurate sensors, which make for better images all around. In addition, auto image stabilization makes up for any shakiness in the hands holding the iPad, and auto-focus has sped up thanks to the super-fast processors being used. Videographers will appreciate the fast frames-per-second capability as well as the slow-motion feature.

To capture a video:

1. Tap the Camera app icon on the Home screen.

   On your iPad, two video cameras are available for capturing video, one in the front and one in the back of the device. (See more about this topic in the next task.)

   The Camera app opens, as shown in **Figure 15-1.**

2. Tap and slide the camera-type options on the lower right of the screen until Video is selected and you see the red record button.

   This is how you switch from the still camera (photo mode) to the video camera (video mode).

3. If you want to switch between the front and back cameras, tap the switch camera icon above the record button (refer to Figure 15-1).

4. Tap the red record button to begin recording the video.

   (The red dot in the middle of this button turns into a red square when the camera is recording.) The duration of your recording is displayed at the top of the screen.

5. Use the Zoom slider to zoom in and out if you need to get closer to or farther away from your subject.

6. When you're finished, tap the record button again.

   Your new video thumbnail is now displayed under the record button.

**Record**

**Switch camera**

**Camera-type options**

FIGURE 15-1

**7.** Tap the video thumbnail to open it and then play, share, or delete it.

In the future, you can find and play the video in your Videos album under Media Types when you open the Photos app.

TIP

Before you start recording, remember where the camera lens is — while holding the iPad and panning, you can easily put your fingers directly over the lens! Also, you can't pause your recording; when you stop, your video is saved, and when you start recording again, you're creating a new video file.

# Edit Videos

The Photos app (where your videos are stored) isn't as full featured as Apple's Final Cut Pro or Adobe's Premier, but it does provide a few handy tools for editing videos.

1. Tap the Photos app icon on the Home screen, locate your video, and tap it to open it.

2. Tap the edit icon (three stacked lines) in the toolbar at the bottom of the screen.

   The Edit screen appears. The one shown in **Figure 15-2** is for a video shot in landscape mode.

**Filters**

**Adjust**

**Intensity slider**

**Auto-enhance**

**Crop**

FIGURE 15-2

3. At this point, you can take several actions with the tools provided. Tap the icon for the following tools to access their sets of options:

- **Crop or rotate:** To crop the video to a portion of its original area, tap the Crop icon. You can then tap any corner or side of the image and drag to remove areas of the video. Tap Done to apply your changes. To rotate or flip the image, tap the Crop icon, and then tap the rotate or flip icon in the upper-left corner (next to Cancel). Tap Done when finished.

- **Filters:** Apply one of nine filters (such as Vivid, Mono, or Noir) to change the look of your video images. These effects adjust the brightness of your video or apply a black-and-white tone to your color videos. Tap the Filters icon and then scroll through the list on the right side to view available filters. Tap one to apply the effect to your video.

- **Enhancements:** Tap the Adjust icon, and then swipe the options to the right of the video to see enhancement options such as Exposure, Brightness, and Saturation. You can use a slew of other tools to tweak contrast, color intensity, shadows, and more.

- **Auto-enhance:** The icon for this feature, which looks like a magic wand, appears when you tap the Adjust icon. Tapping the wand allows your iPad to apply automatic enhancements to your video's exposure, saturation, contrast, and so on.

- **Trim:** Use the trim tool found below the video (if you don't see it, tap the Video icon) to remove parts of your video you no longer want to view.

4. If you're pleased with your edits, tap the Done button.

   A copy of the edited video is saved.

**TIP** Each of the editing features has a Cancel button. If you don't like the changes you made, tap this button (in the upper-left corner) to stop making changes before you save the image. What if you make changes you later regret? Just open the video, tap Edit, and then tap the red Revert button in the upper right to discard changes to the original.

# Play Movies or TV Shows with the TV App

Open the TV app for the first time, and you'll be greeted with a Welcome screen; tap Get Started. You'll be asked to sign in to your television provider, if you haven't done so already.

Signing in allows you to use the TV app to access content in other apps (such as your favorite cable sports or news channels), if such services are supported by your TV provider. This way, you need to use only the TV app — as opposed to using multiple apps — to access content and sign into the services.

TIP

Should you decide to skip signing in to your TV provider and worry about it later (or if you've already opened the TV app and cruised right past this part), you can access the same options by going to Settings ➪ General ➪ TV Provider, tapping the name of your provider, and then entering your account information. If you're not sure of your account information, you'll need to contact your provider for assistance.

The TV app offers a couple of ways to view movies and TV shows: via third-party providers (many require a subscription, such as Hulu, Peacock, and Netflix) or items you've purchased or rented from Apple.

## Content from third-party providers

To access content from providers such as Apple TV+, NBC, ABC, and PBS, open the TV app and tap the Home icon in the sidebar on the left of your screen (see **Figure 15-3**). Swipe to see hit shows and browse by genres such as comedy or action.

Tap a show that interests you, as I did in **Figure 15-4**. Tap an episode to begin playing it, or tap the Details button (you may need to swipe down a bit to find it) to see a description of the episode, as shown in **Figure 15-5**. If you have the app that supports the video, the video will open automatically in the correct app. You may be prompted to connect apps from providers like PBS and ABC to the TV app so you can watch their videos in the TV app. If you want to do so, tap Connect; if not, just tap Not Now. If you don't have the app installed that you need to watch the video, you'll be asked if you'd like to download and install it.

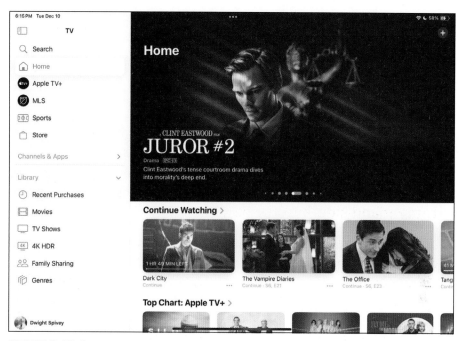

**FIGURE 15-3**

**FIGURE 15-4**

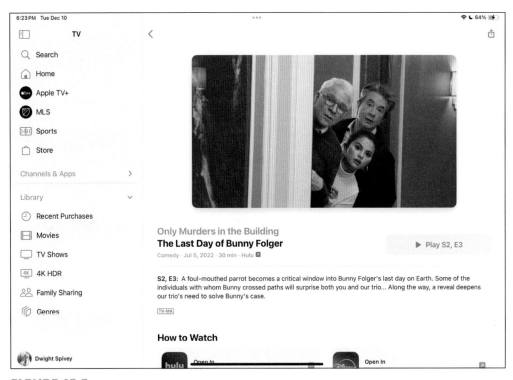

**FIGURE 15-5**

**TIP**

With Home Sharing set up for your iPad and computer, you can stream videos from your computer to your iPad. Check out this Apple Support article for more info regarding Home Sharing and how to set it up for your devices: `https://support.apple.com/en-us/108958`.

## Content from Apple

To access video you've purchased or rented from Apple, follow these steps:

1. Tap the TV app icon on the Home screen to open the application, and then tap Library in the left sidebar to expand it (if it's not already expanded, of course).

2. Tap a selection from the categories listed under Library and a screen similar to the one in **Figure 15-6** appears; tap the video you want to watch.

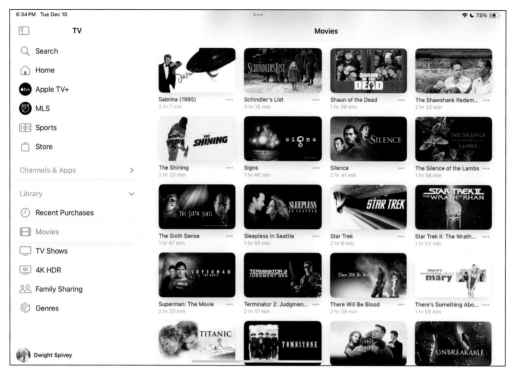

**FIGURE 15-6**

Information about the movie or TV show episodes appears, as shown in **Figure 15-7.**

3. For a TV show, tap the episode that you'd like to play. For a movie, tap the play icon (which appears on the description screen). The movie or TV show begins playing (see **Figure 15-8**).

   If you see a small, cloud-shaped icon instead of a play icon, tap it, and the content will be downloaded from iCloud.

4. With the playback tools displayed (refer to Figure 15-8), take any of these actions:

   • To pause playback, tap the pause icon.

   • To move to a different location in the video playback, drag the video slider or tap one of the buttons labeled 10 to go backward or forward 10 seconds.

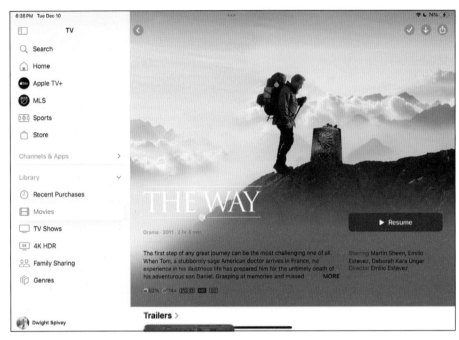

**FIGURE 15-7**

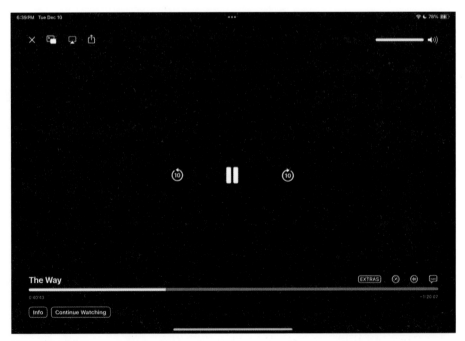

**FIGURE 15-8**

If a video has chapter support, a Scenes button appears for displaying all chapters so you can move more easily from one to another.

- To decrease or increase the volume, tap the end of the lighter section of the volume slider and drag it left or right, respectively.

If your controls disappear during playback, just tap the screen, and they'll reappear.

5. To stop the video and return to the information screen, tap the X in the upper left of the screen.

If you've watched a video and stopped it before the end, it opens by default to the last location you were viewing. To start a video from the beginning, tap the progress bar and drag all the way to the left.

# Turn On Closed-Captioning

The iPad and movies and TV shows sold by Apple offer support for closed-captioning and subtitles. To use this feature, look for the CC logo on media that you download.

Video that you record on your iPad doesn't have this capability.

If a movie has either closed-captioning or subtitles, you can turn on the feature on your iPad.

1. Tap the Settings icon on the Home screen.

2. Tap Accessibility, and then scroll down and tap Subtitles & Captioning in the Hearing section.

3. On the menu that appears, tap the Closed Captions + SDH switch to turn on the feature (the switch toggles to green).

   Now when you play a movie with closed-captioning, you can tap the more icon (three dots) to the right of the playback controls, and then tap Subtitles to manage these features.

# Delete a Video from the iPad

You can buy videos directly from your iPad, or you can sync via iCloud, Finder (a Mac running macOS Catalina or newer), or iTunes (a PC or a Mac running macOS Mojave or earlier) to place content you've bought or created on another device on your iPad.

When you want to get rid of memory-hogging video content on your iPad, do the following:

1. Open the TV app and tap Downloaded in the left sidebar.

2. Tap the more icon (three tiny dots) next to the TV show or movie you want to delete, to display the menu shown in **Figure 15-9.**

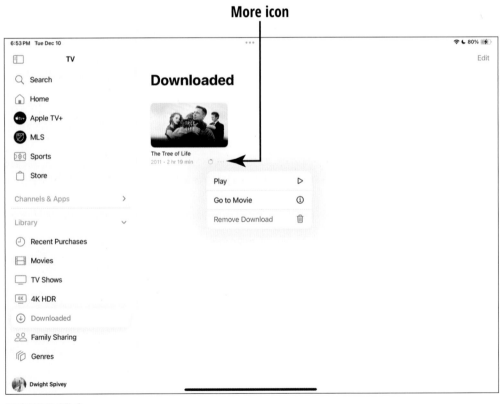

FIGURE 15-9

**3.** Tap Remove Download in the dialog that appears, tap Remove Download again in the confirmation dialog, and the downloaded video is instantly deleted from your iPad.

If you buy a video from Apple using your computer, sync to download it to your iPad, and then delete it from your iPad, it's still saved in your library. You can sync your computer and iPad again to download the video. Remember, however, that when you delete a rented movie, it's gone with the wind. Also, videos — unlike photos and music — don't sync to iCloud.

TIP

If your iPad has only a modest storage capacity, downloading lots of TV shows or movies can fill its storage area quickly. If you don't want to view an item again, delete it to free up space.

# 4

# Living with Your iPad

**IN THIS PART . . .**

Scheduling your life

Managing notifications and creating reminders

Writing notes

Tracking the weather, using the calculator, creating voice memos, measuring distances, managing passwords, and finding devices

Troubleshooting and maintaining your iPad

**IN THIS CHAPTER**

» Add calendar events

» Create a repeating event

» View, search for, and delete events

» Add an alert to an event

» Display clocks

» Set and delete alarms

» Use the Stopwatch and Timers functions

Chapter **16**

# Keeping on Schedule with Calendar and Clock

Whether you're retired or still working, you have a busy life full of activities (perhaps even busier if you're retired, for some unfathomable reason). You need a way to keep on top of all those activities and appointments. The Calendar app on your iPad is a simple, elegant, electronic daybook that helps you do just that.

In addition to being able to enter events and view them in a list or by the day, week, or month, you can set up Calendar to send alerts to remind you of your obligations and search for events by keywords. You can even set up repeating events, such as birthdays, monthly get-togethers with friends, or weekly babysitting appointments with the kids in your life. iPadOS 18 offers the ability to create reminders directly in Calendar, instead of only in the Reminders app (see Chapter 17 for more on Reminders). To help you coordinate calendars on multiple devices, you can also sync events with other calendar accounts. And by taking advantage of the Family Sharing feature, you can create a family calendar that everybody in your family can view and add events to.

Another preinstalled app that can help you stay on schedule is Clock, which enables you to view the time in multiple locations, set alarms, check yourself with a stopwatch feature, and use timers.

In this chapter, you master the simple procedures for getting around your calendar, creating a family calendar, entering and editing events, setting up alerts, syncing, and searching. You also learn the straightforward ins and outs of using Clock.

# View Your Calendar

Calendar offers several ways to view your schedule:

1. Start by tapping the Calendar app icon in the dock or on the Home screen to open the app.

   Depending on what you last had open and the orientation in which you're holding your iPad, you may see today's calendar, list view, the year, the month, the week, an open event, or the Search screen with search results displayed.

2. Tap the Day tab at the top of the screen, and then tap Today in the upper right to display the current date in day view (if it isn't already displayed). Tap the list view icon in the upper left to see all scheduled events for that day.

   The today view with list view, shown in **Figure 16-1,** displays your daily appointments for every day in a list, with times shown to the right of the list pane.

3. Tap an event in the list to get more event details, or tap the list view icon (upper left) to exit list view.

**Calendars**

**Inbox**

**List view**

**Today**

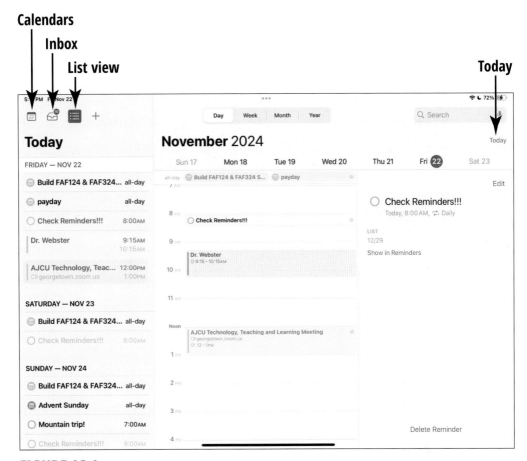

FIGURE 16-1

TIP

If you'd like to display events only from a particular calendar or set of calendars, such as the Birthday or US Holidays calendars, tap the calendars icon in the upper left (refer to Figure 16-1) and select which calendars to view by tapping the circle(s) to the left of the calendar name(s). A check mark in the circle indicates that calendar's items will be displayed. Tap the calendars icon in the upper left again to close the pane.

TIP

Want to know more about a calendar you see listed? Perhaps you've forgotten where it even came from. No fear! Just tap the circled *i* (information) and you'll see a wealth of stuff regarding the calendar in question.

4. Tap the Week tab to view all events for the current week.

   In this view, the left pane shows the appointments and their times, broken up into day sections.

5. Tap the Month tab to get an overview of your busy month (see **Figure 16-2**).

Tap to select a view

**FIGURE 16-2**

In this view, you see the name and timing of each event.

6. Tap the Year tab to see all months in the year so that you can quickly move to one, as shown in **Figure 16-3.**

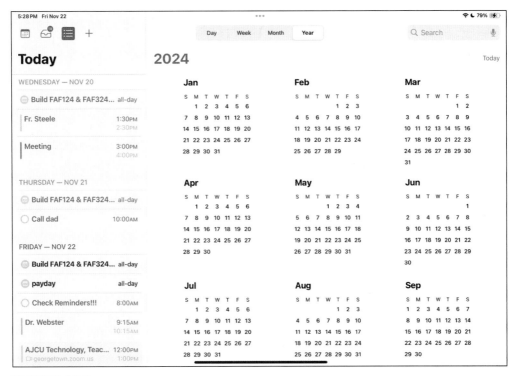

**FIGURE 16-3**

To move from one month or year to the next (depending on which view you're in), you can also scroll up or down the screen with your finger.

7. To jump back to today, tap Today in the upper-right corner of the screen.

Calendar looks slightly different when you hold your iPad in portrait and landscape orientations. Turn your iPad in both directions to see which orientation you prefer to work in, and make sure to try this with each view option. I work in landscape orientation throughout this chapter.

**TIP**

When you accept an invitation, an event is placed on your calendar. Your invitations are displayed on the left of the screen in the Inbox sidebar when you tap the inbox icon in the upper-left corner (refer to Figure 16-1). You can use text within emails (such as a date, flight number, or phone number) to add an event to Calendar. Tap the inbox icon again to close the Inbox sidebar.

# Add Calendar Events and Reminders

Calendars are fun, but adding events and reminders to them makes them *fun*-ctional. (See what I did there?) Note that when you add a reminder in the Calendar app, it's added to the Reminders app as well.

Here's how to add events and reminders to calendars:

1. With any view displayed, tap + (add) in the upper-left corner of the screen to add an event or reminder.

   The New dialog appears.

2. Tap the Event tab or the Reminder tab at the top, depending on which one you'd like to add.

   For this example, I'm adding an event. Steps to add reminders are similar. For more on reminders and how to edit and organize them, visit Chapter 17.

3. Enter a title for the event and, if you want, a location.

4. Set the time for the event:

   - For an all-day event: Tap the All-Day switch to turn it on.

   - To set start and end times for the event: Tap the Starts field. As shown in **Figure 16-4,** dials for setting the day, hour, minutes, and AM/PM appear. Tap the date to select a date to start, and then scroll up or down on the hour, minute, and AM/PM columns to set a time. Repeat for the Ends field.

5. To select which calendar to use for the event, add a note, or change other settings, scroll down in the New dialog and do the following:

   - To select a different calendar, tap the calendars icon and then tap the calendar you'd like to use for this event.

   - To add a related URL or a note, tap in the URL or Notes field and then type your URL or note.

   - To change another setting, tap its button and then tap any options you'd like to adjust.

6. When you're ready, tap Add to save the event.

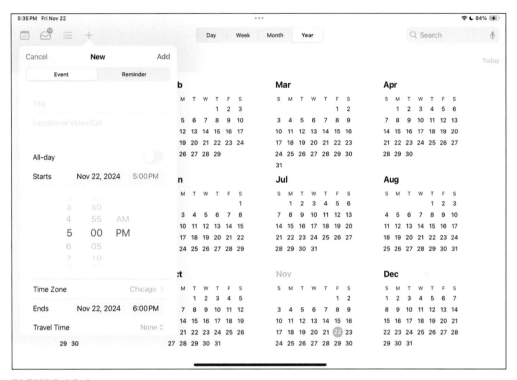

FIGURE 16-4

TIP

You can edit any event or reminder at any time. Simply tap the event or reminder in any calendar view, and when the details are displayed, tap Edit in the upper-right corner. The Edit Event dialog or Reminder Details dialog appears. Make any necessary changes; tap Done to save your changes or tap Cancel to return to the calendar without saving any changes.

# Add Events or Reminders with Siri

Time to play around with Siri and the Calendar app:

1. To engage Siri, press and hold down on the Home button or the top button (depending on your iPad model), or say "Siri" or "Hey Siri."

2. Speak a command, such as "Hey Siri. Create a meeting on October 3rd at 2:30 p.m."

The event is automatically added to Calendar (and Reminders, if you added a reminder instead of an event). You can edit or delete it just as you can other events that you've manually added.

**TIP**

You can use Siri to schedule an event or reminder in several ways:

» Say something like, "Create event." Siri asks you first for a date and then for a time.

» Say something like, "I have a meeting with John on April 1." Siri may respond by saying "I don't find a meeting with John on April 1; shall I create it?" Say "Yes" to have Siri create it.

# Create Repeating Events

If you want an event to repeat, such as a weekly or monthly appointment, you can set a repeating event.

1. With any view displayed, tap + to add an event.

   The New dialog (refer to Figure 16-4) appears.

2. Enter a title and location for the event and set the start and end dates and times, as shown in the previous task, "Add Calendar Events and Reminders."

3. Scroll down the page if necessary, and then tap the Repeat field to display the Repeat menu shown in **Figure 16-5.**

4. Tap a preset time interval — Every Day, Every Week, Every 2 Weeks, Every Month, or Every Year — and you return to the New dialog. Or tap Custom and make the appropriate settings if you want to set any other interval, such as every two months on the 6th of the month.

5. To set an expiration date for the repeated event, tap End Repeat and make the necessary settings.

6. Tap Add (or Done if you're editing an event) and you'll return to the Calendar.

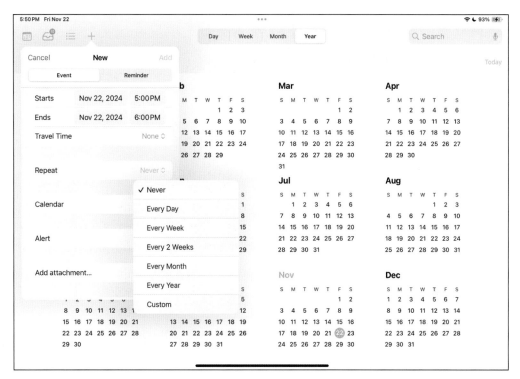

FIGURE 16-5

TIP

Other calendar programs may give you more control over repeating events. If you want a more robust calendar feature, consider setting up your appointments in an application such as the macOS version of Calendar, or Outlook, or Google Calendar and syncing it to your iPad via iCloud.

# View an Event

Tap a Calendar event anywhere — in today, week, month, or list view — to see its details. To make changes to the event you're viewing, tap the Edit button in the upper-right corner.

# Add an Alert to an Event

If you want your iPad to alert you when an event is coming up, you can use the alert feature.

## Select a default Calendar alert

One part of the alert is the sound you hear when you're alerted to an upcoming or occurring event. Follow these steps to select a default sound:

1. Tap the Settings icon on the Home screen and choose Sounds.

2. Scroll down to Calendar Alerts and tap it; then tap an Alert Tone, which causes your iPad to play the tone for you.

3. After you've chosen the alert tone you want, tap Sounds to return to Sounds settings.

## Set up an alert for an event

The other part of an event alert is the text notification you see on your iPad (or other Apple device in which you're signed in to the same iCloud account) when you're alerted of an upcoming or occurring event. Follow these steps to set up this type of alert:

1. Tap the Calendar icon to open the app. Create an event in your calendar or open an existing one for editing, as covered in earlier tasks in this chapter.

2. In the New dialog (refer to Figure 16-4) or Edit Event dialog, tap the Alert field.

   The Alert menu appears, as shown in **Figure 16-6.**

3. Tap any preset interval, and you'll return to the New or Edit Event dialog.

   The Alert setting appears in the dialog, and a Second Alert option appears if you'd like to set one.

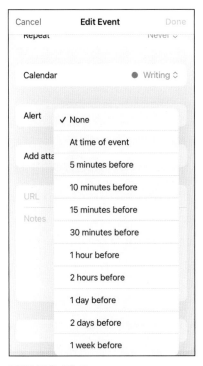

**FIGURE 16-6**

4. Tap Done in the Edit Event dialog or Add in the New dialog to save all settings.

If you work for an organization that uses a Microsoft Exchange account, you can set up your iPad to receive and respond to invitations from colleagues. When someone sends an invitation that you accept, it appears on your calendar. Check with your organization's network administrator (who will jump at the chance to get their hands on your iPad) or the *iPad User Guide* (found at `https://support.apple.com/en-gb/guide/ipad/welcome/ipados`) to set up this feature if it sounds useful to you.

iCloud offers individuals functionality similar to that of Microsoft Exchange.

# Search for an Event

Can't remember what day next week you scheduled that lunch date? You can do a search of your calendars:

**1.** With Calendar open in any view, tap the search field in the top-right corner to display the onscreen keyboard.

**2.** Type a word or words to search by and then tap the blue Search key.

While you type, the Results dialog appears under the search field, as shown in **Figure 16-7**.

Results that appear with a crosshatch pattern are events in the past or invitations to events you haven't yet accepted.

**3.** Tap any result to display the event details.

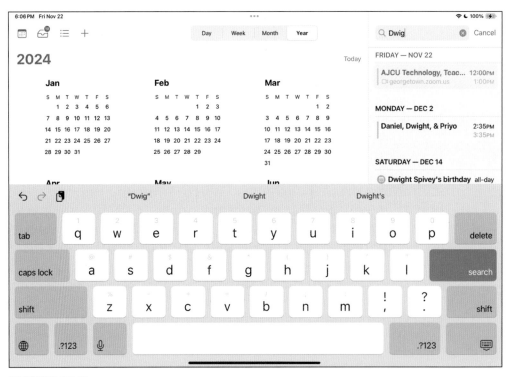

**FIGURE 16-7**

# Add a Calendar Account

If you use a calendar available from an online service, such as Yahoo! or Google, you can read its events on your iPad by adding that calendar to the Calendar app:

1. Tap the Settings icon on the Home screen, and then swipe to the very bottom of the left sidebar and tap Apps.

2. Tap Calendar, and then tap the Calendar Accounts option.

3. Tap Add Account and the Add Account options, shown in **Figure 16-8**, appear.

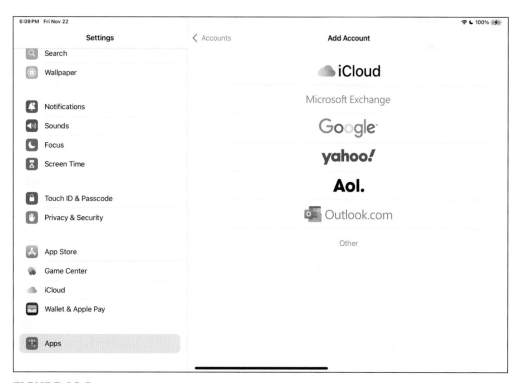

**FIGURE 16-8**

4. Tap a selection, such as Outlook.com, Google, or Yahoo!, depending on the calendar service you'd like to use.

Turn on calendars for other accounts that aren't listed by tapping Other.

5. In the next screen that appears (see **Figure 16-9**), enter your account information for the service.

The screen you see will vary, depending on the service you selected in Step 4. If you don't yet have an account for the service, you'll see onscreen instructions for creating an account. During the last step of the sign-in process, iPad verifies your account information.

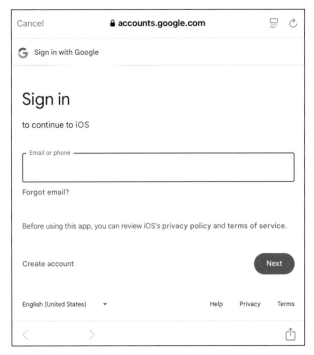

**FIGURE 16-9**

6. On the following screen (see **Figure 16-10**), toggle the switch for the Calendars field on (green).

Your iPad retrieves data from your calendar at the interval you have set to fetch data.

7. Tap Save to save your account settings.

**Toggle to turn calendar syncing on or off**

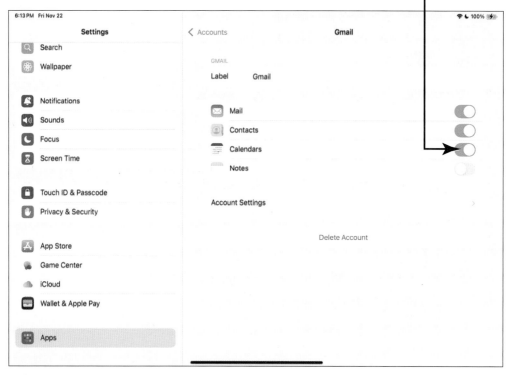

FIGURE 16-10

# Use a Family Calendar

If you set up the Family Sharing feature (see Chapter 11 for how to do this), you create a family calendar that you can use to share family events with up to five other people. After you set up Family Sharing, you have to make sure that the Calendar Sharing feature is on:

1. Tap Settings on the Home screen.

2. Tap the Apple ID (you may need to swipe up to see it on the left) and check that Family Sharing is set up (see **Figure 16-11**).

   You'll see Family if Family Sharing has been set up. If not, go to Chapter 11 for instructions on setting up Family Sharing.

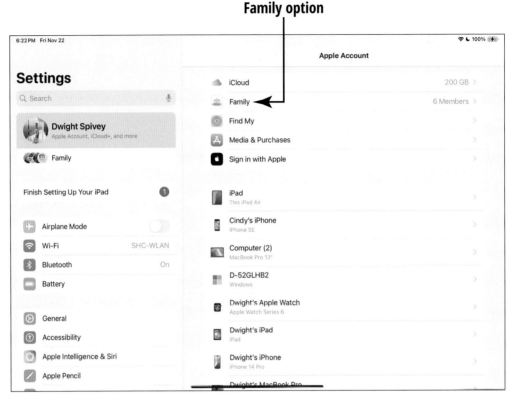

FIGURE 16-11

3. Tap iCloud. In the iCloud settings, tap See All in the Saved to iCloud area, and then tap the switch for Calendar to turn it on if it isn't already.

4. Open the Calendar app, then tap the calendars icon in the upper left of the screen. Scroll down and make sure that Family is selected. Tap the calendars icon again to close the sidebar when finished.

5. Now when you create a new event in the New dialog, tap Calendar and choose Family or one of the other available calendars.

   The details of events contain a notation that an event is from the family calendar.

If you store birthdays for people in the Contacts app, by default the Calendar app displays these when the day comes around so that you won't forget to pass on your congratulations! You can turn off this feature by tapping the calendars icon in the Calendar app and deselecting the Birthdays calendar.

# Delete an Event

When an upcoming luncheon or meeting is canceled, you should delete the appointment:

1. With Calendar open, tap an event.

2. Tap Delete Event at the bottom of the dialog (see **Figure 16-12**), and then tap Delete Event again to confirm (or tap anywhere else on the screen to cancel the deletion).

3. If this is a repeating event, tap to delete only this instance of the event or this and all future instances of the event.

   The event is deleted, and you return to calendar view.

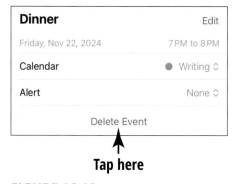

**Tap here**

FIGURE 16-12

If an event is moved but not canceled, you don't have to delete the old one and create a new one. Simply edit the existing event to change the day and time in the Edit Event dialog (tap the event and then tap Edit).

# Display the Clock App

Clock is a preinstalled app that resides on the Home screen along with other preinstalled apps, such as Books and Camera.

1. Tap the Clock app to open it.

2. If the World Clock tab (see **Figure 16-13**) isn't displayed, tap the tab at the top.

   You can add a clock for many (but not all) locations around the world.

**FIGURE 16-13**

3. Tap + (add) in the upper-right corner.

4. Tap a city in the list, or tap a letter on the right side to display locations that begin with that letter (see **Figure 16-14**) and then tap a city.

**FIGURE 16-14**

You can also tap in the search field and begin to type a city name; when the name appears in the results list, tap it.

The new clock appears at the end of the World Clock list.

# Delete a Clock

Maybe you no longer need to know what time it is in San Francisco, which is one of the default clocks on your iPad. You can delete that clock if you want:

**1.** To remove a location, tap Edit in the top-left corner of the World Clock screen.

**2.** Tap the minus symbol next to a location to delete it (see **Figure 16-15**).

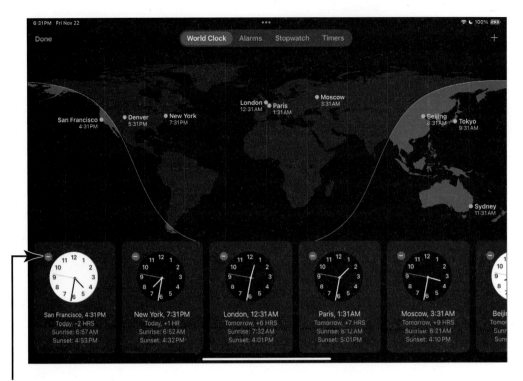

**Delete button**

FIGURE 16-15

# Set an Alarm

It seems like nobody has a bedside alarm clock anymore; every-one uses their smart device instead. Here's how you set an alarm on your iPad:

**1.** With the Clock app displayed, tap the Alarms tab at the top of the screen.

**2.** Tap + in the upper-right corner.

**3.** In the Add Alarm dialog that appears (shown in **Figure 16-16),** take any of the following actions, tapping Back after you make each setting to return to the Add Alarm dialog:

- Tap Repeat if you want the alarm to repeat at a regular interval, such as every Monday or every Sunday.

**FIGURE 16-16**

- Tap Label if you want to name the alarm, such as "Leave to get kids" or "Call Glenn."
- Tap Sound to choose the tune the alarm will play.
- Tap the switch for Snooze if you want to use the snooze feature.

4. Place your finger on any of the three columns at the top of the dialog and scroll to set the time you want the alarm to occur (don't forget to verify AM or PM!); then tap Save.

   The alarm appears in the Alarms tab.

TIP

To delete an alarm, tap the Alarms tab and tap Edit. All alarms appear. Tap the delete icon (the red circle with a minus in it), and the alarm is deleted. Be careful: When you tap the delete icon, the alarm is unretrievable and will need to be re-created from scratch if you mistakenly removed it.

# Use Stopwatch and Timer

Sometimes life seems like a countdown or a ticking clock counting the minutes you've spent on a certain activity. You can use the Timer and Stopwatch tabs of the Clock app to do a countdown to a specific time, such as the moment when your chocolate chip cookies are done baking, or to time an activity, such as reading.

These two features work similarly: Tap the Stopwatch or Timers tab at the top the Clock's screen and then tap the Start button (see **Figure 16-17**). When you set a timer, your iPad uses a sound to notify you when the time's up. When you start a stopwatch, you have to tap the Stop button when the activity is done.

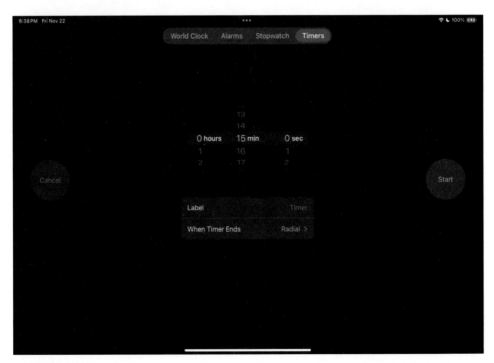

FIGURE 16-17

**TIP**

Stopwatch allows you to log intermediate timings, such as a lap in the pool or the periods of a timed game. With Stopwatch running, just tap the Lap button, and the first interval of time is recorded. Tap Lap again to record a second interval, and so forth.

**IN THIS CHAPTER**

» **Make and edit reminders and lists**

» **Schedule a reminder**

» **Sync reminders and lists**

» **Complete or delete reminders**

» **Set notification types**

» **View notifications and use Notification Center**

» **Set up and turn on a focus**

Chapter **17**

# Working with Reminders and Notifications

The Reminders app and Notification Center warm the hearts of those who need help remembering all the details of their lives.

Reminders is a kind of to-do list that lets you create tasks and set reminders so that you don't forget important commitments. You can even be reminded to do things when you arrive at a location, leave it, or receive a message from someone. For example, you can set a reminder so that when your iPad detects that you've left the location of your golf game, an alert reminds you to pick up your grandchildren, or when you arrive at your cabin, the iPad reminds you to turn on the water . . . you get the idea. Tags for reminders, such as #groceries or #kids, help you organize and find reminders quickly.

iPadOS 18 includes a nifty feature: Your grocery list automatically sorts items into categories, which of course you can modify to your heart's content. iPadOS 18 also allows you to create reminders from the Calendar app; check out Chapter 16 for more info.

Notification Center allows you to review all the things you should be aware of in one place, such as mail messages, text messages, calendar appointments, and alerts.

If you occasionally need to escape all your obligations, or focus on only certain tasks, try the Focus and Notification Summary features. Turn on these features, and you won't be bothered with alerts and notifications until you're ready to be.

In this chapter, you discover how to set up and view tasks in Reminders, as well as how Notification Center can centralize all your alerts in one easy-to-find place.

## Create a Reminder

Creating an event in Reminders is pretty darn simple:

1. Tap Reminders on the Home screen.

2. Tap the New Reminder button with a plus sign to the left of it at the bottom of the screen to add a reminder (see **Figure 17-1**).

   The New Reminder screen appears in the Reminders list, together with the onscreen keyboard.

3. Enter a task name or description using the onscreen keyboard, and then tap Done in the upper-right corner to create the reminder.

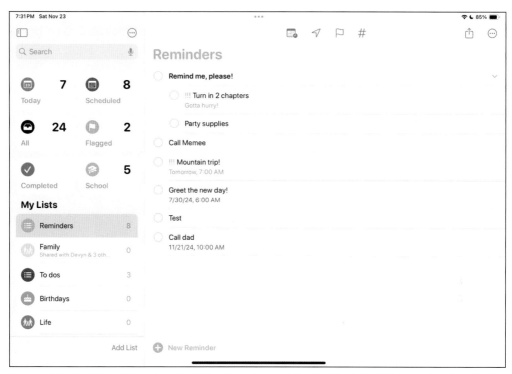

FIGURE 17-1

# Edit Reminder Details

The following task shows you how to add specifics about an event for which you've created a reminder.

1. Tap a reminder and then tap the details icon (an *i* in a circle) that appears to the right of the reminder to open the Details dialog shown in **Figure 17-2.**

   I deal with reminder settings in the following task.

2. To enter notes about the event or to enter a URL for a related website, tap the Notes field or URL field, respectively, and enter any notes about the event using the onscreen keyboard.

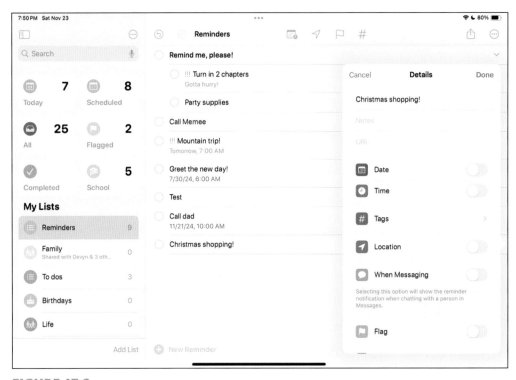

**FIGURE 17-2**

**3.** Toggle the Flag switch to enable or disable a flag for the reminder.

> **TIP** Swipe up or down within the Details dialog if you don't see the Flag switch (or any other options discussed in this section) upon first glance.

Flags help denote the most important events.

**4.** Tap Priority and then tap None, Low (!), Medium (!!), or High (!!!) from the choices that appear.

> **TIP** Priority settings display the associated number of exclamation points associated with an event in a list to remind you of its importance.

**5.** Tap List and then tap which list you want the reminder saved to, such as your calendar, iCloud, Exchange, or a category of reminders that you've created (see **Figure 17-3**).

**6.** Tap Done in the upper right of the Details dialog to save the changes you made to the event.

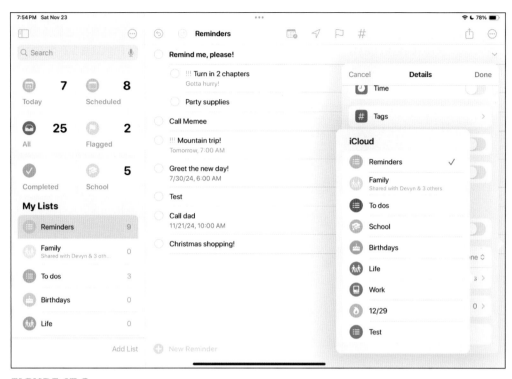

**FIGURE 17-3**

TIP

For some text fields, Reminders now includes a quick toolbar that appears in the upper right of the screen (refer to Figure 17-1), which allows you to quickly add a time, location, tags, a flag, or images to the reminder you've tapped in a list. Just tap the icon for whichever item you want to activate, and make the appropriate settings as prompted.

# Schedule a Reminder by Time, Location, or When Messaging

One of the major purposes of Reminders is to remind you of upcoming tasks. To set options for a reminder, follow these steps:

1. Tap a task and then tap the details icon (a small *i* in a circle) that appears to the right of the task.

2. In the dialog that appears (refer to Figure 17-2), toggle the Date switch on (green). In the calendar that appears (see **Figure 17-4**), select a date for your task.

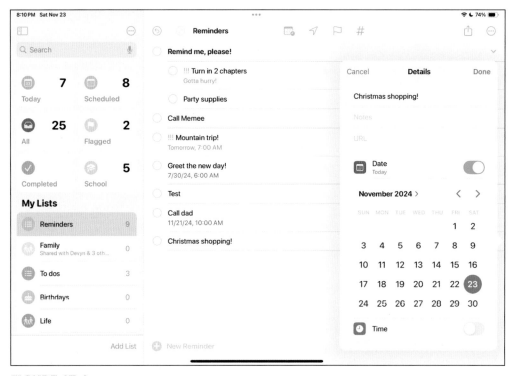

**FIGURE 17-4**

3. Toggle the Time switch on (green) to display the hour and minute dials (see **Figure 17-5**). Use the dials to select a time for the reminder. Select AM or PM as appropriate.

4. If you'd like to be reminded of this task earlier, tap Early Reminder and select an option from the list, or tap Custom to create your own early reminder.

5. If this is something you frequently need to be reminded of, tap Repeat and select an appropriate option.

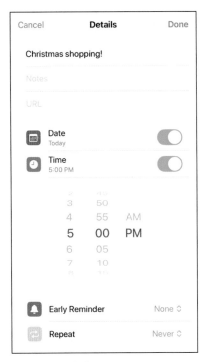

**FIGURE 17-5**

6. Tap the Tags button and add as many tags as you like to your reminder.

   To add a tag, just type the word using the onscreen keyboard and tap Return. There's no need to add a hashtag (#) in front of the word for your tag; Reminders automatically adds it.

7. Toggle the Location switch on (green), and then tap one of the buttons to set a location for your task. Or use the Custom field to enter a location manually.

**TIP**

   If you're not connected to Wi-Fi, you have to be in range of a GPS signal for the location reminder to work properly.

8. Scroll down if necessary and then toggle the When Messaging switch on (green). Then tap Choose Person and select a person or group from your Contacts.

This option will remind you of the item when you're engaged in messaging with the person or group selected. This is a super helpful tool if you, like I, have trouble remembering to share information with people.

9. Add subtasks to this task by tapping the Subtasks option near the bottom of the screen.

10. To attach an image from your photo library, scan a document, or take a photo, tap the Add Image option at the very bottom of the Details dialog. To attach the image, follow the necessary steps based on the option you selected.

11. When you're finished, tap the Done button in the upper-right corner.

# Create a List

The Reminders app starts you off with a single list simply called Reminders, but you can create your own lists of tasks to help you keep different parts of your life organized and even edit the tasks in the list in list view.

1. Tap Reminders on the Home screen to open the app.

2. Tap Add List at the bottom of the screen to display the New List dialog shown in **Figure 17-6.**

3. Tap the List Name text field and enter a name for the list.

4. Tap a color; the list name will appear in that color in list view.

5. Tap an icon to customize the icon for the list.

   This feature helps you to better organize your lists by using icons for birthdays, medications, groceries, and a host of other occasions and subjects (see **Figure 17-7**).

6. Tap Done in the upper-right corner to save the list. Tap the New Reminder button to enter a task.

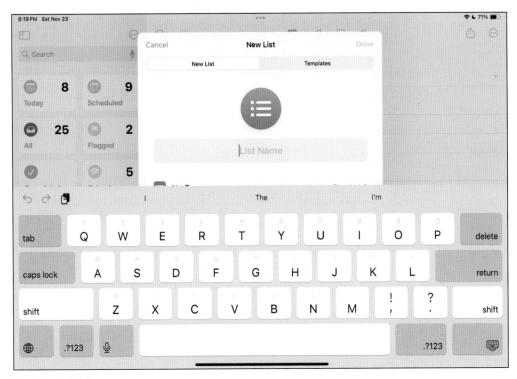

**FIGURE 17-6**

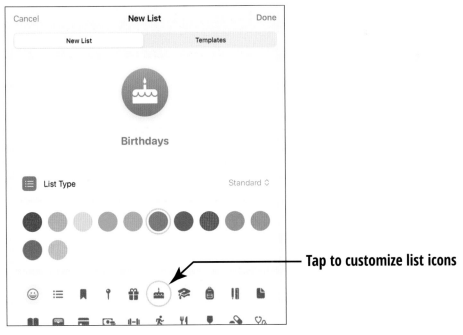

Tap to customize list icons

**FIGURE 17-7**

# Sync with Other Devices and Calendars

To make all these settings work, you need to set up your default calendar and enable reminders in your iCloud account.

**TIP**

Your default Calendar account is also your default Reminders account.

1. To determine which tasks are brought over from other calendars (such as Outlook or Yahoo!), tap Settings on the Home screen.

2. Tap your Apple Account, tap iCloud, and then tap the See All button in the Saved to iCloud section of the iCloud screen. In the next screen, be sure that Reminders is set on (green).

3. In the main Settings list on the left, tap Apps, find and tap Calendar, and then tap Calendar Accounts.

4. Tap the account you want to sync Reminders with and then toggle the Reminders switch on, if available (as shown in **Figure 17-8**).

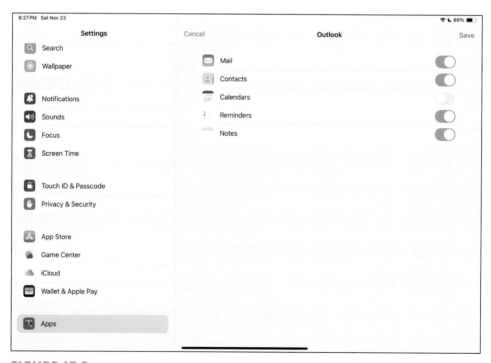

**FIGURE 17-8**

# Mark as Complete or Delete a Reminder

You may want to mark a task as completed or just delete it entirely:

1. With Reminders open and a list of tasks displayed, tap the circle to the left of a task to mark it as complete.

   The completed task disappears from the list in a second or two.

2. To view completed tasks, tap the more icon (blue circle with three dots) in the upper right and then tap Show Completed in the options that appear (see **Figure 17-9**). To hide completed tasks, just tap the more icon and then tap Hide Completed.

**TIP**

   You can also tap the Completed button in the left sidebar to see only completed tasks.

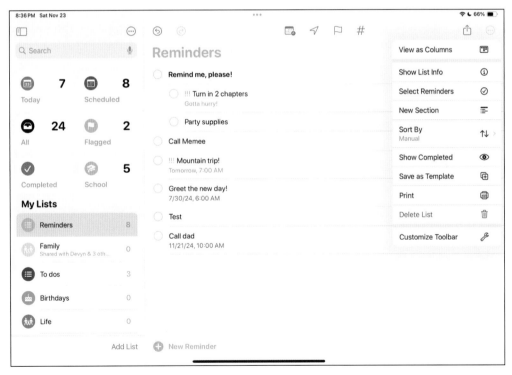

**FIGURE 17-9**

**3.** To delete a single task, make sure the list of tasks is displayed, and then swipe the task you want to delete to the left. Tap the red Delete button to the right of the task (see **Figure 17-10**) and it will disappear from your list.

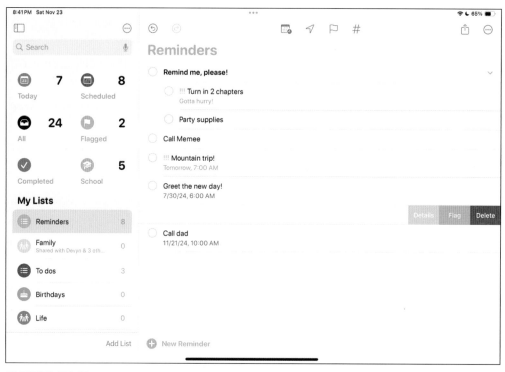

**FIGURE 17-10**

**TIP**

In previous iterations of Reminders, a task was gone for good. Thanks to iPadOS 18, Reminders now has a Recently Deleted option at the bottom of the My Lists section. Deleted tasks reside there for 30 days before being automatically removed forever. You can recover deleted tasks by going to Recently Deleted and tapping a task. If you simply want to remove the item from a list without deleting it, mark it as completed, as instructed in Step 1.

**4.** To delete more than one task, display the list of tasks, tap the more icon in the upper right and tap Select Reminders in the options. In the screen shown in **Figure 17-11,** tap the circle to the left of the tasks you want to select, and then tap the delete icon (trash can) at the bottom of the screen.

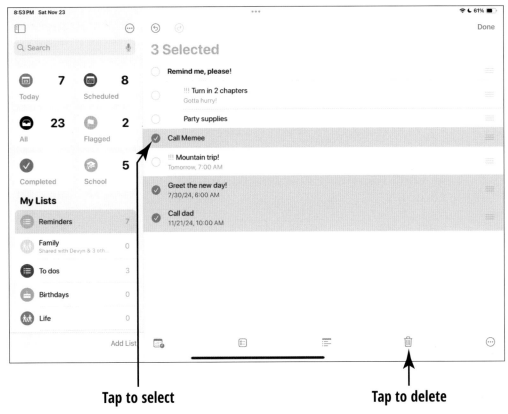

**Tap to select**

**Tap to delete**

FIGURE 17-11

# Get Notified!

Notification Center is a list of various alerts and scheduled events; it even provides information (such as stock quotes) that you can display by swiping down from the top of your iPad screen. Notification Center is on by default, but you don't have to include every type of notification there if you don't want to. For example, you may never want to be notified of incoming messages but always want to have reminders listed here — it's up to you.

Notifications are enabled for every app when they're installed, so once you start using your iPad, you could spend half your day reading or dismissing notifications that you could've waited to see later. To your rescue comes the much-loved Notification Summary feature, which allows you to set up notifications so that you receive them for only some apps as a summary at scheduled times during your day.

Let's jump right in.

## Notification summaries

Since notification summaries are such a cool thing, let's take a look at enabling them and determining which apps are included in the summary.

To enable the Notification Summary feature (if it's not enabled already):

1. Open Settings, tap Notifications, and then tap Scheduled Summary.

2. Toggle the Scheduled Summary switch on (green), as shown in **Figure 17-12.** If this is the first time you're setting this, you'll walk through several prompts to set up this feature.

3. Adjust your schedules, if you like.

   By default, you get two summaries a day: one at 8 AM and another at 6 PM. From the Schedule section of the Scheduled Summary window, you can

   - Tap the + in a green circle (Add Summary) to add another schedule.

   - Tap the minus sign (–) in a red circle (delete), and then tap the red Delete button to delete a schedule.

   - Tap a time to the right of a schedule to adjust when the schedule occurs.

4. To add apps to Notification Summary:

   **(a)** Scroll down to the Apps in Summary section of the Scheduled Summary screen.

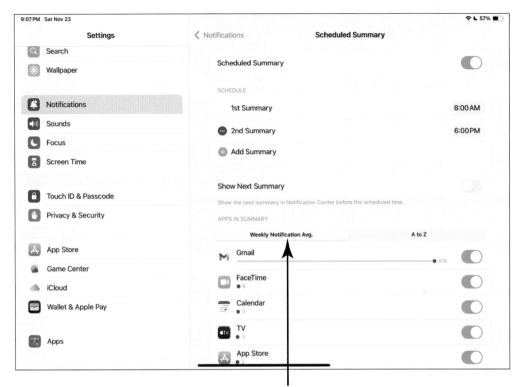

**Weekly Notification Avg. tab**

FIGURE 17-12

**(b)** Tap the Weekly Notification Avg. tab (refer to Figure 17-12) or the A to Z tab to see a list of apps sorted by the average of how many notifications you receive from them or by alphabetical order, respectively.

**(c)** Toggle the switch on (green) for each app that you want to appear in the notification summary.

Note the line with the red dot below each app in the Weekly Notification Avg. tab is simply an indicator of the daily average of notifications that the app generates.

**TIP** You can feel comfortable adding all your apps to Notification Summary, if you like, although that could make the summary lengthy. Time-sensitive messages, such as phone calls and texts, will break through anyway.

# Set notification types

Some Notification Center settings let you control what types of notifications are included:

1. Tap Settings and then tap Notifications.

   The Notification Style section lists the apps included in Notification Center. The app's state is listed directly under its name. For example, *Immediate, Announce* appears below Find My in **Figure 17-13,** indicating the method of notifications enabled for that app.

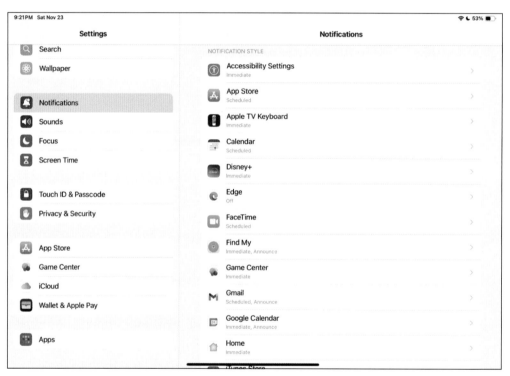

FIGURE 17-13

2. Tap any app to open its settings.

3. Set an app's Allow Notifications switch (see **Figure 17-14**) on (green) or off (white), to include or exclude it, respectively, from Notification Center.

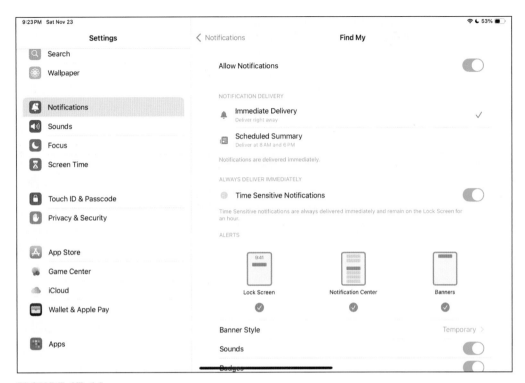

**FIGURE 17-14**

4. In the Notification Delivery section, tap Immediate Delivery (to receive notifications for this app immediately) or Scheduled Summary (to add the app to the notification summary; see the preceding task in this chapter for more info).

5. In the Alerts section, you can choose to display alerts on the lock screen, in Notification Center, as banners, or as a combination of these. If you don't want any alerts, simply don't make a selection.

**TIP**

If you enable banners, choose a style by tapping the Banner Style option. Banners will appear and then disappear automatically if you tap the Temporary style. If you choose Persistent, you have to take an action to dismiss the alert when it appears (such as swiping it up to dismiss it or tapping to view it). Tap the name of the app at the top of the screen to return to the previous screen.

6. Toggle the Sounds and Badges switches on or off to suit your taste.

7. Scroll down and tap Show Previews to determine when or if previews of notifications should be displayed on your iPad's screen.

Options are Always, When Unlocked (previews appear only when your iPad is unlocked), or Never. Tap the name of the app at the top of the screen to go to the previous screen.

8. Select a Notification Grouping option.

This feature enables you to group notifications if you like, which can keep things much cleaner, as opposed to seeing every single notification listed. Options are

- **Automatic:** Notifications are grouped according to their originating app, but they may also be sorted based on various criteria. For example, you may see more than one group for Mail if you receive multiple emails from an individual; those email notifications may merit their own grouping.

- **By App:** Notifications are grouped according to their originating app — period. You'll see only one grouping for the app, not multiple groups based on the varying criteria, as described for the Automatic setting.

- **Off:** All notifications for this app will be listed individually.

Tap the name of the app at the top of the screen to return to the previous screen.

9. Tap Notifications at the top of the screen to return to the main Notifications settings screen. When you've finished making settings, press the Home or top button or swipe up from the bottom of the screen.

## View Notification Center

After you've made settings for what should appear in Notification Center, you'll want to take a look at those alerts and reminders regularly.

1. Swipe down from the top of any screen to display Notification Center (see **Figure 17-15**).

2. To close Notification Center, swipe upward from the bottom of the screen.

**FIGURE 17-15**

To determine what is displayed in Notification Center, see the preceding task.

There are two sections in Notification Center for you to play with: Notification Center and Today.

1. Swipe down from the top of the screen to open Notification Center.

   Notifications are displayed by default.

2. Swipe from left to right on the date/time at the top of Notification Center to access the Today section. Here you can view information in widgets that pertain to today, such as reminders, weather, stock prices, news, calendar items, and other items you've selected to display in Notification Center (see the preceding task).

You can select which widgets appear on the Today screen. From the first Home screen, swipe from left to right to access the Today screen, and then touch and hold on an empty space on the screen until the widgets begin to jiggle. You can remove a widget by tapping the – in the upper-left corner of its icon or resize it by dragging the handle found in the lower-right corner of its icon. To add a widget, tap + upper-left corner of the screen. In the Widgets window, tap an app, select a widget for the app, and then tap the Add Widget button. Tap Done in the upper-right corner to finish customizing your Today screen.

3. Swipe from right to left anywhere in the Today screen to go back to the Notifications section to see all notifications that you set up in the Settings app.

   You'll see only notifications that you haven't responded to, haven't deleted in the Notifications section, or haven't viewed in their originating app.

# Stay Focused and Undisturbed

The Focus feature is really an extension of (and incorporates) the ever-popular Do Not Disturb feature.

Focus keeps you from being disturbed by incoming calls and notifications during various times and tasks. You can customize a list of people or apps that can still contact or notify you, even when a focus is enabled. When you turn on a focus for your iPad, it's automatically turned on for every other Apple device that you're signed into using the same Apple ID.

Do Not Disturb is a simple but useful setting that you can use to stop alerts, phone calls, text messages, and FaceTime calls from appearing or making a sound. You can make settings to allow calls from certain people or several repeat calls from the same person in a short time to come through. (The assumption here is that such repeat calls may signal an emergency or an urgent need to get through to you.)

# Set up a focus

**To set up a focus:**

1.  Go to Settings and tap Focus.

2.  Tap either Do Not Disturb or the particular focus you'd like to edit.

3.  In the Allow Notifications section (see **Figure 17-16**), tap People or Apps to customize who or what app can contact or notify you, even when Do Not Disturb or the particular focus is on.

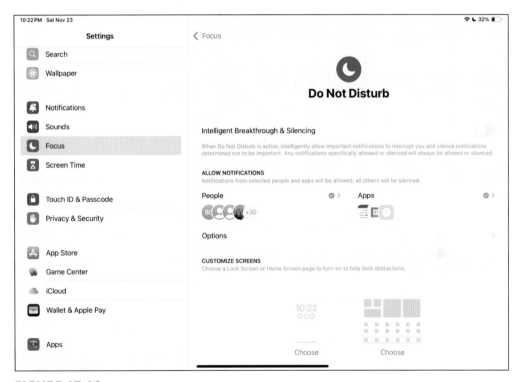

**FIGURE 17-16**

4.  Tap the Add People or Add Apps button.

5.  Tap the names of people or apps for which you want to allow exceptions, and then tap Done in the upper-right corner.

    The Allowed People or Allowed Apps area displays the people or apps for which you've allowed exceptions, as shown in **Figure 17-17.**

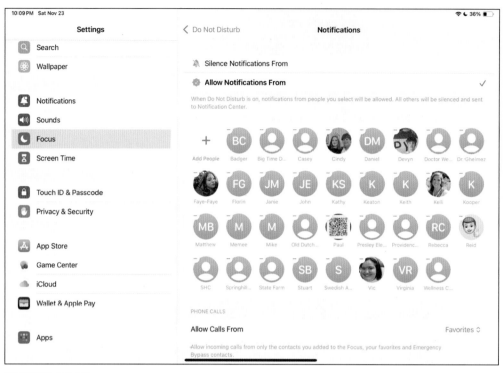

**FIGURE 17-17**

6. Tap the minus sign (–) in the upper-left corner of an icon to remove an individual person or app from the list.

7. To exit, tap the name of the focus in the upper middle of the screen.

If you prefer to turn on the focus at a specific time, use the options in the Set a Schedule section to set a schedule.

## Turn on a focus

To turn on a focus:

1. Open Control Center by swiping down from the upper-right corner of your screen.

2. Tap the text on the focus button.

**3.** Tap a focus in the list to turn it on.

When a focus is on, its button is white, as shown in **Figure 17-18, left**.

**4.** Tap the more icon (three dots) to the right of a focus name to access more options, as shown in **Figure 17-18, right.**

These options may vary, depending on the focus.

**FIGURE 17-18**

**IN THIS CHAPTER**

» **Create notes**

» **Copy and paste**

» **Insert pictures**

» **Add drawings and text styles**

» **Create checklists**

» **Delete notes**

» **Create Quick Notes**

Chapter **18**

# Making Notes

N otes is the app that you can use to do everything from jotting down notes at meetings to keeping to-do lists. It isn't (yet) a robust word processor (such as Apple Pages or Microsoft Word), but for taking notes on the fly, jotting down shopping lists, or writing a few pages of your novel-in-progress while you sip a cup of coffee on your deck, it's becoming an increasingly useful tool with each new iteration.

In this chapter, you see how to enter and edit text in Notes and how to manage those notes by navigating among them, searching for content, and sharing or deleting them. I also help you explore the shortcut menu that allows you to create bulleted checklists, add pictures and drawings to notes, and apply styles to text in a note.

iPadOS also includes Quick Notes, which is a feature that allows you to — you guessed it!— quickly create notes. The unique part is that you can do so from anywhere and any app on your iPad; you don't have to be in the Notes app to make a Quick Note.

Time to get started!

# Open a Blank Note

To open a blank note:

1. To get started with Notes, tap the Notes app icon on the dock or the Home screen.

   If you've never used Notes, it opens with a blank Notes list displayed. (If you have used Notes, it opens to the last note you were working on. If that's the case, you may want to jump to the next task to display a new, blank note.) You see the view shown in **Figure 18-1.**

**New note**

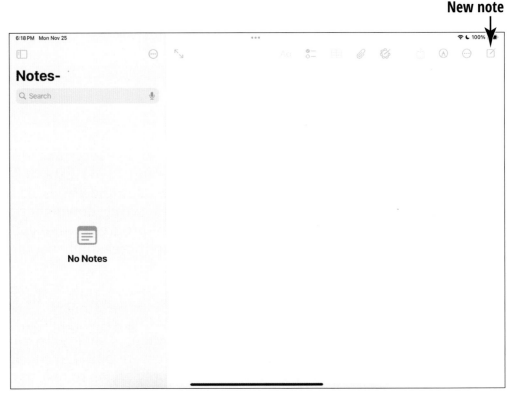

FIGURE 18-1

2. Tap the new note icon (labeled in Figure 18-1) in the upper-right corner of the open note.

A blank note opens and displays the onscreen keyboard, shown in **Figure 18-2.**

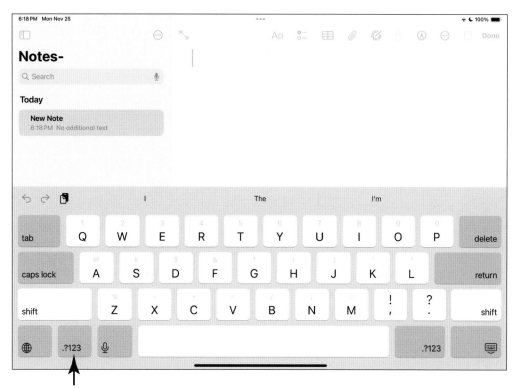

**Tap to open numeric keyboard**

FIGURE 18-2

**TIP**

Notes can be shared among Apple devices via iCloud. In Settings, both devices must have Notes turned on under iCloud. New notes are shared instantaneously if both devices are connected to the internet; this makes it easy to begin a note on one device and move to another device, picking up right where you left off.

3. Tap keys on the keyboard to enter text or, with Siri enabled, tap the dictation key (the microphone) to speak your text.

If you want to enter numbers or symbols, tap the key labeled .?123 on the keyboard (refer to Figure 18-2). The numeric keyboard, shown in **Figure 18-3,** appears. To return to the alphabetic keyboard, tap the key labeled ABC.

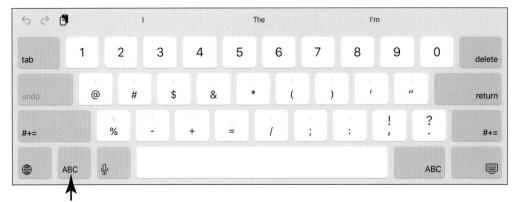

**Tap for alphabetic keyboard**

FIGURE 18-3

TIP

When the numeric keyboard is displayed, you can tap the key labeled #+= to access even more symbols, such as the percentage sign or the euro symbol, or additional bracket styles.

TIP

Allow me to introduce you to a cool keyboard trick: the ability to access alternate characters on a key with a simple pull-down. For example, if you need to type the number 4, simply touch the R key, quickly pull down on it, and then release, as opposed to engaging the numerical keyboard.

4. To capitalize a letter, tap one of the shift keys (refer to Figure 18-2), and then tap the letter. Tap a shift key again to turn the feature off.

TIP

Caps lock should be enabled by default. If it's not, go to Settings ⇨ General ⇨ Keyboard and toggle the Enable Caps Lock switch on (green).

5. When you want to start a new paragraph or a new item in a list, tap the Return key (refer to Figure 18-2).

6. To edit text, tap to the right of the text you want to edit and either use the delete key (refer to Figure 18-2) to delete text to the left of the cursor or enter new text. No need to save a note — it's kept automatically until you delete it.

TIP

You can press a spot on your note and, from the menu that appears, choose Select or Select All. Then you can tap the Format button to apply bold, italic, underline, or strikethrough formatting.

# Use Copy and Paste

The Notes app includes two essential editing tools that you're probably familiar with from using other smart devices and computers: copy and paste.

**1.** With a note displayed, press and hold your finger on a word.

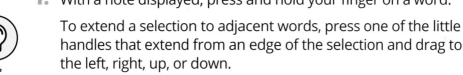

TIP

To extend a selection to adjacent words, press one of the little handles that extend from an edge of the selection and drag to the left, right, up, or down.

**2.** Tap Select or Select All in the options that appear.

**3.** On the next toolbar that appears (see **Figure 18-4**), tap the Copy button.

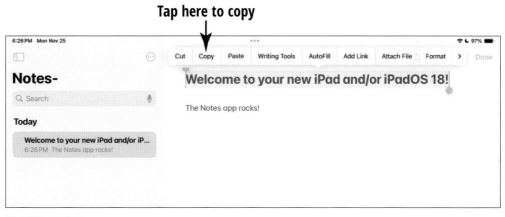

FIGURE 18-4

4. Tap in the document where you want the copied text to go and then press and hold your finger on the screen.

5. On the toolbar that appears (see **Figure 18-5**), tap the Paste button.

   The copied text appears (see **Figure 18-6**).

Tap here to paste

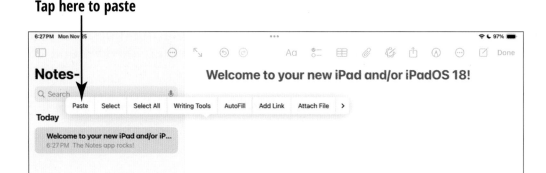

FIGURE 18-5

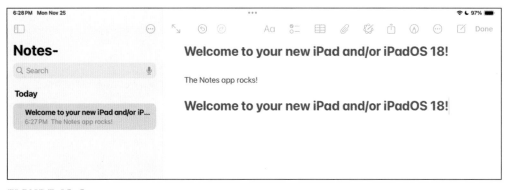

FIGURE 18-6

TIP

If you want to select all text in a note to either delete or copy it, tap the Select All button on the toolbar shown in Figure 18-5. All text is selected, and then you use the Cut or Copy command on the toolbar, shown in Figure 18-4, to cut or copy the selected text. You can also tap the delete key on the keyboard to delete selected text.

# Insert Attachments

iPadOS allows you to add attachments — such as scanned documents, photos, videos, audio recordings, or files — to your notes. I show you how to insert a photo, but the steps are similar for other types of attachments.

To insert a photo into a note:

**1.** Tap the attachment icon (paperclip) in the toolbar at the top of the note. In the menu that appears, tap Choose Photo or Video (see **Figure 18-7**).

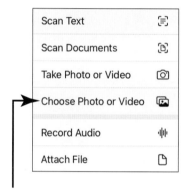

**Tap here**

FIGURE 18-7

**2.** Tap to choose the photos you want to insert, as shown in **Figure 18-8.**

**3.** Tap Add, and the photos are inserted into your note.

**TIP**

If you want to take a photo or video, tap Take Photo or Video in Step 2 and take a new photo or video. Tap Use Photo (lower-right corner) to insert it into your note, or tap Retake (lower-left corner) to start over.

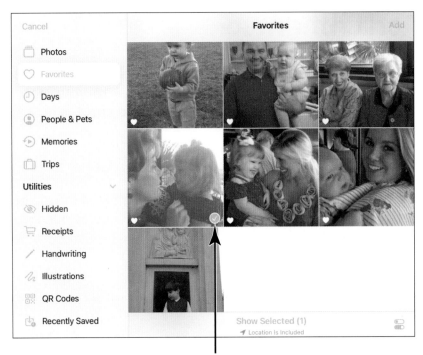

**Selected photo**

FIGURE 18-8

# Add a Drawing or Handwriting

Notes allows you to create drawings and add handwriting in your notes.

1. With a note open, tap the markup icon (a marker) in the toolbar at the top of the screen, and the drawing and writing tools appear.

2. Tap a drawing and writing tool (pen, marker, or pencil).

   The selected tool will be the tallest among the group.

3. Tap a color button in the color palette to display a list of available colors.

4. Tap a color in the list and then draw on the screen using your finger (or with a stylus, such as an Apple Pencil), as shown in **Figure 18-9.**

5. When you've finished drawing or writing, tap the markup icon.

**FIGURE 18-9**

You can delete a drawing or writing from a note by pressing and holding it until the toolbar appears. Tap the Delete button, shown in **Figure 18-10,** to remove the drawing.

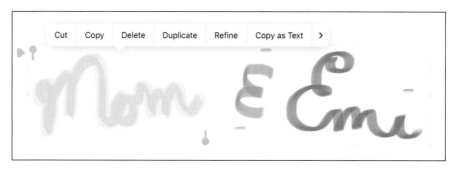

**FIGURE 18-10**

TIP

Tapping the ruler tool (refer to Figure 18-9) places a ruler-shaped item onscreen that you can use to help you draw straight lines. Use two fingers on the screen to rotate the ruler. Tap the ruler tool again to dismiss it when you're finished using it.

TIP

Is your handwriting a mess? If so, let iPadOS help make things a bit more legible. Select your handwriting by pressing and holding it until the toolbar appears, and then tap the Refine button (refer to Figure 18-10); your chicken scratch magically becomes readable to the rest of humanity!

# Apply a Text Style

Text styles, including Title, Heading, Subheading, Body, Monostyled, Bulleted List, Dashed List, and Numbered List, are available on the shortcut toolbar (which is just sitting on the top right of the screen). With a note open, press on the text and choose Select or Select All.

Tap the text style icon (labeled with Aa) in the toolbar at the top of the screen and then tap to choose a style from the options, shown in **Figure 18-11.**

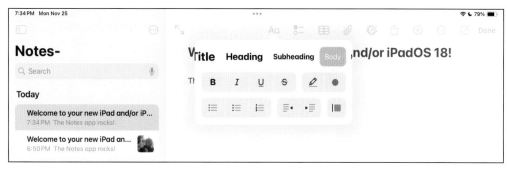

**FIGURE 18-11**

**TIP**

Notes is a great application and is getting better with every iOS iteration, but it's limited when compared to full-blown word-processing apps. So if you've made some notes and want to graduate to building a more robust document in a word processor, you have a couple of options. One way is to download the Pages word-processor app for iPad (it's free) from the App Store (if it's not already installed) and copy your note into it (using the copy-and-paste feature discussed earlier in this chapter). Alternatively, you can send the note to yourself in an email message, sync it to your computer, or use the share icon to send it to your computer via AirDrop. Open the note and copy and paste its text into a full-fledged word processor, and you're good to go.

# Create a Checklist

The checklist formatting feature in Notes allows you to add circular buttons in front of text and then tap those buttons to check off completed items on a checklist.

1. With a note open, tap the checklist icon (two circles with dashes next to them; one circle contains a check mark) in the toolbar at the top of the note.

2. Enter text and tap Return on the keyboard.

   A second checklist bullet appears.

**3.** Continue adding checklist bullets. When you've finished, tap the checklist icon again (or press Return twice) to turn off the feature.

You can apply checklist formatting to existing text by pressing on the text, tapping Select or Select All, and then tapping the checklist icon.

Now that your checklist is completed, simply tap the circle next to completed items in the checklist to place a check in them, marking them complete, as shown in **Figure 18-12.**

**Checklist icon**

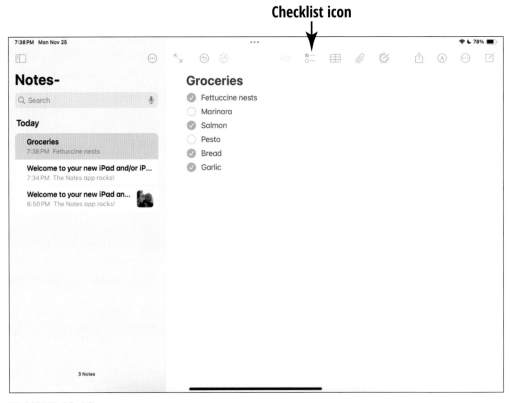

FIGURE 18-12

You can allow Notes to automatically sort checked items in your list by moving them to the bottom of the list. Doing so keeps the remaining items from getting lost in the shuffle. The first time you use the checklist feature, your iPad will ask if you want to automatically sort items. To enable or disable this at some other time, go to Settings ⇨ Apps ⇨ Notes ⇨ Sort Checked Items and tap Automatically or Manually, respectively.

# Delete a Note

There's no sense in letting your Notes list get cluttered, making it harder to find the ones you need. When you're done with a note, it's time to delete it:

1. Tap Notes on the Home screen to open Notes.

2. Tap a note in the Notes list to open the note.

3. Tap the more icon (a circle with three dots) in the upper-right corner of the note, and then tap the Delete button in the drop-down menu that appears (see **Figure 18-13**).

   The note is deleted.

An alternative way to delete a note is to swipe to the left on a note in the Notes list and then tap the delete icon (trash can) that appears. You can also move the note to another folder or share it with someone via Messages or Mail.

Should you like to retrieve a note you've deleted, tap the sidebar icon in the upper-left corner of the screen to see the Folders list, and then tap Recently Deleted. Tap the Edit button above the Recently Deleted list, tap the circle to the left of the note or notes you'd like to recover, tap Move in the lower-left corner, and then select a folder to relocate the selected items. Notes not removed from Recently Deleted will be permanently deleted in 30 days.

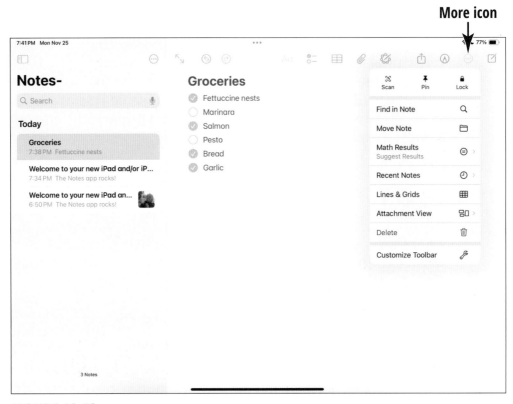

**FIGURE 18-13**

# Speeding Along with Quick Notes

Sometimes a thought strikes and you just have to immediately jot it down before you forget it (which is happening to me more frequently with each passing day). I'm guessing that those kinds of fleeting thoughts were behind Apple's motivation for Quick Notes.

From the Home screen or in most apps, a simple diagonal swipe up from the right corner to the center of the screen with your Apple Pencil opens a Quick Note like the one shown in **Figure 18-14,** where you can type, scribble, or draw until you get that idea down. To accomplish the same thing with your finger, go to Settings ⇨ Multitasking & Gestures and toggle the switch for Swipe Finger from Corner on (green). Then tap the option for Bottom Right Corner and make sure it's set to Quick Note.

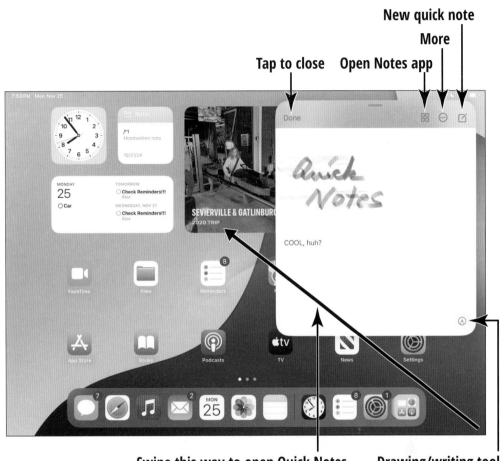

**New quick note**

**More**

**Tap to close**   **Open Notes app**

Swipe this way to open Quick Notes     Drawing/writing tool

FIGURE 18-14

While working within a Quick Note, you can

» Tap the drawing and writing tool icon in the lower right of the window (refer to Figure 18-14) to open the tools to change writing instruments and colors, as well as to access other tools.

» Tap the more icon (a circle containing three dots; refer to Figure 18-14) in the upper-right corner to share or delete your note, or to add a screenshot.

- » Tap the new note icon (refer to Figure 18-14) to open a new note in the Quick Notes window.

- » Swipe right or left in the Quick Notes window to move from note to note.

- » Drag the Quick Notes window to anywhere on the screen where you want to position it.

- » Tap the notes icon (a two-by-two stack of boxes), to open the Quick Notes folder in the Notes app.

- » Tap Done in the upper-left corner of the window to close Quick Notes.

Your Quick Notes are stored in the Quick Notes folder in the Notes app. You can find and organize them all there. You can also move them to other folders in Notes, but doing so will change the Quick Note to a regular note.

**TIP**

You can't lock Quick Notes, so if you want to lock a note you created in that app, just move it to a different folder in the Notes app.

# Smarten Things Up

The Smart Folder feature for Notes provides a quick way to search your notes by filters. Any note that matches a filter in a Smart Folder will be found easily by simply visiting that Smart Folder.

To create a Smart Folder:

1. Open the Notes app, and then open the sidebar by tapping the sidebar icon in the upper-left corner (if the sidebar isn't already open).

2. Tap the add folder icon (folder with +) in the lower-left corner.

3. In the New Folder field, enter a descriptive name for your Smart Folder.

4. Tap the Make Into Smart Folder button.

5. Tap the menu to the right of each option in the Filters window (shown in **Figure 18-15**) to select and customize the option.

6. When finished, tap the Done menu in the upper-right corner of the Filters window, and then tap Done again in the upper-right of the New Smart Folder window.

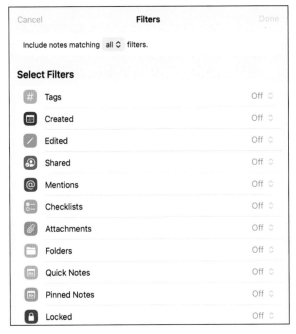

Cancel                     **Filters**                     Done

Include notes matching  all ↕  filters.

**Select Filters**

| # | Tags | Off ↕ |
| 🗓 | Created | Off ↕ |
| ✏️ | Edited | Off ↕ |
| 💬 | Shared | Off ↕ |
| @ | Mentions | Off ↕ |
| ☑ | Checklists | Off ↕ |
| 📎 | Attachments | Off ↕ |
| 📁 | Folders | Off ↕ |
| 📷 | Quick Notes | Off ↕ |
| 📌 | Pinned Notes | Off ↕ |
| 🔒 | Locked | Off ↕ |

**FIGURE 18-15**

IN THIS CHAPTER

» Use the Calculator app

» Record a voice memo

» Measure a distance

» Find a lost Apple device

» Keep tabs on the weather

» Translate words and phrases

» Keep track of passwords
   and codes

Chapter **19**

# Using Utilities

I n this chapter, you find out how to use the Calculator app to keep your numbers in line, make recordings using the Voice Memos app, and take measurements with the Measure app in iPadOS. Also, in case you lose your iPad, I tell you about a feature that helps you find it, mark it as lost, or even disable it if it has fallen into the wrong hands. I also offer a quick introduction to the Weather and Translate apps, as well as the new Passwords app, which helps us keep on top of the myriad passwords and other codes we all collect over time.

## Use the Calculator App

New to iPadOS 18, the Calculator app works like just about every calculator app (or actual calculator, for that matter). Follow these steps:

1. Tap the Calculator app icon to open it.

2. Tap a few numbers (see **Figure 19-1**), and then use any of these functions and additional numbers to perform calculations:

- **+, –, ×, and ÷:** These familiar buttons add, subtract, multiply, and divide, respectively, the number you've entered.

- **+/–:** If the calculator is displaying a negative result, tap this to change it to a positive result, and vice versa.

- **AC:** This is the clear button; tap it to clear all entries. You'll see a backspace button here if you're entering numbers, but it will appear as AC the rest of the time.

- **=:** Tap this to produce the result of the calculation you entered.

**FIGURE 19-1**

**TIP**

If you have a true mathematical bent, you'll be delighted to see that the iPadOS 18 version of Calculator offers an easy way to turn the basic calculator into a scientific calculator (see **Figure 19-2**). Simply tap the calculator type icon (calculator) in the lower left and then tap Scientific to see a ton of new options. Now you can play with calculations involving cosines, square roots, tangents, and other fun stuff. You can also use memory functions to work with stored calculations.

**FIGURE 19-2**

Calculator keeps up with your history of calculations, too. Simply tap the History icon in the upper-left corner to see your previous calculations listed.

Another new feature is the capability to make conversions right in the app; you no longer need a third-party app cluttered with ads to handle such things. Tap the aforementioned calculator type icon in the lower left and then tap the Convert switch to see conversion types at the top of the screen. Convert until you can't convert anymore!

Math Notes is by far the coolest feature of Calculator. Tap the calculator type icon in the lower left and then select Math Notes; you'll see a list of previous notes on the left side of the screen and the contents of the selected note on the right side. Tap the new icon (pencil in a square) in the upper right and either type your math equation using the keyboard or — and this is where the cool stuff comes in — use your Apple Pencil or your finger to draw your equation. For example, in **Figure 19-3,** I drew the equation and an equal sign (=) and Calculator automatically supplied the answer!

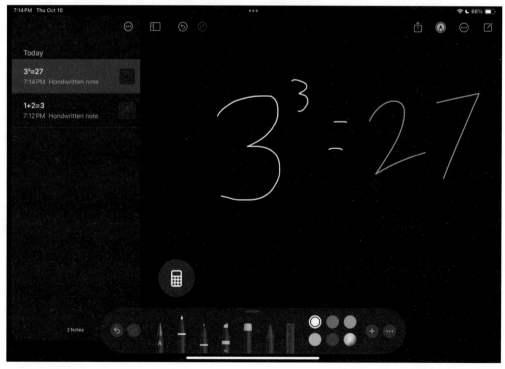

**FIGURE 19-3**

# Record Voice Memos

The Voice Memos app allows you to record memos, edit memos by trimming them, share memos through email or instant message with Messages, synchronize recordings and edits across Apple devices (iPad, iPhone, and Mac), and label recordings so that you find them easily. You can also organize recordings by creating folders in the app, and speed playback.

**TIP**

If you use iCloud with Voice Memos, the memos you record on your iPhone, iPad, Mac, or Apple Watch will sync with all your Apple devices (if they're signed into iCloud with your Apple ID). Bear this in mind should you want to keep your memos private but share your devices with others.

To record a voice memo, follow these steps:

1. Tap the Voice Memos icon (on the second Home screen page, by default) to open the app.

2. In the Voice Memos app (see **Figure 19-4**), tap the red record button in the bottom left of the screen to record a memo.

   This button changes to a red pause button when you're recording, and the screen changes to show you the recording in progress. A red waveform moving from right to left indicates that you're in recording mode (see **Figure 19-5**).

3. While recording, you can

   - Tap the name of the recording (called New Recording by default) to give it a more descriptive name.

   - Tap the red pause button to pause the recording; then tap Resume to continue recording. While paused, you can also tap the play icon to play what you've recorded so far, and then tap Resume to continue recording.

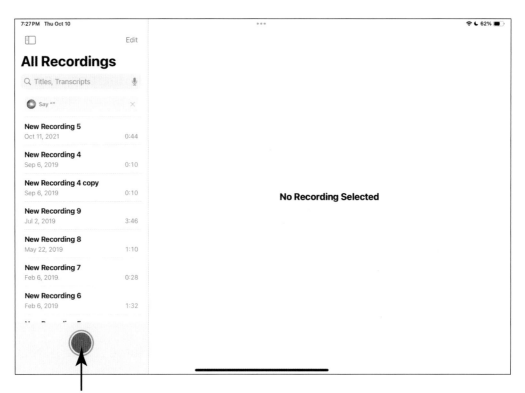

**Tap to record**

FIGURE 19-4

- While paused, drag the waveform to a place in the recording you'd like to record over and then tap the Replace button to begin recording from there.

- Tap Done to stop recording, and the new recording appears in the Voice Memos list.

4. Tap a recording in the All Recordings list (in the left sidebar) to open its controls. From here you can

- Tap the play icon to play back the recording.

- Tap the forward or reverse icons to move forward or backward, respectively, 15 seconds in the recording.

**FIGURE 19-5**

- Tap the trash can icon (at the top of the screen) to delete the recording.

- Tap the name of the recording to rename it.

5. Tap the Options icon in the upper-right corner in the recording playback controls to display the following options (shown in **Figure 19-6**):

- **Playback Speed:** Drag the slider to slow down or speed up playback.

- **Skip Silence:** Toggle this switch on (green) to have playback skip any gaps in the audio.

- **Enhance Recording:** Toggle this switch on to remove background noise from the recording.

Tap the blue Reset in the upper-left corner of the Options pane to return to the default settings, if you like.

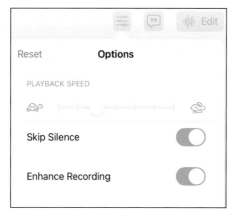

FIGURE 19-6

TIP

Deleted voice memos are kept for 30 days in the Recently Deleted folder in the Voice Memos list. To retrieve a deleted memo, tap the Recently Deleted button, tap the name of the memo you want to retrieve, and then tap Recover.

# Measure Distances

iPadOS uses the latest advancements in augmented reality (AR) and your iPad's camera to offer you a cool new way to ditch your measuring tape: the Measure app! This app allows you to use your iPad to measure distances and objects simply by pointing your iPad at them. This app is fun to play with and surprisingly accurate to boot (although you still may want to hang onto your trusty measuring tape).

TIP

To increase the accuracy of your measurements when using the Measure app, make sure you have plenty of light.

1. Open the Measure app by tapping its icon.

2. When prompted, calibrate the Measure app by panning your iPad so that the camera gets a good look at your surroundings.

**3.** Add the first reference point for your measurement. Do so by aiming the white targeting dot in the center of the screen to the location of your first reference point, as shown in **Figure 19-7.** Tap the add a point icon (white button containing +) to mark the point.

FIGURE 19-7

**4.** Next, mark the second reference point by placing the targeting dot on the location and tapping the add a point icon (+) again.

TIP

Should you make a mistake or simply want to start afresh, tap the Clear button in the upper-right corner to clear your reference points and begin again.

The length of your measurement is displayed as a white line, with the distance in the middle of the line (see **Figure 19-8**).

**Capture**

**Add a point**

FIGURE 19-8

5. You can continue to make measurements by aiming the targeting dot at a previous reference point, tapping the add a point icon, and moving your iPad to the next reference point, where you again tap the add a point icon to make a new measurement (as shown in **Figure 19-9**).

6. When you've finished measuring, tap the white capture icon (just above the add a point icon) to save an image of your measurements to the Camera Roll in the Photos app.

Measure is a handy app and is only going to get more useful as Apple updates it.

FIGURE 19-9

# Find a Missing Apple Device

The Find My app can pinpoint the location of your Apple devices and your Apple-using friends. This app is extremely handy if you forget where you left your iPad or someone absconds with it. Find My not only lets you track down the critter but also lets you wipe out the data contained in it if you have no way to get the iPad (or other Apple device) back.

You must have an Apple Account to use Find My. If you don't have an Apple Account, see Chapter 3 to find out how to set one up.

If you're using Family Sharing, someone in your family can find your device and play a sound. This works even if the volume on the device is turned down. See Chapter 11 for more about Family Sharing. Also, see Apple's support article called "Share your location with your family" at `https://support.apple.com/en-us/105107` for help with this service.

Follow these steps to set up the Find My feature for your iPad:

1. Tap Settings on the Home screen.

2. In Settings, tap your Apple ID at the top of the screen and then tap Find My.

3. In the Find My settings, tap Find My iPad and then tap the switch for Find My iPad to turn the feature on (see **Figure 19-10**).

FIGURE 19-10

TIP

You may also want to turn on the Find My Network option. This feature allows Apple devices to be found using their built-in Bluetooth technology, even when not connected to Wi-Fi or a cellular network. When you mark your device as missing on `www.icloud.com` and another Apple device is near the device, the two devices connect anonymously via Bluetooth and you're notified of its location. It's pretty cool stuff and completely private for all involved parties.

TIP

You may also want to enable the Send Last Location switch, which lets your iPad send its location to Apple just as its battery is running low.

From now on, if your iPad is lost or stolen, you can go to www.icloud.com from your computer, iPhone, or another iPad and enter your Apple ID and password. You can also use the Find My app on an iPad, iPhone, or Mac.

4. In the iCloud Launchpad screen of your computer's browser, locate and click the Find My button to display a map of your device's location and some helpful tools (see **Figure 19-11**).

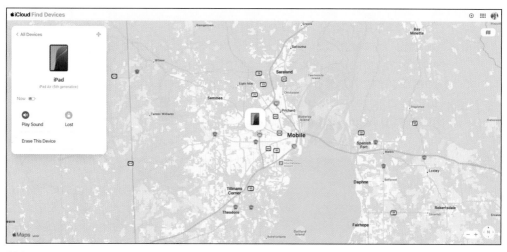

**FIGURE 19-11**

5. In the All Devices list on the left, click your iPad. In the window that appears, choose one of three options:

- *Play Sound:* Plays a ping sound that might help you locate it if you're in its vicinity.

- *Lost:* Locks the iPad so others can't access it. You can send a note to whoever has your iPad with details on how to return it to you.

- *Erase This Device:* Wipes information from the iPad.

TIP

The Erase iPad option deletes all data from your iPad, including contact information and content (such as music and photos). However, even after you've erased your iPad, it can display your phone number on the lock screen along with a message so that any Good Samaritan who finds it can contact you (you'll be prompted to add your phone number, message, or both after you initiate the erasure). If you've created an iTunes or iCloud backup, you can restore your iPad's contents from those sources.

# Get the Latest Weather Updates and Alerts

The Weather app, shown in **Figure 19-12,** is your one-stop shop for all things weather related. You can glean information from a bevy of weather categories, and tapping any of the category boxes will help you dig even further into the topic. For example, tapping the map in the Precipitation box will display a map of your region. Tap the Done button in the upper-left corner to exit the expanded info.

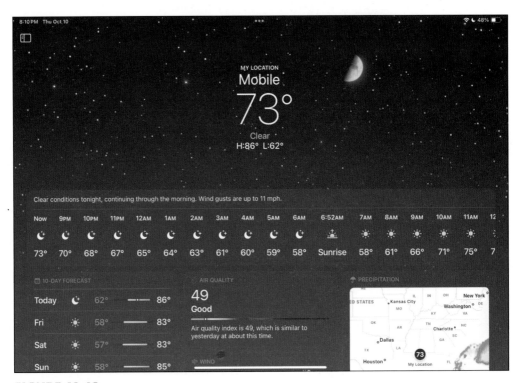

**FIGURE 19-12**

To add locations or make other modifications to the Weather app, tap the sidebar icon in the top-left corner to open the sidebar, and then tap the more icon to see the list of options shown in **Figure 19-13.** Tap Edit List to search for and add locations, or to edit or reorganize your current list of locations. From here you can:

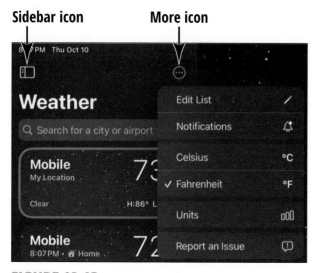

**Sidebar icon**          **More icon**

FIGURE 19-13

» Rearrange the locations in your list by dragging the handles of a location (see **Figure 19-14**) to wherever you want it to reside and then removing your finger from the screen.

» Delete a location from the list by tapping the delete icon (red circle to the left of a location), and then tapping the confirmation icon (red square containing a white trash can) that appears to the right of the location name.

TIP

Weather can let you know when severe weather alerts are issued in your area. You may be prompted by Weather to enable the feature. Or you can enable it manually by opening the Weather sidebar, tapping the more icon, and then tapping Notifications (refer to Figure 19-13). You can also enable these alerts on a location-by-location basis, instead of globally, if you prefer.

Search field      Confirmation button

Delete icon      Handles

FIGURE 19-14

# Translate Words and Phrases

Translate allows you to, well, translate words and phrases from one language into another, supporting 21 languages. Translate even helps you engage in conversations on the fly with its Conversation mode.

**TIP**

Translate currently supports English (U.S. and U.K.), Spanish (Spain), Mandarin Chinese (Simplified and Traditional), Arabic, Portuguese (Brazil), Russian, Korean, Italian, German, French, Turkish, Dutch, Thai, Polish, Vietnamese, Indonesian, Ukrainian, Hindi, and Japanese.

## To start translating:

**1.** Tap the Translate app icon to open the app.

You're presented with a box that's split in two.

**2.** Tap the language button in the left half, and then tap to select the language you want translated.

**3.** Tap the language button in the right half and tap to select the language you want your words or phrases translated to.

**4.** Enter your words or phrases either by tapping the Enter Text area and typing or pasting your text or by tapping the microphone icon and speaking your text.

Translate displays your original text in white or black (depending on whether your phone is using light or dark mode) and the translated text in blue, as shown in **Figure 19-15.**

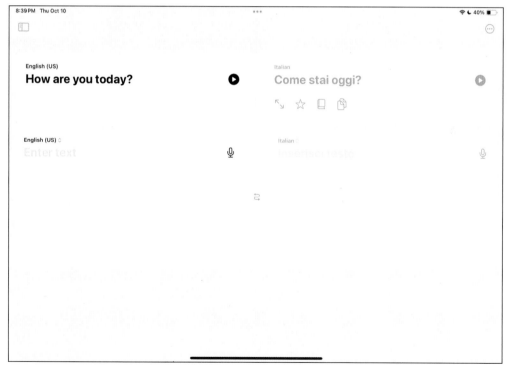

**FIGURE 19-15**

5. To hear the word or phrase spoken, tap the blue play icon next to the translated text.

6. To save the translation to your Favorites, which is helpful if the translation is a common phrase that you'll need to refer to often, tap the star under the translated text.

   To access your Favorites list, just tap All Favorites in the sidebar on the left (you may need to tap the sidebar icon in the upper left to open the sidebar).

7. If you'd like to see a comprehensive definition of a word, complete with usage examples, tap the word in the translation to highlight it, and then tap the dictionary icon below it. After you're read the definition, tap the X in the upper right of the Dictionary sheet to close it.

**TIP**

Tap the Camera icon in the Translate sidebar to allow Translate to translate text from images. This feature is handy when trying to translate road signs, restaurant menus, books, you name it!

Conversation mode allows you to carry on a conversation with someone who speaks a different language, and you both can see the translations in real time. Here's how to make that happen:

1. With the Translate app open, simply tap the Conversation icon in the sidebar on the left. Conversation mode opens, as shown in **Figure 19-16.**

   By default, Translate automatically detects the language being spoken by each participant in the conversation.

2. Take turns tapping the microphone icon and speaking.

   When the speaker stops, the word or phrase is translated so that the other participant can read what the speaker said.

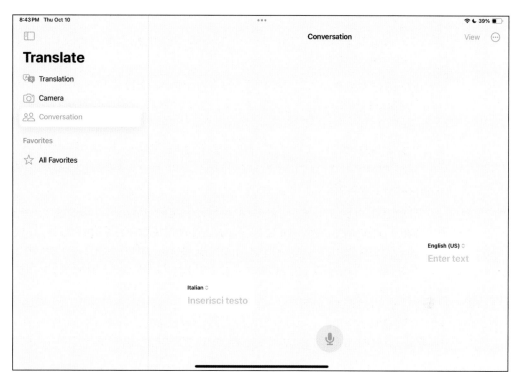

**FIGURE 19-16**

**3.** Tap View in the upper-right corner (see Figure 19-16) to decide whether you and the person you're speaking with would like to translate the conversation side by side (the default shown in Figure 19-16) or face to face (shown in **Figure 19-17**). Tap the X in the upper-left corner to return to a side-by-side conversation.

TIP

If the language isn't properly being detected or if the translation isn't quite right, you can disable the Auto Translate and Detect Language settings for a possibly more accurate translation. Tap the more icon (three dots) and then tap Auto Translate or Detect Language to enable or disable each feature.

FIGURE 19-17

# Manage Passwords and Other Stuff

Keeping up with all the passwords, codes, and other security measures taken by websites, networks, and the like can be quite the task.
Most of us build a formidable list of these passwords and codes, and
managing or remembering them isn't in the cards. iPadOS 18 introduces the Passwords app to help you find your passwords and such
in one secure location. What's more, Passwords is synced across all
of your Apple devices signed in to your Apple Account, as well as the
iCloud for Windows app on PCs.

By default, Passwords is located on the second Home Screen page.
Tap to open it and you'll see that Passwords is organized into categories, as shown in **Figure 19-18.** If you don't see the Passwords list,
just tap the sidebar icon in the upper left to open it.

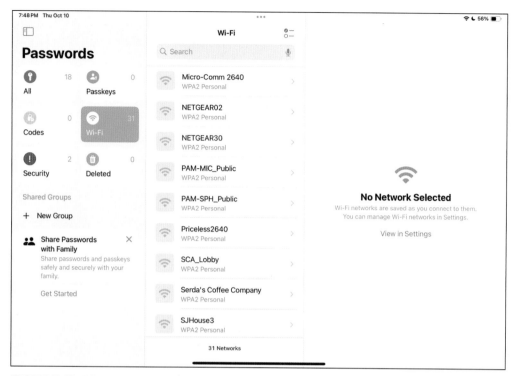

**FIGURE 19-18**

You can search for passwords by using the search field or tap a category to see lists of all the items in it. Passwords and other codes are stored in the Passwords app when you use them for a website, a Wi-Fi network, two-factor authentication, and the like. You can also add passwords manually for sites or apps by tapping the add icon (+) in the lower-right corner.

Passwords allows you to easily share passwords and such with trusted family and friends. You have total control over who you share with and what you share with them, such as a Wi-Fi password or a door lock code. Click the Get Started button in the Share Passwords with Family box to set up password sharing.

IN THIS CHAPTER

» Clean and protect your iPad

» Fix a nonresponsive iPad

» Update the iPadOS software

» Get support

» Back up your iPad

Chapter **20**

# Troubleshooting and Maintaining Your iPad

Pads don't grow on trees — none of them are cheap and some cost a pretty penny. That's why you should learn how to take care of your iPad and troubleshoot many of the problems it might have so that you get the most out of it.

In this chapter, I provide some advice about the care and maintenance of your iPad, tips for solving common problems, and steps for updating your iPad system software (iPadOS) and even resetting the iPad if something goes seriously wrong. Finally, you get information about backing up your iPad settings and content using iCloud.

# Keep the iPad Screen Clean

If you've been playing with your iPad, you know that it can be a fingerprint magnet (even though Apple claims that the iPad has a fingerprint-resistant screen). Here are some tips for cleaning your iPad screen:

» **Use a dry, soft cloth.** You can remove most fingerprints with a dry, soft cloth, such as the one you use to clean your eyeglasses or a lint-free and chemical-free cleaning tissue. Or try products used to clean lenses in labs, such as Kimwipes (which you can get from several major retailers, such as Amazon, Walmart, and office supply stores).

» **Use a slightly dampened soft cloth.** This may sound counter-intuitive to the preceding tip, but to get the surface even cleaner, very (and I stress *very*) slightly dampen the soft cloth. Again, make sure that whatever cloth material you use is free of lint.

TIP

Don't use premoistened lens-cleaning tissues to clean your iPad screen! Most brands of wipes contain alcohol, which can damage the screen's coating. Be sure that whatever cleaner you do use states that it's compatible with your model iPad, because there are differences in screen technology between models.

» **Remove the cables.** Turn off your iPad and unplug any cables from it before cleaning the screen with a moistened cloth, even a very slightly moistened one.

» **Avoid too much moisture.** Avoid getting too much moisture around the edges of the screen, where it can seep into the unit. It isn't so much the glass surface you should worry about, as it is the Home button (if your iPad is equipped with one) and the speaker holes on the top and bottom of the iPad.

» **Don't use your fingers!** That's right, by using a stylus (preferably an Apple Pencil) rather than your finger, you avoid smearing oil from your skin or cheese from your pizza on the screen. Besides the Apple Pencil, a number of top-notch styluses are out there; just search Amazon for *iPad stylus,* and you'll be greeted with a multitude of them, most of which are priced reasonably.

» **Never use household cleaners.** They can degrade the coating that keeps the iPad screen from absorbing oil from your fingers. Plus, you simply don't need to use such cleaners because the screen cleans easily with little or no moisture.

TIP

How about disinfecting your iPad? According to Apple, it's okay to use Clorox Disinfecting Wipes, a 75 percent ethyl alcohol wipe, or a 70 percent isopropyl alcohol wipe to disinfect your iPad. However, be very gentle and be careful not to squeeze liquid into the openings. Always and forever avoid using anything that contains bleach or hydrogen peroxide! And one more thing: For the sake of all that is good in this world, do not ever submerge your iPad in any kind of cleaning agent. Neither you nor your iPad will be happy about the result.

# Protect Your Gadget with a Case

Your screen isn't the only element on the iPad that can be damaged, so consider getting a case for it so that you can carry it around the house or travel with it safely. Besides providing a bit of padding if you drop the device, a case makes the iPad less slippery in your hands, offering a better grip when working with it.

Many types of covers and cases are available, but be sure to get one that will fit your model of iPad because the dimensions and button placements may differ, and some models have slightly different thicknesses. Covers and cases aren't the same thing:

» **Covers tend to be more for decoration than overall protection.** Although they do provide minimal protection, they're generally thin and not well-padded.

» **Cases are more solid and protect most, if not all, of your iPad.** They're usually a bit bulky and provide more padding than covers.

# Extend Your iPad's Battery Life

The much-touted battery life of the iPad is a wonderful feature, but you can do some things to extend it even further. Here are a few tips to consider:

» **Keep tabs on remaining battery life.** You can view the amount of remaining battery life by looking at the battery icon on the far-right end of the status bar, at the top of your screen. You can get a more accurate idea by displaying the battery percentage in the icon; go to Settings ⇨ Battery ⇨ Battery Percentage and toggle the switch on.

» **Keep iPadOS up to date.** You can find out how in "Update the iPadOS Software," later in this chapter.

» **Use standard accessories to charge your iPad most effectively.** When connected to a recent-model Mac or Windows computer for charging, the iPad can slowly charge. However, the most effective way to charge your iPad is to plug it into a wall outlet using the Lightning-to-USB-C or USB-C cable and the USB power adapter that come with your iPad.

A third-party charging cable (the cable, not the block) usually works just fine, but some are less reliable than others. If you use a third-party cable and notice that your iPad is taking longer than usual to charge, try another cable. I also recommend steering clear of the super-inexpensive cables you may come across; they're that cheap for a reason and could potentially cause harm to your iPad.

» **The fastest way to charge your iPad is to turn it off while charging it.** If turning your iPad completely off doesn't sound like the best idea for you, you can disable Wi-Fi or Bluetooth to facilitate a faster recharge.

Activate airplane mode to turn both Wi-Fi and Bluetooth off at the same time.

» **Dim the screen, or use auto-brightness, which automatically adjusts the brightness of your screen according to external lighting conditions.** Auto-brightness can be enabled or disabled by toggling its switch on (green) or off (gray) at Settings ⇨ Accessibility ⇨ Display & Text Size ⇨ Auto-Brightness.

» **The battery icon on the status bar indicates when the charging is complete.**

Be careful not to use your iPad in ambient temperatures higher than 95° Fahrenheit (35° Celsius) because doing so may damage your battery. Damage of this kind may also not be covered under warranty. Charging in high temperatures may damage the battery even more. Although you can safely use your iPad within a wide range of temperatures, the optimal temps are between 62–72° Fahrenheit (16–22° Celsius).

If you notice that your battery won't charge more than 80 percent, it could be getting too warm. Unplug the iPad from the charger and try again after it has cooled down a bit. If getting too warm becomes a recurring issue, be sure that you're using a genuine Apple charger block and cable.

Your iPad battery is sealed in the unit, so you can't replace it yourself the way you can with some devices. If the battery is out of warranty, you have to fork over $99 or more (depending on your iPad model) to have Apple install a new one. See the "Get Support" section, later in this chapter, to find out where to get a replacement battery.

## CHECK YOUR BATTERY'S STATISTICS AND HEALTH

iPadOS 18 has a great way to keep track of your iPad's battery health and how it's being used. Go to Settings ⇨ Battery to view stats about your battery over the last 24 hours and last 10 days. You can also enable low power mode, which temporarily disables some non-essential activities that may zap your battery's charge until you can give it some more juice.

Apple offers AppleCare+. Starting at $149 for iPad Pro models and $69 for all other iPad models, you get an extra year of coverage (on top of the original one-year warranty that comes with your iPad, extending coverage to two years from the date of purchase), which even covers you if you drop or spill liquids on your iPad. You can purchase AppleCare+ when you buy your iPad or within 60 days of the date of purchase. Visit `www.apple.com/support/products/ipad` for more details.

# What to Do with a Nonresponsive iPad

If your iPad goes dead on you, it's most likely a power issue, so the first thing to do is to plug the Lightning-to-USB, Lightning-to-USB-C, or USB-C cable (depending on your iPad model) into the USB or USB-C power adapter, plug the power adapter into a wall outlet, plug the other end of the cable into your iPad, and charge the battery.

You can always use the tried-and-true reboot procedure: For iPads without a Home button, press the top button and either volume button until the power off slider appears. Drag the slider to the right to turn off your iPad. After a few moments, press the top button to boot up the little guy again. On iPads with a Home button, press the top button until the power off slider appears.

If the situation seems drastic and none of these ideas works, try to force restart your iPad. For iPads without a Home button, press the volume up button once, press the volume down button once, and then press and hold down the top button until the Apple logo appears. For iPads with a Home button, press and hold down the top button and the Home button at the same time for at least ten seconds until the Apple logo appears onscreen.

**TIP**

If your iPad has this problem often, try closing some active apps that may be running in the background and using too much memory. For iPads without a Home button, swipe up from the bottom of the screen and pause momentarily until the active apps appear. Then swipe an app upward to close it. To do this on iPads with a Home button, press the Home button twice, and then from the screen showing active apps, tap and drag an app upward to close it. Also check to see that you haven't loaded your iPad with too much content, such as videos, which could be slowing its performance.

# Update the iPadOS Software

Apple occasionally updates the iPad system software, known as iPadOS, to fix problems or offer enhanced features. You should check for an updated version every month or so. You can check by connecting your iPad to a recognized computer (that is, a computer you've used before to sign into your Apple account), but it's even easier to just update from iPad Settings, though it can be a tad slower:

1. Tap Settings from the Home screen.

2. Tap General and then tap Software Update (see **Figure 20-1**).

   A message tells you whether your software is up to date.

3. If your software isn't up to date, follow the prompts to update to the latest iPadOS version.

**TIP**

If you're having problems with your iPad, you can use the Reset feature to try to restore the natural balance. To do so, go to Settings ➪ General ➪ Transfer or Reset iPad ➪ Reset, and then tap the function you want to reset when prompted.

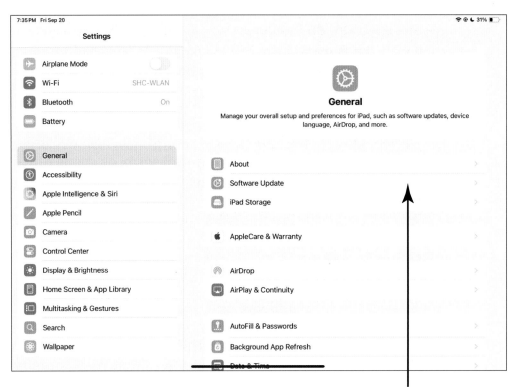

Tap here to check for iPadOS updates

**FIGURE 20-1**

# Restore the Sound

My wife frequently has trouble with the sound on her iPad, so we've learned quite a bit about troubleshooting sound issues, enabling us to pass our knowledge on to you. Make sure that

>> **You haven't touched the volume control buttons on the side of your iPad:** Be sure not to touch the volume down button and inadvertently lower the sound to a point where you can't hear it. Note that pushing the volume buttons will have no effect if the iPad is sleeping.

- » **The speaker isn't covered up:** No, really — it may be covered in a way that muffles the sound (perhaps by a case or stand).

- » **A headset isn't plugged in:** Sound doesn't play over the speaker and the headset at the same time.

- » **The Reduce Loud Audio option is set on:** You can set the decibel level limit for headphones to control how loudly audio can play through them. Tap Settings on the Home screen and, on the screen that displays, tap Sounds, tap Headphone Safety, and then toggle the Reduce Loud Audio switch on (green). Use the slider that appears (shown in **Figure 20-2**) to set the decibel level limit.

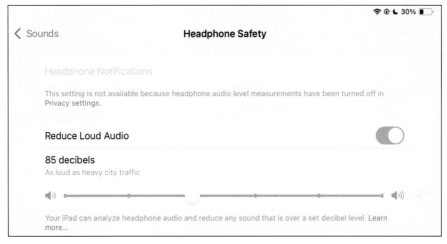

**FIGURE 20-2**

When all else fails, reboot.

TIP

# Get Support

Every new iPad comes with a year's coverage for repair of the hardware and 90 days of free technical support. Apple is known for its high level of customer support, so if you're stuck, I definitely recommend that you give them a try. Here are a few options for getting help that you can explore:

» **Apple Store:** Go to your local Apple Store (if one's nearby) to see what the folks there might know about your problem. Call first and make an appointment with the Genius Bar to be sure you get prompt service. To find your local Apple Store, visit www.apple.com/retail and enter your ZIP code.

» **Apple support website:** It's at https://support.apple.com/ipad. You can find online manuals, discussion forums, and downloads, and you can use the Apple Expert feature to contact a live support person by phone.

» **iPad User Guide:** You can download the free manual that is available through Apple Books from the Apple Book Store. Be sure to download the one for iPadOS! See Chapter 12 for more about Apple Books.

» **Apple battery replacement service:** If you need repair or service for your battery, visit www.apple.com/batteries/service-and-recycling and scroll down to the iPad Owners section. Note that your warranty provides free battery replacement if the battery is defective during the warranty period. If you purchase the AppleCare+ service agreement, the period is extended to two years.

TIP

Apple recommends that you have your iPad battery replaced only by an Apple authorized service provider. Please don't take this warning lightly; you don't want to trust the inner workings of your iPad to just anyone who says they can work on it.

## Back Up to iCloud

Since Apple's introduction of iCloud, you can back up your iPad via a Wi-Fi network to your iCloud storage. You get 5GB of storage for free. You can pay for increased storage: a total of 50GB for $0.99 per month, 200GB for $2.99 per month, 2TB for $9.99 per month, 6TB for $29.99 per month, or 12TB for $59.99 per month. The 6TB and

12TB options are overkill for the vast majority of us, unless you have a multitude of folks on your iCloud plan and everyone uploads lots of massive video files.

**TIP**

You must have an iCloud account to back up to iCloud. If you don't have an iCloud account, see Chapter 3 to find out how to get one.

To perform a backup to iCloud:

1. Tap Settings from the Home screen and then tap your Apple ID at the top of the screen to view your Apple Account.

2. Tap iCloud and then tap iCloud Backup (see **Figure 20-3**).

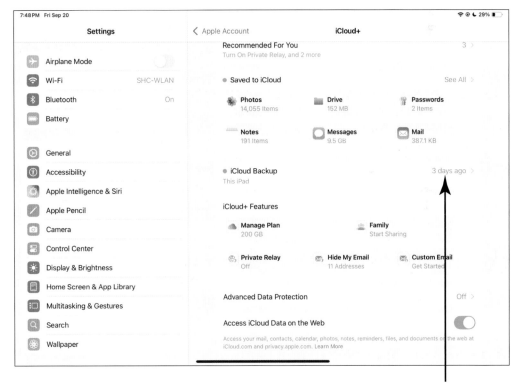

**FIGURE 20-3**

**Tap here**

3. In the pane that appears (see **Figure 20-4**), tap the Back Up This iPad switch to enable automatic backups. Or to perform a manual backup, tap Back Up Now.

A progress bar shows how your backup is moving along.

Toggle this switch

FIGURE 20-4

TIP

If you've been backing up your iPad to iCloud, you can get your content back if you erased it all (perhaps if the iPad was lost). Just enter your Apple ID and password, and you can reactivate it.

TIP

You can back up your iPad also by using Finder (for Macs running macOS 10.15 or newer) or iTunes (for all PCs or for Macs running macOS 10.14 or older). This method saves more types of content than an iCloud backup, and if you have encryption turned on in iTunes, it can save your passwords as well. However, you must connect to a computer to perform the backup. If you do back up and get a new iPad at some point in the future, you can easily restore all your data from your computer to the new iPad.

## APPLE ACCOUNT AND PASSWORD SUPPORT

In today's technology-driven society, it seems like you need a username and password to wake up in the morning! Remembering usernames and passwords can be a daunting task, and your Apple Account and password are no exceptions. Thankfully, Apple is at the ready with your solution. Whether you've forgotten your Apple Account, can't remember your password, your Apple Account is locked, or you've encountered some other issue, Apple has your answer at `https://support.apple.com/apple-account`. If you can't find what you're looking for by using any of the links on the site, scroll down to the bottom and click or tap the Start Now link under the Get Support section to connect with Apple's stellar support team.

# Index

## A

accessibility
  additional physical and motor settings, 106
  AssistiveTouch, 103–105
  Books app options, 261–263
  customizing on per-app basis, 114–116
  Eye Tracking, 111–113
  Guided Access, 106–108
  hearing aids, using iPad with, 98–99
  Live Speech and Personal Voice, 102–103
  Magnifier, 84–86
  Night Shift, 87–88
  screen brightness, setting, 86–88
  subtitles and captioning, 100–101
  Vision features, 95–98
  Vocal Shortcuts, 113–114
  Voice Control, 109–111
  VoiceOver
    setting up, 90–93
    using, 93–95
  volume settings, 99–100
  wallpaper, changing, 88–90
Accessibility Shortcut setting, 93
accessories for iPads, 18
accounts
  Apple, 68–70, 419
  email, adding, 214–216
  email, manually setting up, 216–218
  Facebook, 166, 187–188
  iMessage, 172–174
  Instagram, 166, 189–190
  X app, 166, 188–189
AirDrop, sharing photos with, 300
AirPlay, streaming music via, 279
AirPods, 277–278
AirPrint technology, 300
alarms, setting, 340–341
albums, creating, 296–297
alerts for events, 330–331
Amazon Kindle e-reader app, 253–254
app library, browsing, 36–40
App Store
  downloading Kindle app from, 253–254
  getting apps from, 138–139
  installing social media apps, 186–187
  overview, 62
  purchasing and downloading games, 147–149
  searching, 136–137
  updating apps, 145–147
App Switcher, 47
Apple account, 68–70, 419
Apple Arcade, 146–147
Apple battery replacement service, 416
Apple Digital AV Adapter, 18
Apple Intelligence, 10, 118
Apple Music Sing, 275
Apple One, 147
Apple Pay, 245–246
Apple Pencil, 9, 18, 376, 408
Apple Store, 416

Apple support website, 416

Apple TV app

Family Sharing, 246–247

overview, 239

renting or buying movies and TV shows, 243–245

Apple Wallet, 245–246

AppleCare+, 412

apps

accessibility settings for, 114–116

deleting, 143–144

getting from App Store, 138–139

organizing in folders, 142–143

organizing on Home screen pages, 139–141

preinstalled, 11, 60–63

purchasing and downloading games, 147–149

removing from Home screen, 38

searching App Store, 136–137

switching between, 47–48

updating, 145–147

Arcade, Apple, 146–147

Archive folder, 232–233

artificial intelligence, 10

asking Siri for facts, 130

AssistiveTouch, 103–105

attachments, inserting in notes, 373–374

Audio Descriptions option, 98

audio messages, 181

auto-enhancement

of photos, 296

of videos, 309

automatic updates, 66, 146

**B**

backing up to iCloud, 416–419

barometric sensor, 10

battery

Apple battery replacement service, 416

charging, 67

extending battery life, 410–412

Beats by Dr. Dre, 277

Bluefire Reader, 253–254

Bluetooth earbuds, 277

Bold Text setting, 96

Book Store, 250–253, 255–256

bookmarks, Safari, 204–207

Books app

accessibility and layout options in, 261–263

buying books in, 255–256

customizing, 259–263

finding books in Book Store, 250–253

fonts in, 260–261

navigating books in, 256–259

other e-book sources, 253–255

overview, 62, 249

themes in, 259–260

box contents, 19

browsing history, Safari, 202–203

browsing iPad files, 77–80

Button Shapes setting, 96–97

buying iPads

accessories for, 18

choose right iPad for you, 12–13

contents of box, 19

deciding on amount of storage, 13–15

hardware features, 19–23

Internet access for iPad, 15–16

newest models and OS, 8–11

pairing iPads with computers, 16

Wi-Fi only versus Wi-Fi + cellular options, 16–17

## C

Calculator app, 385–388

Calendar app

  adding calendar accounts, 333–335

  adding events and reminders, 326–327

  adding events or reminders with Siri, 127, 327–328

  alerts for events, 330–331

  creating events from email, 231–232

  creating repeating events, 328–329

  deleting events, 337

  events, adding with Siri, 127

  overview, 60, 321–322

  searching for events, 332

  using family calendars, 335–337

  viewing calendar, 322–325

  viewing events, 329

Call Audio Routing feature, 106

calling contacts with Siri, 125–126

Camera app

  capturing video, 306–307

  live photos, 10

  overview, 52, 61

  taking photos, 288–292

cameras

  overview, 21, 52

  switching during FaceTime calls, 172

capital letters, typing, 43

captioning, 100–101

carousel, 292

cases for iPads, 18, 409

cellular networks

  connecting to internet, 192–193

  making FaceTime calls over, 168–170

  Wi-Fi + Cellular models, 12–13, 16–17

charging cable, 410

charging iPads, 67, 410, 412

checklists, creating, 377–379

child accounts, 247

cleaning screen, 25–26, 408–409

clearing conversations, 177

Clock app

  deleting clocks, 339–340

  displaying, 338–339

  overview, 61, 322

  setting alarms, 340–341

  using stopwatch, 342

  using timer, 342

closed captioning, 100–101

Color Filters, 95

computers

  charging battery with, 67

  pairing iPads with, 16

  syncing wirelessly, 71–72

  syncing with, 26–27

Contacts app

  adding contacts, 152–155

  adding photos to contacts, 157–159

  calling contacts with Siri, 125–126

  deleting contacts, 163

  designating related people, 160–161

  Facetime calls via Siri, 125–126

  linked contacts, 160

  overview, 62

  setting ringtones and text tones, 161–162

  syncing contacts with iCloud, 155–157

contrast setting, 96

control center, 52–55

Conversation mode, Translate app, 402–404

conversions with Calculator app, 388

copying and pasting in notes, 371–372

covers for iPads, 18, 409

cropping
photos, 296
videos, 309

## D

deleted files, retrieving, 80

deleting
apps, 143–144
clocks, 339–340
contacts, 163
email, 232–233
events, 337
notes, 379–380
photos, 302–303
videos, 316–317

dictation with Siri, 131–132

Digital Touch, 179–180

dimensions of iPads, 8

directions, asking Siri for, 129–130

disinfecting iPads, 409

Do Not Disturb feature, 170, 362–365

dock, 28–29, 40

documents, copying photos into, 299

Dolby Atmos, 277–278

downloading
files in Safari, 210–211
games from App Store, 147–149
movies from Apple TV app, 243
music from iTunes Store, 243

drawings, adding to notes, 374–376

duplicate photos, merging, 298

Dwell Control settings, 113

## E

earbuds, listening to music with, 276–277

earphones, 277–278

e-books
accessibility & layout options in, 261–263
buying, 255–256
customizing, 259–263
finding in Apple Book Store, 250–253
fonts in, 260–261
navigating, 256–259
other e-book sources, 253–255
overview, 249
themes in, 259–260

editing
photos, 295–296
videos, 308–309

email
adding accounts, 214–216
alternative apps for, 227
creating and sending, 222–223
creating events from contents of, 231–232
creating VIP list, 235–236
deleting, 232–233
flagging for follow-up, 229–231
formatting, 224–227
manually setting up accounts, 216–218
marking as unread, 229–231
muting threads, 231
notifications of, 231
opening and reading, 218–220
organizing, 233–234

precautions with, 222

replying to or forwarding, 220–222

searching, 228–229

sending with Siri, 131

Undo Send option, 223

emoji keyboard, 43–44

emojis, 178–179

enhancements

for photos, 296

for videos, 309

Erase iPad option, 397–398

e-readers, 253–255. *See also* Books app

events

adding to calendar, 326–327

adding to calendar with Siri, 127, 327–328

alerts for, 330–331

creating from email contents, 231–232

deleting, 337

repeating events, creating, 328–329

searching for, 332

viewing, 329

exploring iPad

App Library, browsing, 36–40

cameras, 52

Control Center, discovering, 52–55

the dock, 40

Face ID, 56–57

gestures, 31–35

locking iPad, 63–64

locking screen rotation, 57

multitouch screen, 28–31

onscreen keyboard

displaying and using, 40–41

keyboard shortcuts, 42–44

QuickPath, 44

preinstalled apps, 60–63

search feature, 46–47

Slide Over feature, 48–50

small keyboard feature, 44–45

Split View feature, 48, 50–52

status bar, 58

switching between apps, 47–48

touch ID, 55–56

turning iPad off, 63–64

turning on iPad for first time, 26–27

unlocking iPad, 63–64

what you need to use iPad, 26

widgets, 59–60

extending battery life, 410–412

external storage devices, 77–78

Eye Tracking, 111–113

**F**

Face ID, 9, 56–57, 64

Facebook app

creating account, 166, 187–188

sharing photos, 298–299

FaceTime

accepting, enjoying, and ending calls, 170–172

device and information needed for, 166–167

general discussion, 167–168

group calls, 172

making calls with Wi-Fi or cellular connections, 168–169

muting sound in calls, 171

overview, 61, 165–166

switching views, 172

turning on feature, 167

using memojis, 170

using Siri to call contacts, 125–126

facial recognition, 9, 56–57

facts, asking Siri for, 130

Family Sharing
  Calendar Sharing, 335–337
  finding devices with, 395–396
  media content, 246–247

Files app, 61, 77–80

files on iPad, browsing, 77–80

filters
  for photos, 296
  for videos, 309

Find My app, 63, 395–398

Find My iPad feature, 77

Find My Network option, 396

fingerprint sensor. *See* Touch ID

flagging email for follow-up, 229–231

flash settings, 290

flash storage, 14

flicking, 32

Focus feature, 362–365

folders
  deleting, 144
  in Mail app, 233–234
  organizing apps in, 142–143
  Smart Folder feature for notes, 382–383

fonts, in Books app, 260–261

forcing iPad off, 64, 412

formatting email, 224–227

forwarding email, 220–222

Freeform app, 63

## G

games
  Apple Arcade, 146–147
  purchasing and downloading, 147–149

gestures, 31–35, 94

gigabytes (GB), 14–15

Google search engine, 204

group FaceTime calls, 172

group messaging, 183–184

Guided Access, 106–108

## H

handwriting, adding to notes, 374–376

hearing aids, using iPad with, 98–99

hiding Home screens, 39

High Dynamic Range (HDR) feature, 290

Home app, 62

Home button
  accessibility settings for, 106
  activating Siri with, 120

Home screens
  customizing, 31
  exploring, 29–30
  hiding, 39
  organizing apps in, 139–141
  overview, 28–29
  playing music from, 271
  removing apps from, 38
  wallpaper, changing, 88–90
  widgets, adding, 59–60

Home Sharing, 272, 312

## I

iCloud
  backing up to, 416–419
  general discussion, 72–74
  information to back up on, 73–74
  overview, 65
  Photo Sharing feature, 291, 300–301

sharing notes, 369
storage capacity, 73
sync settings, setting up, 76–77
syncing contacts with, 155–157
syncing with computer, 26–27
upgrading storage, 74
iCloud Drive, 65, 75
iMessage, 166, 172–174
Instagram app, 166, 189–190
instant messaging (IM), 166, 172–174
internet
adding and using bookmarks, 204–207
connecting to, 26, 192–193
downloading files, 210–211
exploring Safari, 193–195
navigating web pages, 195–197
private browsing, 209
public hotspots, 193
saving content to Reading List, 208–209
searching web, 204
Sign In with Apple feature, 70
tab groups, 199–202
tabbed browsing, 197–198
translating web pages, 211–212
viewing browsing history, 202–203
web searches with Siri, 130–131
Wi-Fi only versus Wi-Fi + Cellular models, 12–13, 16–17
Invert Colors feature, 96
iPad Air, 8, 13

**K**

keyboards
displaying and using, 40–41
keyboard shortcuts, 42–44
Magic Keyboards, 44

QuickPath, 44
small, 44–45
Smart Keyboard, 10, 18
Kindle e-reader app, 253–254

**L**

languages
for Siri, 120
Translate app, 400–404
translating web pages, 211–212
translation with Siri, 125, 132–133
VoiceOver settings, 92
Larger Text feature, 96
layout options, Books app, 261–263
Lightning/USB-C Connector slot, 20
linked contacts, 160
Liquid Retina display, 9
lists, creating, 350–351
live photos, 10, 290
Live Speech, 102–103
location
getting directions from Siri, 129
scheduling reminders by, 347–350
sharing in Messages app, 182–183
lock screen rotation, 57
locking iPad, 63–64

**M**

Macs. *See* computers
Magic Keyboards, 44
Magnifier app, 62, 84–86
Mail app
adding email accounts, 214–216
creating and sending new messages, 222–223

Mail app *(continued)*

  creating events from email contents, 231–232

  creating VIP list, 235–236

  deleting email, 232–233

  flagging email for follow-up, 229–231

  formatting email, 224–227

  manually setting up email accounts, 216–218

  marking email as unread, 229–231

  muting threads, 231

  notifications of, 231

  opening and reading messages, 218–220

  organizing email, 233–234

  overview, 60, 213

  replying to or forwarding email, 220–222

  searching email, 228–229

  sharing photos, 298–299

  Trash versus Archive folders, 232–233

  Undo Send option, 223

maintaining iPad

  cleaning screen, 408–409

  covers and cases, 409

  extending battery life, 410–412

  overview, 407

Maps app, 61, 129–130

marking email as unread, 229–231

Math Notes in Calculator app, 388

Measure app, 62, 392–395

memojis, 170

memory of iPads, 12–13

Messages app

  addressing, creating, and sending messages, 174–175

  apps and tools in, 179–180

  audio messages, 181

  clearing conversations, 177

  Digital Touch, 179–180

  group messaging, 183–184

  overview, 60

  reading messages, 176

  scheduling reminders by messaging, 347–350

  sending emojis with text, 178–179

  sending messages later, 175

  sending messages with Siri, 131

  sending photos or videos, 181–182

  setting up iMessage account, 172–174

  sharing location in, 182–183

microphones, 22

Microsoft Exchange, 331

models of iPads, 8–13

motion, reducing, 33, 98

motor settings, 106

movies

  Apple account, signing in to, 68–70

  closed-captioning and subtitles for, 315

  playing with TV app

    content from Apple, 312–315

    content from third-party providers, 310–312

  renting or buying, 243–245

  streaming, 14

multitouch screen, 28–31

music

  Apple account, signing in to, 68–70

  exploring iTunes Store, 240–241

  Family Sharing, 246–247

  iTunes Match, 268

  playing with Siri, 128

  purchasing in iTunes Store, 242–243

  streaming, 14

Music app
  Apple Music Sing, 275
  creating playlists, 269–270
  Family Sharing, 276
  iTunes Match, 268
  listening with earbuds, 276–277
  listening with spatial audio, 277–279
  overview, 60, 265
  playing music, 271–276
  playing music with radio, 279–281
  searching for music, 270–271
  shuffling music, 276
  using AirPlay, 279
  using Siri with, 128
  viewing lyrics, 275–276
  viewing Music Library, 266–268
Music Library
  searching for music, 270–271
  viewing, 266–268

## N
Neural Engine, 9
News app, 62
Night Shift, 87–88
nonresponsive iPads, troubleshooting, 412–413
Notes app
  adding drawings or handwriting, 374–376
  copying and pasting in, 371–372
  creating checklists, 377–379
  deleting notes, 379–380
  formatting text, 371
  inserting attachments, 373–374
  opening blank notes, 368–371
  overview, 11, 61, 367

  Quick Notes, 380–382
  ruler tool, 376
  Smart Folder feature, 382–383
  text styles in, 376–377
Notification Center
  Do Not Disturb feature, 362–365
  Focus feature, 362–365
  notification summaries, 356–357
  overview, 344, 355–356
  setting notification types, 358–360
  viewing, 360–362
notification summaries, 356–357
numbers, typing, 42

## O
One, Apple, 147
On/Off Labels, 96
onscreen keyboard
  displaying and using, 40–41
  keyboard shortcuts, 42–44
  QuickPath, 44
operating system (OS)
  Apple Intelligence, 10–11, 118
  updating, 27, 66, 146, 413–414
organizing email, 233–234
organizing photos, 296–298

## P
Pages app, 299, 376
pairing iPads with computers, 16
panoramic photos, 289
parallax, 33, 98
password support, 419
Passwords app, 63, 404–405
Pay, Apple, 245–246

PC free feature, 27

Pencil, Apple, 9, 18, 376, 408

per-app accessibility settings, 114–116

Personal Voice, 102–103

Photo Booth app, 62

Photo Sharing feature, iCloud, 291, 298–299

photos
  adding to contacts, 157–159
  inserting in notes, 373–374
  live photos, 10, 290
  sending in Messages app, 181–182
  taking with iPad, 288–292

Photos app
  albums, creating, 296–297
  cropping photos, 296
  deleting photos, 302–303
  duplicate photos, merging, 298
  editing photos, 295–296
  editing video, 308–309
  enhancing photos, 296
  filters, 296
  time delay for photos, 290

## Q

Quick Notes, 380–382

QuickPath, 44

QuickType, 41

## R

Radio app, 279–281

Reading List, Safari, 208–209

reboot procedure, 412

recording voice memos, 389–392

Reduce Loud Audio option, 415

Reduce Motion setting, 98

Reduce Transparency setting, 96

Reduce White Point feature, 95

registering iPads, 15, 27

related contacts, designating, 160–161

Reminders app
  adding reminders to calendar, 326–327
  adding reminders to calendar with Siri, 327–328
  creating lists, 350–351
  creating reminders, 126–127, 344–345
  deleting reminders, 353–355
  editing reminder details, 345–347
  marking reminders as complete, 353–355
  overview, 62, 343–344
  scheduling reminders by time, location, or when messaging, 347–350
  syncing with other devices and calendars, 352
  using Siri with, 126–127

renting or buying movies and TV shows, 243–245

repeating events, creating, 328–329

replacement charger cables or power adapters, 67

replying to email, 220–222

resetting iPad, 413

restoring sound, 414–415

ringtones, 154, 161–162, 240

## S

Safari
  adding and using bookmarks, 204–207
  connecting to internet, 192–193
  downloading files, 210–211
  enabling private browsing, 209
  exploring, 193–195

navigating web pages, 195–197

overview, 60, 191–192

saving content to Reading List, 208–209

searching web, 204

setting as default browser, 194

tab groups, 199–202

tabbed browsing, 197–198

translating web pages, 211–212

viewing browsing history, 202–203

scheduling reminders, 347–350

scientific calculator, 387

screen

cleaning, 25–26, 408–409

touchscreen technology, 29

Ultra Retina XDR display, 9

screen brightness, setting, 86–88

screen rotation feature, 30, 57

search feature, 46–47

searching

email, 228–229

for events, 332

web, 204

web with Siri, 130–131

Settings app, 63

severe weather alerts, 399

sharing photos

overview, 291

using AirDrop, 300

using iCloud Photo Sharing, 300–301

via Mail, social media, or other apps,
298–299

Shazam app, 128

Shortcuts app, 63

shuffling music, 276

Sign In with Apple, 70

SIM tray, 21

Siri

activating, 119–121

adding events to calendar with, 127

asking for facts, 130

calling contacts via Facetime, 125–126

cancelling requests, 126

customizing, 120–121

functions of, 121–125

getting directions, 129–130

getting suggestions, 125

language translation, 125, 132–133

nationality and voice options, 121

overview, 117–118

playing music, 128, 272

reminders and alerts, creating, 126–127

searching web, 130–131

sending email, messages, or tweets
with, 131

using dictation, 131–132

sleep mode, 63

Slide Over feature, 48–50

small keyboard feature, 44–45

Smart Connector, 10, 21

Smart Folder feature, 382–383

Smart Keyboard, 10, 18

social media apps

dos and don'ts of using, 185

Facebook account, creating, 187–188

finding and installing, 185–187

Instagram account, creating, 189–190

overview, 166

sharing photos, 298–299

X account, creating, 188–189

software updates, 66

sound, restoring, 414–415

Sounds settings, 99–100

spatial audio, 277–279

speakers, 21

Split View feature, 48, 50–52

Spoken Content, 95

square photos, 289

status bar, 32, 58

Stocks app, 62

stopwatch, 342

storage, choosing amount of, 13–15

streaming, 14

subscribing to podcasts, 281–284

subtitles, 100–101

suggestions, asking Siri for, 125

swiping, 31

Switch Control feature, 106

switching between apps, 47–48

switching cameras during calls, 172

symbols, typing, 42

sync settings, iCloud, 76–77

syncing

  with computers, 26–27

  contacts with iCloud, 155–157

  reminders, 352

  wirelessly, 71–72

## T

tab groups, Safari, 199–202

tabbed browsing in Safari, 197–198

Talk & Type to Siri options, 119–120

tap and swipe gesture, 31–35

tap method, 31

tap-twice method, 31

technical support, 415–416

terabytes (TB), 15

text messages. *See* Messages app

text styles in notes, 376–377

text tones, setting, 154, 161–162

themes, Books app, 259–260

three-finger tap, 31

time, scheduling reminders by, 347–350

time delay for photos, 290

timer, 342

Top button, 20

Touch ID, 9, 20, 55–56, 64

touchscreen technology, 29

Translate app

  Conversation mode, 402–404

  languages supported, 400

  overview, 62

  translating text, 401–402

  translating text from images, 402

translating

  with Siri, 132–133

  web pages, 211–212

transparency effects, 96

Trash folder, 232–233

trimming videos, 309

troubleshooting

  backing up to iCloud, 416–419

  getting support, 415–416

  nonresponsive iPads, 412–413

  overview, 407

  restoring sound, 414–415

  updating software, 413–414

turning iPad off, 63–64

turning on iPad for first time, 26–27

TV app
  overview, 61, 305
  playing content from Apple, 312–315
  playing content from third-party providers,
    310–312
  signing in to TV provider, 310
TV shows
  closed-captioning and subtitles, 315
  playing with TV app
    content from Apple, 312–315
    content from third-party providers,
      310–312
  renting or buying, 243–245
tweets, sending with Siri, 131
Twitter app. *See* X app

## U

Ultra Retina XDR display, 9
Undo Send option, 223
unlocking iPad, 63–64
updating apps, 145–147
updating operating system, 27, 66, 146,
  413–414
USB-C cable, 19
USB-C Connector slot, 20
USB-C power adapter, 19
User Guide, iPad, 416
utilities
  calculator, 385–388
  finding missing devices, 395–398
  managing passwords, 404–405
  measuring distances, 392–395
  overview, 385
  translating words and phrases, 400–404

voice memos, 389–392
weather updates and alerts, 398–400

## V

video calls
  accepting, enjoying, and ending calls,
    170–172
  device and information needed for,
    166–167
  general discussion, 167–168
  group calls, 172
  making calls with Wi-Fi or cellular
    connections, 168–169
  muting sound in calls, 171
  overview, 61, 165–166
  switching views, 172
  turning on feature, 167
  using memojis, 170
  using Siri to call contacts, 125–126
videos
  capturing with iPad cameras, 306–307
  closed-captioning and subtitles, 315
  deleting, 316–317
  editing in Photos app, 308–309
  inserting in notes, 373–374
  overview, 305
  playing movies or TV shows with TV app
    content from Apple, 312–315
    content from third-party providers,
      310–312
  sending in Messages app, 181–182
viewing events, 329
VIP list, creating, 235–236
Vision features, 95–98

Vocal Shortcuts, 113–114

Voice Control, 109–111

Voice Memos app, 62, 389–392

VoiceOver
  gestures for, 94–95
  setting up, 90–93
  tutorial, 94
  using, 93–95

volume rocker, 22

volume settings, 99–100

# W

Wallet, Apple, 245–246

wallpaper, changing, 31, 88–90

Weather app, 61, 398–400

web browser. *See* Safari

web pages
  adding and using bookmarks, 204–207
  downloading files, 210–211
  enabling private browsing, 209
  navigating, 195–197
  saving to Reading List, 208–209
  searching web, 204

searching web with Siri, 130–131

tab groups, 199–202

tabbed browsing, 197–198

translating, 211–212

viewing browsing history, 202–203

white point, reducing, 95

widgets, 29, 59–60

Wi-Fi + Cellular models, 12–13, 16–17

Wi-Fi networks
  connecting to, 192–193
  making FaceTime calls over, 168–170
  public hotspots, 193

Wi-Fi only models, 12–13, 16–17

wireless syncing, 71–72

# X

X app
  creating account, 166, 188–189
  sending tweets with Siri, 131
  sharing photos, 298–299

# Z

Zoom feature, 95

# About the Author

Dwight Spivey has been a technical author and editor for over a decade, but he's been a bona fide technophile for more than three of them. He's the author of *Apple Watch For Seniors For Dummies* (Wiley), *iPhone For Seniors For Dummies* (Wiley), *Idiot's Guide to Apple Watch* (Alpha), *Home Automation For Dummies* (Wiley), *How to Do Everything Pages, Keynote & Numbers* (McGraw-Hill), and many more books covering the tech gamut.

Dwight is also the Director of Educational Technology at Spring Hill College. His technology experience is extensive, consisting of macOS, iOS, Android, Linux, and Windows operating systems in general, educational technology, learning management systems, desktop publishing software, laser printers and drivers, color and color management, and networking.

Dwight lives on the Gulf Coast of Alabama with his wife, Cindy, their four children, Victoria, Devyn, Emi, and Reid, and their pets Rocky, Penny, and Mirri.

# Dedication

This one's for you, Uncle Kenneth. Your laugh was one-of-a-kind, and your heart was a hundred times larger than those beautiful cowboy hats you loved to wear. No one rocked a bolo tie like you, either. The world feels emptier without you in it. I so much look forward to seeing you again. We love you.

# Author's Acknowledgments

Massive thanks to my agent, Carole Jelen. It is such a joy to have you in my corner!

Sincere gratitude goes to Steve Hayes, Susan Pink (the best project editor I've ever worked with), and Guy Hart-Davis (the best technical editor on either side of the Atlantic). And of course, the editors, designers, and other wonderful Wiley professionals who are absolutely critical to the completion of these books I'm so blessed to write. I sincerely want every individual involved at every level to know how appreciative I am of their dedication, hard work, and patience in putting together this book.

## Publisher's Acknowledgments

**Executive Editor:** Elizabeth Stilwell

**Managing Editor:** Sofia Malik

**Project Editor:** Susan Pink

**Production Editor:** Tamilmani Varadharaj

**Technical Reviewer:** Guy Hart-Davis

**Proofreader:** Debbye Butler

**Cover Image:** © Moon Safari/ Getty Images